YUTKA

And the Voyage of the Parita

YUTKA

And the Voyage of the Parita

MARCIA BREECE

Publishing Partners
2024

Copyright © 2024 Marcia Breece
Publishing Partners
www.publishing-partners.com
Port Townsend, WA
marcia@marciabreece.com

All rights reserved. No part of this book may be reproduced, stored in, or introduced into a retrieval system or transmitted in any form or by any means (electronic, mechanical, photocopying, recording, or otherwise) without the prior written permission of the author.

Creative nonfiction
The events in this work of authorship are historically accurate. The dialogue and other details have been created by the author for the purpose of story telling.

Library of Congress Number: 2024935490

ISBN: 978-1-944887-80-3
eISBN: 978-1-944887-68-1
B&N ISBN: 978-1-944887-87-2

Frontispiece: When the *Parita* landed on the sandbar, 500 refugees fled to safety camouflaged by the Tel Avivians who crowded the shoreline. Then the British cordoned off the beach and arrested the 300 passengers still onboard.

Figure 27, photo of Sam and Batia by Rich Breshears, Kennewick, WA. www.breshearsphoto.com

Contents

Other books by Marcia Breece vii
Maps viii
Character Chart xi
Dedication xiii
Prologue xvii
Poland, 1897 xvii

PART ONE

Chapter 1 - Tel Aviv, August 1939 5
Chapter 2 - Poland, November 1938 6
Chapter 3 - Uncle Srulik Emigrates, 1934 9
Chapter 4 - Discussing Emigration, 1939 11
Chapter 5 - *Yutka's Decision,* April *1939* 13
Chapter 6 - Next Meeting, 1939 18
Chapter 7 - Letter to Uncle Srulik and Aunt Zipporah, 1939 21
Chapter 8 - Packing for the Journey, Poland, 1939 23
Chapter 9 - Marseille, France, March 1939 29
Chapter 10 - France 1939 32
Chapter 11 - *Shabbat* Dinner, July 1939 37
Chapter 12 - The Telegram 42
Chapter 13 - Train to Constanța 47
Chapter 14 - Constanța, Rumania, July 12, 1939 52
Chapter 15 - Boarding the *Parita* 56
Chapter 16 - Elsa's Story 67
Chapter 17 - The first few days at sea, July 1939 74
Chapter 18 - Day 6 at Sea, July 19, 1939 83
Chapter 19 - Yutka and Yaakov meet on the *Parita* 87
Chapter 20 - Yaakov 90
Chapter 21 - July 23, 1939 93
Chapter 22 - July 25, 1939 96
Chapter 23 - Bread and Water 99
Chapter 24 - The *Marco Polo* 101
Chapter 25 - Entertaining the children 105
Chapter 26 - Levivots 111
Chapter 27 - *Ekmek ve su,* Izmir, August 8th 115
Chapter 28 - Zosia and Channah 118
Chapter 29 - Serioja's dreidel game 127
Chapter 30 - Mama's Books 131
Chapter 31 - Back to Constantinople 137
Chapter 32 - Mutiny, August 20, 1939 142
Chapter 33 - Tel Aviv Beach, August 22, 1939 147

PART TWO
Chapter 34 - Tel Aviv, August 20, 1939 154
Chapter 35 - Yaakov in Tel Aviv 157
Chapter 36 - Tel Aviv 159
Chapter 37 - September 1939 166
Chapter 38 - Jezreel Valley, November 1939 171
Chapter 39 - Hanukkah, 1939 175
Chapter 40 - Tel Aviv, January 1940 178
Chapter 41 - Returning the Mandolin, February 1940 183
Chapter 42 - Sabbath at the Vineyard 189
Chapter 43 - Postcards, April 1940 191
Chapter 44 - September 1940 193
Chapter 45 - March 1941 195
Chapter 46 - The Proposal, April 1941 202
Chapter 47 - Yutka and Yaakov's Wedding, April 1941 207
Chapter 48 - A Married Couple, May 1941 211
Chapter 49 - Last Letter, March 1942 214
Chapter 50 - End of WWII, May 8, 1945 216
Chapter 51 - Tel Aviv, October 1945 218
Chapter 52 - Yaakov's Sister, 1946 224
Chapter 53 - The Vote, November 29, 1947 231
Chapter 54 - Hadassah Convoy, April 13, 1948 235
Chapter 55 - Israeli War for Independence, May 14, 1948 239
Chapter 56 - End of the War for Independence, March 1949 247
Chapter 57 - Hope, 1949 251
Chapter 58 - Holocaust Remembrance Day 254
Epilogue 257
Photos 261
Chronology 271
Author's Note 273
Acknowledgments 281
Bibliography 283
Glossary 285
Recipes 299
About the Author 301
Book Club Discussion Questions 303

Other books by Marcia Breece

>*Finding This place*
>*Secrets Lost*
>*Kala's Choice*
>*Last Bottle of Burgundy* (coming soon)

Maps

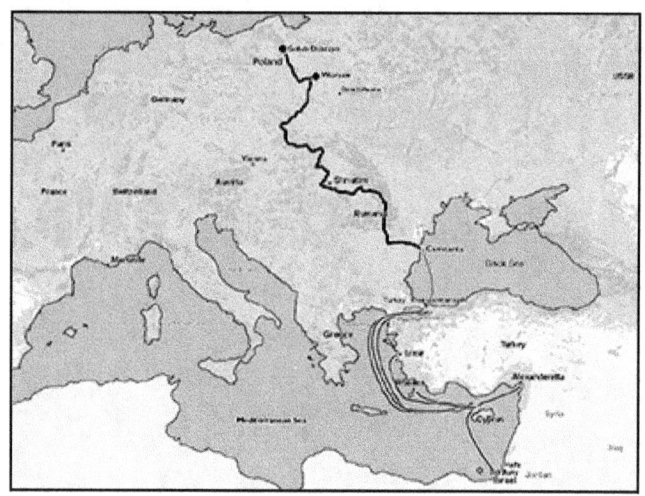

Figure 1
Yutka Lipka's route from her home in
Dobrzyn, Poland to *Eretz* Israel in 1939

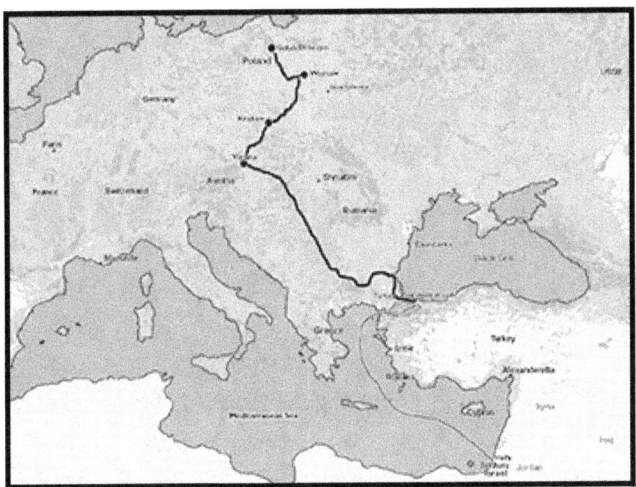

Figure 2
Yutka's grandfather, Fiebush Lipka's route from his home in
Dobrzyń, Poland to Ottoman Palestine in 1909

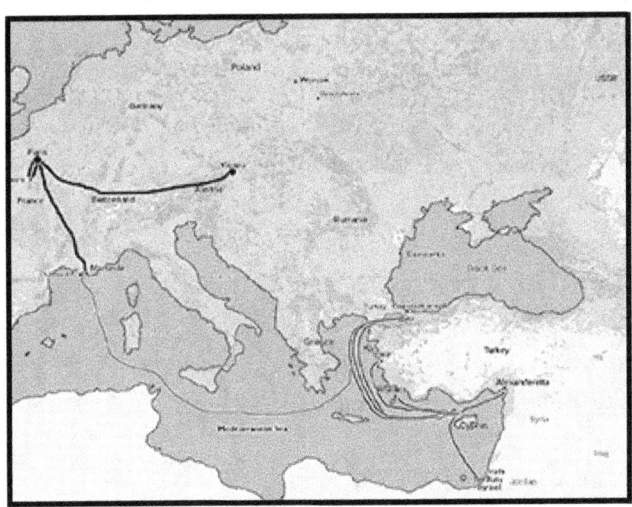

Figure 3
Elsa's escape route from her home in
Vienna, Austria to *Eretz* Israel in 1939

Character Chart

CHARACTER	RELATIONSHIP	DOB in story	DOD
YUTKA LIPKA*		1921	2010
Mordechai Lipka*	father	1878	1942
Bluma Cohen Lipka*	mother	1883	1942
Shmuel*	son (actual 1942)	1947	
Chaya*	daughter (actual 1944)	1948	
Fiebush Lipka*	paternal grandfather	1842	1921
Rozka Lipka Hirsch*	sister	1914	1942
Heniek Lipka*	brother	1913	1942
Sonya (Heniek's wife)*	sister-in-law		1942
Josip (Heniek's son)*	nephew	1942	1942
Zigi Hirsch (Rozka's husband)*	brother-in law	1914	1942
Dr. Max Hirsch*	sister Rozka's brother-in-law		
Jerzyk Hirsch (Rozka's son)*	nephew	1937	1942
Rebekah Hirsch (Rozka's daughter)	niece	1939	1942
Srulik Lipka	father's brother		
Moshe Lipka	father's brother	1903	
Zipporah Lipka	Srulik's wife		
Yaakov Polonecki*	husband	1907	1981
Arie Polonecki (Yaakov's brother)*	brother-in-law	1905	
Sara Polonecki (Arie's wife)*	sister-in-law	1910	
Mala (Yaakov's sister)*	sister-in-law	1915	
Halina (Yaakov's niece)*	niece	1937	

* Indicates Yutka's actual relatives

PARITA PASSENGERS

Elsa (French)	Yutka's friend	1920	
Nikos (Greek)**	cook	1921	
Oshrah (Romanian)**	married Nikos (cook)	1921	
Serioja (Russian)*	second engineer, the angel		
Jacob Ariel (Polish)*	Betar operative		
Elijaha Even (Polish)*	Betar operative		
Emmanuel Solchansky (Polish)*	15-year-old stowaway	1924	2006
Mr. Edelman (French)	oldest man on *Parita*	1899	
Mrs. Joséphine Edelman (French)	mother of two girls	1911	
Priscilla Edelman (French)	4-year-old passenger	1935	
Rochelle Edelman (French)	3-year-old passenger	1936	
Erwin Leibovitz*[1]	*Parita's* Betar Commander	1919	1954
Vladimir Mikhailovich*	Parita's captain		

OTHERS

René Goldhacht (French)	Elsa's husband	1919	1948
Dr. Reuben Hecht (Swiss)*	Aliya Bet rep in Europe	1909	1993
Herschel Waxman (French)**	Retrofit Parita in France		
Adras Alexopoulos (Greek)**	Supplied food to Parita		
Ze'ev Jabotinsky (Russian Empire)*	Founder of Betar 1880	1940	
Eri Jabotinsky (Russian Empire)*	Betar founder's son	1910	1969
Mr. Minakoulis (Greek)*	Parita's Greek owner		
Mr. Bender (Polish)*	Hired Yaakov at barbershop		
Mr. and Mrs. Newman**	Rented room to Yutka and Yaakov		
Mr. and Mrs Goldfarb**	Tourists on *Marco Polo* in Rhodes		

* Indicates actual passengers and other characters
** Indicates real people but actual name unknown

---

1. "Erwin" was Leibovitz's Betari nickname. He was born Itzhak Leibovitz, but later changed his name to Itzhak (Isaac) Ariel.

Dedication

In memory of Yutka Lipka Polonecki
And the survivors of the voyage of the *Parita*

Figure 4
Commemorative plaque near the site where the *Parita* landed

The best perfume in the world could not even compete with the whiff coming from the hay, the cut lumber, and the flower bed at the back of our home.

—*Yutka Lipka Polonecki*

Figure 5
Fiebush Lipka 1842 - 1921

Prologue

Poland, 1897

"I agree with Herzl," insisted Reb Fiebush Lipka after reading *Der Judenstaat (The State of the Jews)* by Zionist, Theodor Herzl. "European Jews should purchase land in Ottoman Palestine and work to establish the free state of Israel."

"But Fiebush, what Herzl proposes would create an apartheid state. We should wait for the coming of the messiah," argued his orthodox friend, Saul.

"No Saul, establishing a state where Jews govern themselves is the only way we can live without threat of exile and put an end to the pogroms."

So inspired by Herzl's book, Fiebush Lipka traveled to Switzerland to attend the first Zionist Congress in Basel.

Herzl climbed to the dais and looked out over Stadtcasino Basel concert hall filled with two hundred thirty formally dressed international attendees, including seventeen women.

"Zionism seeks to establish a home for the Jewish people in Palestine secured under public law," Herzl began.

The crowd roared its approval.

✡

In 1909, after twenty years of preaching in favor of Zionism, Fiebush transferred responsibility for running his many successful businesses to his two oldest sons, Mordechai and Srulik. Then, sixty-seven-year-old Fiebush took a year-long journey to Ottoman Palestine.

The train from Warsaw to Krakow passed rippling wheat fields, green pastures dotted with beef cattle, and rolling hills covered in dense Scots pine forests. On the sleeper train from Krakow to Vienna, Fiebush nibbled at his dinner. The food was not kosher and not at all satisfying. On the Orient Express from Vienna to Constantinople the meals were not kosher but the food was tasty. He ate his meals and slept soundly in the comfortable sleeping car.

He ferried over the Bosphorus Strait from European Turkey to Asian Turkey, and spent weeks in Constantinople meeting with Zionists leaders, and discussing Herzl's book. Then he chartered a ship for transport across the Mediterranean Sea to the port at Haifa, Palestine, controlled by the Turks since 1516.

Exploring Haifa and discussing his ideas for creating a business manufacturing crates and boxes and exporting oranges occupied weeks of his time until he boarded a train to the Jezreel Valley. The great iron wheels turned, and steam quickly evaporated in the hot, dry desert air as the train slowly traversed the valley toward the Carmel mountain range. Fiebush had plenty of time to study the territory. He told a fellow passenger, "Even at my age I should walk faster than this train!"

In Afula, a hot, dry breeze ruffled his frizzy, white beard. Fertile farmland had attracted inhabitants to this region since prehistoric times. He knew the history of this valley, positioned to control the major east-west and north-south highways. According to the Hebrew Bible, great wars were fought here. Gideon led the Israelites to victory against the Midianites, the Amalekites, and various nomadic desert-dwelling tribes. Later, the Philistines defeated the Israelites led by King Saul.[2]

A quote from the Hebrew Bible inspired Fiebush to buy land where his descendants would plant a vineyard and fulfill the biblical prophecy; *But every man shall sit under his grapevine or fig tree with no one to disturb him (Micah 4:4).*

Bending slightly due to rheumatism, he gazed into the gnarled branches of a one-thousand-year-old fig tree. At last, Fiebush had found the property he was seeking. At the base of the Gilboa mountain ridge, he purchased thousands of dunams of fertile land. Peering through the wire-rimmed spectacles that rested at the end of his generous nose, he inspected the documents then folded them into his pocket, closed his eyes and prayed that in the not-too-distant future, his descendants would find their way from Europe to this historic, fertile valley. He knew his dream would not be fulfilled in his lifetime, but he was certain someday The Land of Israel would become an independent Jewish state where his clan would live in peace.

---

2. An Israeli is a citizen of the state of Israel as it exists today. "Israelites" were physical ancestors of the twelve tribes called 'the Children of Israel'. They were a group of Semitic-speaking tribes in the ancient Near East who inhabited a part of Canaan (currently Israel, the West Bank and Gaza, Jordan, and the southern portions of Syria and Lebanon) during the Iron Age (1200 to 500 B.C.E.). The name "Israel" first appears in the Merneptah Stele (first known Biblical reference) of ancient Egypt, dated to about 1200 BCE. See Genesis 32:22-32

PART ONE
The *SS Parita*

Chapter 1

Tel Aviv, August 1939

Yutka looked over her shoulder at the listing *Parita* lodged on a sandbar fifty meters from Tel Aviv beach. She raised her chin, but her knees gave way beneath her. Foamy saltwater streamed over her legs as she knelt on the warm, white sand. She'd survived forty-two days at sea with little food or water and achieved her goal to immigrate to *Eretz* Israel.[3] Brushing the wet sand from her legs, however, her heart split in two. She had finally reached *Eretz* Israel, while her family faced the violence in Poland.

As she scanned the gathering crowd, hoping her aunt and uncle would find her, she remembered Ze'ev Jabotinsky's presentation to her Betar Youth Group nine months before, her ultimate motivation to immigrate to *Eretz* Israel.

"Listen to my remarks at the twelfth hour," Ze'ev Jabotinsky warned. His owlish eyes squinting behind round-framed spectacles, his chin jutting, his fist pounding the table. "For God's sake, may each one save his life while there is still time. And time is short."

---

3. Eretz is Hebrew for 'the land of'

Chapter 2

Poland, November 1938

Ze'ev Jabotinsky's warning ricocheted in Yutka's thoughts. She hurried past the family lumber yard where the scent of fresh-cut pine filled the bitterly cold breeze. Horses' breath turned to silver clouds. Harnesses and chains clanked as she avoided horse-drawn wagons hauling lumber off to constructions sites across Poland. Yutka's fur-lined boots stomped through fresh snowfall and her breath burst into clouds of vapor.

At home in the narrow entrance hall, seventeen-year-old Yutka took off her boots, unwrapped the blue wool scarf Mama had knitted for her and hung her matching cloche hat and long black wool coat on pegs. Warm air and the welcoming aroma of potatoes, onions and cabbage frying in goose fat met her at the door.

As always, Papa asked, "How was your meeting today, *bubbala*?"

"More bad news Papa. Rioters in Germany destroyed Jewish homes, businesses and synagogues. Ze'ev Jabotinsky says we should leave Poland while we still can." Her voice became sharp and penetrating, "Papa, Jabotinsky is right," she put her hand over her heart, "I feel it. He's right. Hitler's army will march into Poland, and they'll burn our synagogues, steal everything, and take us to work camps… or worse. Poland isn't safe for us."

"Why should German soldiers bother us?" replied Mordechai. "My electric plant supplies power, and the country depends on my forest lands and lumber mill." He waved his hand as if shooing a fly.

"Oh, Papa, they will seize your businesses. Hitler blames Jews for all bad things that ever happened. He wants to eliminate all Jews." Yutka paced back and forth in front of the fire in her soundless stocking feet. Static-charged black curls encircled her round face, escaping the deep waves she had pressed into place that morning. She looked wild and unhinged.

"Police just watched the violence. Jewish homes and shops burned. Then the authorities herded thousands of Jews like cattle onto trains and took them to German camps." The pitch of her voice spiraled higher. Despite her efforts to stay composed, her arms waved like a plover defending its nest. "The *Gazeta Polska* newspaper called the riot *Kristallnacht* because of all the broken glass in the streets. At the meeting today, our leaders showed us photographs of doctors, lawyers, and business owners, like you Papa, scrubbing the sidewalks in Berlin, crawling in the broken glass on their hands and knees wearing their handsome suits and fedoras while soldiers pointed guns at them."

"Yutka, these Betar meetings have ignited your Zionist's passion since you were thirteen, but it is not like you to become hysterical. Come, sit by the fire with me before dinner."

Yutka sat on the rug next to his rocking chair. She faced the crackling fire with her arms around her shins, her chin resting on her bent knees. Her small hands mindlessly tugged at the top button of her dark navy blue Betar uniform. Papa rested his hand on the top of her head and gently patted to comfort her. She tried to speak softly, "This is different Papa, and I'm not hysterical. The *Kristallnacht* was terrifying. The same will happen to us if we don't leave Poland…." She paused to breathe deeply and calm her voice. She knew how her papa would react to her next suggestion. She looked up at him, "At the meeting they said Betar has organized an *Aliyah Bet*. They're chartering ships to take Jews to *Eretz* Israel. Whatever the cost, we should go."

"You know how I feel about *Aliyah Bet*. How should illegal immigration be the right answer?" Mordechai barked. "We must cooperate with the British Mandate and the rules they have established."

"Papa, aren't you a *Zionist* like *Saba* Fiebush?"

"Of course. Diaspora Jews must return to the Land of Israel. I hope to go one day myself and join my brother Srulik, but…" deep creases formed between his bushy brows, "breaking the law is not our way."

"But Papa! Illegal immigration is the *only* way," she closed her eyes and took a deep breath, still struggling to keep her voice calm. "They told us the British Empire needs Arab oil. Since Arabs don't want us there, the British set immigration limits to keep the Arabs satisfied. We can't hope for an independent state if Arabs outnumber Jews."

"Nonsense, there is no reason Arabs and Jews can't live in Israel just as Catholics and Jews live together in Dobrzyń. We must follow the law. When I am ready, we will apply for immigration certificates."

Exasperated, Yutka ignored his dismissive tone, "Papa, even if you applied today, it would take months or even years for them to issue your immigration certificates. Uncle Srulik waited over a year and then immigrated illegally. We should go to *Eretz* Israel and help Uncle Srulik work the land *Saba* Fiebush left you."

"Srulik and Zipporah were lucky," said Mordechai. "British authorities allowed them to stay, but that was four years ago. The British are no longer so generous."

Chapter 3

Uncle Srulik Emigrates, 1934

"Since Hitler became chancellor a year ago, anti-Semitism is escalating and violence against Jews grows worse," said Srulik.

"This is the way it has always been. Things get better. Things get worse. Such is the life of a Jew in Poland," Yutka's father, Mordechai, tilted his head, lifted his palm and shrugged his shoulders.

"The Zionist movement is working to establish a free Jewish State in *Eretz* Israel, a place where Jews will rule themselves," said Yutka's Uncle Srulik. "My German friends are among 350 Jews who are chartering a small steamer called the *Vallos* to take them to *Eretz* Israel. Zipporah and I have the opportunity to join them."

"You have received your immigration certificates?"

"No, we have not. We applied over a year ago but hear nothing from the British embassy."

"Do you have the proper travel documents?"

"I have arranged for forged papers."

"So! You should break the law and immigrate illegally?" Mordechai loudly grumbled. "Have you gone *meshugge*? What if the authorities discover your papers are counterfeit?"

"I will wait no longer. Papa bought the land in the Jezreel Valley over twenty years ago. One of us must pursue his dream. I am a vintner; it makes sense I should develop the land Papa left to me."

"Srulik! What a risk you take! If the British catch you, the consequences will be dire. They could shoot you, sink the *Vallos* or turn the ship away."

"Zipporah and I have discussed the danger. It is a risk we are willing to take. You know Papa was an unyielding Zionist. How will the free state of Israel be built if Jews stay in Europe? I must fulfill his dream."

"What about your vineyard here in Poland?" boomed Mordechai. "Have you worked hard for years just to throw it all away?"

"Zipporah and I will work just as hard to plant a vineyard in the Jezreel Valley. Moshe will manage the vineyard here in Poland. He's been working with me long enough to know the business," Srulik spoke more softly. "Mordechai, I'm hoping you should help him if Moshe needs advice."

Giving himself time to think, Mordechai clicked open his tin tobacco canister. He carefully loaded the bowl of his pipe with fresh tobacco, took a test puff, struck a wooden match on the sole of his shoe, and pulled deeply. The spicy scent of pipe tobacco filled the room. His wooden rocking chair squeaked as he leaned back, stared into the fire, and stroked his clean-shaven chin. "I do not agree with your decision to immigrate illegally Srulik," Mordechai sighed heavily. "However, if your decision is made, I promise to help Moshe if he needs me. But you must know, I think you make a terrible mistake."

"Uncle, are you going far away?" asked Yutka after listening from the kitchen.

"Yes, Auntie and I will plant a vineyard on the land your *Saba* Fiebush left to us in *Eretz* Israel." He put his arm over her shoulder, "My sweet *liebling*, I will miss you, but I must do this. It is my destiny."

"Take me with you, Uncle," begged thirteen-year-old Yutka. "Israel is my destiny too."

Chapter 4

Discussing Emigration, 1939

As the snow turned to slush and buds on cherry trees swelled, Yutka lounged on the floor by the fire arguing with her brother, Heniek, who was seven years older. Papa sat in his rocking chair reading and listening to them, while Mama and Heniek's wife, Sonya, prepared dinner.

"Fascists are tearing Europe apart, and Hitler's just getting started. We should all emigrate while we still can!" Yutka pleaded. "If not *Eretz* Israel, then somewhere safe from Nazis!"

"That Betar youth group has made you into an idealist," her older brother chided. "You think you're a pioneer looking for adventure, but you will find only trouble."

"Heniek, didn't boys treat you roughly because you're a Jew?"

"This is the way it has always been," he shrugged.

She grumbled with exasperation, "How can you be so satisfied with the way Jews are treated? We can find a better way! We can be free in a Jewish state in *Eretz* Israel!"

"By breaking the law?" he barked. "If we abide by the law, why should they kill Jews? It isn't logical."

"*Oy vey*, Heniek!" Her arms waved like a bird taking flight. "War is never logical!" Her shrill voice bounced from the papered walls. "Do you really think Hitler's idea of an Aryan nation should be logical? Have you read the newspapers? Have you seen the pictures?"

"It's ridiculous to believe the Nazis should try to kill all the Jews in Europe, there are millions of us," Heniek scolded. "Ze'ev Jabotinsky is out of touch with the real world, he's a melodramatic old fool."

Yutka saw the corners of her papa's mouth curl up slightly, "Heniek, Jabotinsky is fifty-eight years old. Ah, I suppose to you that is ancient?" He shook his head and returned to reading his *Torah*.

In her bed that night, in that space between consciousness and sleep, Yutka clearly saw the future of Poland....

> *German soldiers march into Dobrzyń[4] from the east. They run into the synagogue carrying flaming torches. The beautifully polished solid oak woodwork turns orange in the inferno. Flames lap at the elaborate carvings of animals, birds and plants adorning the Holy Ark. The sacred scrolls flash into ashes.*
>
> *The rioters set homes on fire. They kill residents, even Catholic Poles. They kidnap blond, blue eyed, racially suitable, Aryan-looking children after killing their Catholic parents. Kicking in Rozka's front door, they rip the wedding portrait of Rozka and her husband off the wall and smash it to bits.... They shoot Jewish babies like her nephew Jerzyk. They kill pregnant women like her sister....*
>
> *Yutka sat up, breathing heavily through her dry, gaping mouth as if a scream could erupt at any moment. Sweat soaked her flannel nightgown. She told herself, Papa would say what I imagine is far worse than reality could ever be. I wish Papa were right, but I know...*

---

4. *Dobrzyń became Golub-Dobrzyń in 1951*

Chapter 5

Yutka's Decision, April 1939

One Friday evening in April, Yutka stood at the kitchen door, contemplating the living room where the family gathered after Sabbath dinner. A large, framed painting of Mama, Heniek and Rozka hung on the wall above the fireplace, painted before Yutka was born. Below, family photos, gathered since 1888 when Papa was a toddler, crowded the thick, live edge mantel. Shadows from a candle flickered, competing with the light from the fire and the brass lamp next to Papa's chair. Yutka noticed faint scribbles on the wallpaper behind Papa where, when she was three, Yutka had drawn their family of stick people. Mama never washed it away.

The fragrances of cabbage, onions and cloves lingered from the *gołąbki* Mama had served for dinner. Mama sat in her rocking chair, sewing a button on Papa's shirt. Yutka's brother, Heniek, sat on the sofa next to his wife, Sonya, both reading a book. The spicey scent of juniper berries from Papa's pipe tobacco drifted toward the fire as he gazed into the flames.

For months they had argued about illegal immigration, the potential consequences as Hitler advanced in Europe, and Yutka's desire to emigrate. She could argue no more.

Yutka filled her lungs with the scent of home, slowly walked across the rug and stood in front of the brass andirons. The faces of those she loved most turned toward her. She took a trembling breath, lifted her chin, and announced, "I have decided to immigrate to the Land of Israel on Betar's boat. If you must take the risk of staying, I will travel alone."

Mordechai bellowed, "I have asked before, how do you plan to pay for this adventure?"

For the first time in her seventeen years, Yutka did not allow Papa's deep, loud voice to intimidate her. She looked into his angry black eyes. Keeping her chin high, she said, "If you refuse to help me, I will find a way. I must do this, Papa."

"My money will not support this idealistic escapade," he growled. As Mordechai stood up, Heniek and Sonya went to their bedroom and Mama disappeared into the kitchen. The lamp wobbled on the side table next to Mordechai's rocking chair as he stormed out of the house into the cool April evening, his favorite pipe clinched in his teeth, smoke wafting behind him in the night air.

"I'm not doing this to hurt you," Yutka whispered as the door slammed. She stood alone by the crackling fire, trembling as if chilled. She looked around at Heniek's book on the sofa, Mama's mending basket on the floor. A whiff of pipe tobacco still lingered. She knew how deeply her plans hurt her dear parents and brother. "I'm not doing this to hurt you," she whispered to no one. "Please, come with me."

The next day, Yutka rode her bicycle a few blocks to her sister's house, knowing her future depended on her brother-in-law's generosity. She passed rows of three-story brick townhouses but didn't notice the white snowdrops and purple crocus poking through the damp soil or the willow tree branches with swollen buds lining the street. She tapped the brass door knocker, touched the *mezuzah*, then kissed her fingers. As always, she opened the door without waiting. Her nephew dropped the wooden truck his papa had carved for him and ran into her arms.

"*Tata oo, Tata oo,*" he squealed, his two-year-old's tongue unable to pronounce *Tante* Yutka.

"Jerzyk, you're getting so big. You look more like your papa every day." Hugging him in her arms more firmly than usual, she kissed his plump, dimpled cheeks and inhaled the fresh scent of soap, baby powder, and innocence. For a moment, Yutka envied the simplicity of her little nephew's life, still unaware of prevailing anti-Semitism in the world, no awareness or fear of the pending war. His happy giggle filled the room with joy.

Her insides twisted, wondering how old he would be…. Her mind refused to accept that she may never see her family again. She squatted down beside him on the rug, picked up the wooden truck and made a *brrrumm* sound, rolling the wheels across the floor. Then she stood, patted his soft black curls, and faced her pregnant sister. "Looks like that baby is ready to join us," she said. "April is a good month for having a baby." The sisters hugged with Rozka's enormous belly between them as if Yutka hugged the baby too.

Rozka was inches taller than Yutka, and even before pregnancy, Rozka was much stouter, but both had a pretty round face with a low forehead below raven-black, unmanageably wavy hair. The sisters had easy, wide smiles, dark penetrating eyes, and beautifully clear, olive skin.

"It will be very soon, God willing," said Rozka.

"*Shalom*, Yutka," Zigi kissed his sister-in-law on both cheeks as he joined them in the living room.

"*Shalom*, Zigi." She smiled at Zigi and Rozka standing arm in arm. The sun shone on a portrait hanging on the wall behind them. Zigi's father had commissioned the popular artist, Bolesław Barbacki to paint a formal portrait of Rozka and Zigi after their wedding. Barbacki painted a stunningly beautiful likeness, capturing their happiness and spirit with fine strokes and muted tones.

She thought, *I hope what I saw was only a nightmare and not….* Yutka tore her eyes from the painting and drew a breath, reminding herself why she'd come. "I have something to tell you.... I have decided to immigrate to *Eretz* Israel as soon as Betar's boat is ready."

Rozka threw her arms around her younger sister and hugged even tighter despite of her extended belly. "I knew you would decide to go.... You are far braver than I have ever been." She stood back and wiped tears from her face with both hands.

"I'm not brave. I'm afraid to stay. You should come too." She looked from Rozka to Zigi.

"We have discussed it," Rozka's black eyes glanced toward Zigi, "but I will not be traveling for a while." Rozka placed her hands on both sides of her belly. Yutka watched her sister's face glow with love, while Zigi beamed with pride.

"There is one problem." Yutka looked at her shoes as if they might give her strength, then took a deep breath, lifted her heart and raised her chin. "Papa refuses to support the trip and I have not saved enough." Yutka hated to ask for help, but she knew it would not be a burden for her brother-in-law. The Hirsch family owned acres of wheat fields, the grain mill, and several bakeries. And they were the sole importer of tractors, plows, fertilizers, and cement mixing machines. Zigi ran the import branch of the family business while his brother, Max, was a well-respected medical doctor in Dobrzyń.

"I have heard of Jabotinsky's plea for Jews to leave Poland," said Zigi. "If you must go, I will sponsor your trip. When the new baby is old enough to travel, we will take the next boat and join you in *Eretz* Israel. Perhaps by then, the others can be persuaded to join us."

Rozka's voice caught in her throat, "We will need someone to greet us when we arrive in *Eretz* Israel." She took a deep breath. "I will miss you little sister, more than you know," she said in a hoarse whisper.

"Where will you live?" asked Zigi.

"I posted a letter to Uncle Srulik and Aunt Zipporah, but

I couldn't write that I'm immigrating illegally. God forbid the letter should fall into the wrong hands. And I couldn't tell them when I'll arrive."

"Do you know when you will leave Poland?"

"No, the date and location are top-secret. It could take Betar operatives months to charter a ship."

"You will have friends traveling with you?" Rozka wanted to know.

"Yes, Tova, Ester, Lala and Jonas are planning to go"

"Ah, it is good you will not be traveling only with strangers."

Chapter 6

Next Betar Meeting, 1939

Yutka knew she would board the train in Dobrzyń for a port of departure, probably on the Black Sea, then board a boat and navigate to *Eretz* Israel, but beyond that her plans were a mystery.

She and her friends had studied the map pinned to the wall in the Betar meeting room. "How long will the trip take us," one of her friends had contemplated.

"A week I should think," said another, "depending on the port of departure."

"Military-like organization and discipline are absolutely necessary with a group of young immigrants on an over-crowded ship," announced their leader.

Yutka expected crowded conditions, snug, uncomfortable sleeping arrangements and unappetizing, non-kosher meals, but she had not considered the conduct of her fellow passengers. Now she realized that anticipation, mixed with fear and raw emotions triggered by separation from family, would cause tension and anxiety. Since joining Betar at age thirteen, she had worn her Betar uniform and participated in military-like drills, but the necessity for military discipline on the boat hadn't entered her mind.

"You will be divided into platoons of fifty; each will have a platoon leader. We will assign platoon leadership positions to Betar members who have been with us for over four years. Platoon leaders will be responsible for daily roll call, during which complaints and requests can be submitted. These will be reported to the commander who will make decisions within twenty-four hours. There will be no smoking below decks and firearms are strictly prohibited. Misbehavior will be punished; first offence with a private reprimand, next offence with a public reprimand, three-time offenders will be assigned to special work detail. With a fourth transgression, the offender will be tied to a post for up to twelve hours, and if there is a fifth offense, the repeat offender will be removed from the ship at the next port or sent back when the ship returns."

Misbehavior? Who would dare misbehave? We are like-minded refugees fleeing the coming violence, thought Yutka.

"Your assigned bunk will not be comfortable. Please bring your own blanket, soap, towel, and toilet paper. Women and men will be assigned separate compartments. We are considering a family compartment for married Betar members who have young families. The decision will be based on the number of families with children in the final group."

Afterward, Yutka took the leader aside, "I'm concerned about the punishment you outlined. Would you really send a Jew back to the Nazis because he misbehaved on the ship?"

"Ah, kind and thoughtful Yutka. No Betar member would ever follow through with this extreme punishment, however, the threat might help maintain order. But," he put his finger to his lips, "*sha, sha,* don't speak of it."

Before they left the meeting hall, Yutka, Tova, Ester, Lala, and Jonas paid for their passage, and their Betar leader gave them instructions. "Betar officials are searching for an appropriate vessel. It could take days, weeks or months to charter and retrofit but once the ship is ready to smuggle passengers, you will receive a telegram. When it arrives, you will purchase a train ticket to the destination specified. If asked, say you are visiting a sick aunt or going to a cousin's wedding. Most importantly, behave normally, as if this were a routine trip. A Betar member will meet you when you disembark at the appointed destination. He or she will greet you like a family member, and you must play along. We have no idea who might be watching. The Betar member will give you forged travel documents and train tickets to your destination. Go home, pack and be ready."

Chapter 7

Letter to Uncle Srulik and Aunt Zipporah, 1939

Yutka wrote to her uncle Srulik, hoping when she arrived in *Eretz* Israel she could live and work at his vineyard. The letter Yutka mailed in late March finally reached Srulik and Zipporah in June. As Srulik read the letter, deep ridges formed between his heavy eyebrows. He handed it to Zipporah.

Dear Uncle Srulik and Aunt Zipporah,
 How are you?
 I've been busy with school and I attend Betar Youth Group meetings every Wednesday. They keep us up to date on various political activities around the world.
 How do you like living in the Land of Israel? Mama said that you grow grapes and make fine wine to sell in Tel Aviv and you have a big garden to grow food. Maybe there is a job for me there? I look forward to tasting your wine and helping you work in the garden and prepare meals with your produce. But it is a long trip from Poland to Israel over land by train and the sea by boat. The British allow very few immigration certificates.
 Mama sends her love,
 Your loving niece,
 Yutka

"Yutka's letter sounds different. She mentions a long trip and working here? Is she planning to immigrate?" He rubbed his heavy black beard as if it were a genie's lamp that could offer wisdom. "Yutka has always been a strong-willed girl.... She wrote this letter to us in March, three months ago. If illegal immigration is her plan, she can't tell us in case the authorities are reading the mail." He paused for a moment, still stroking his beard. "I've heard of boats filled with Jews making the trip. Some have ended badly. Let us hope she was not on one of the apprehended boats."

"She has our address, but we will watch for news of boats arriving," said Zipporah. "I only hope the rest of the family escapes before Hitler occupies Poland."

Chapter 8

Packing for the Journey, Poland, 1939

Yutka pulled her khaki canvas knapsack from the floor of her wardrobe, removed the schoolbooks, and carried them downstairs to the bookcase in the living room. Her parents, especially Mama, loved the volumes packed on the shelves. As if listening to Mama's soft voice reading poetry aloud, Yutka's fingers danced over the spines of each treasured book until she came to *Pan Tadeusz* by the Polish bard, Adam Mickiewicz. She gently tugged it from the shelf, held the book in both hands and breathed in the scent of leather, ink and paper. Finally, she pushed the leather bound volume back into its place on the shelf and returned to her packing.

As she climbed the stairs back to her room, automatically avoiding the squeaky third step, Yutka remembered the bright resonance of Mama's voice seemed to emerge from her heart as she read the epic poem aloud.

> *Meanwhile, bare my soul heavy with yearning's dull pain,*
> *To those soft woodland hillocks, those meadows, green, gleaming,*
> *Spread wide along each side of the blue-flowing Niemen,*
> *To those fields, which by various grain painted, there lie*
> *Shimmering, with wheat gilded, and silvered with rye;*

> *Where grows the amber mustard, buckwheat white as snow,*
> *Where, with maidenly blushes, clover flowers glow,*
> *And all as if beribboned by green strips of land,*
> *The balks, upon which scattered quiet pear trees stand.*

Adam Mickiewicz told a story of love and conflict between two families, at a time in history when Poland/Lithuania was wiped from the map of Europe, divided between Russia, Prussia, and Austria; a story of revolt against the Russian occupiers and the struggle for independence. Yutka knew she and her comrades would face similar circumstances in the course of creating an independent state of Israel.

On her neatly made bed, Yutka placed a dark blue rain jacket, three summer blouses and skirts, an extra pair of shoes, stockings, underwear, pajamas, toothbrush, tooth powder, a roll of toilet paper, a comb, a hairbrush, and a matchbox filled with pins for her hair. She crossed the hall to the cabinet and gathered a towel, a washcloth, a small wool blanket Mama never used anymore, and a bar of lavender soap she and her mama made together. She smiled as she breathed in the fresh lavender scent.

In the pantry off the kitchen, she found a basket of empty tobacco tins Mama had collected. Yutka picked up a tin, clicked the lid open with her thumbs, and sniffed the residual aroma left from Papa's tobacco, then filled the tin with soap flakes. Returning to her room, she wondered if her laundry would smell like tobacco instead of sunshine.

A cloth bag of clean rags she used for her monthly cycle rested in her top drawer. She hoped she wouldn't need them during the trip. Never considering she would find other uses for the rags during the voyage, she tucked the cloth bag into the bottom of her knapsack.

She took a deep breath and pondered the display across her bed; the sum of possessions she would take to her new homeland. With her back to the art déco dressing table and round-framed mirror, she sat on the padded bench as she gazed at the matching dresser; its drawers filled with fine cotton underwear, silk scarves, woolen socks, flannel nightgowns, and hand-knitted sweaters.

Heniek knocked on the open door and stepped into her room. "I have something for your trip." He handed her an orange canvas package, tied with a twill ribbon.

"What is this Heniek?"

"Look inside," he said. "It's the First Aid Kit Papa gave me when I joined Scouts. I hope you have room in your knapsack."

Yutka untied the twill ribbon and unrolled the canvas package. Inside, she found pockets containing sticky plasters, sachets of ointment, safety pins, gauze, antiseptic, surgical tape, smelling salts, and a small pair of scissors. "You should have this on the boat, in case something happens and maybe when you arrive…."

Yutka stood speechless for a moment. "I will make room for it. This is kind of you, Heniek. Thank you."

She hugged her brother, who was eight years older and several inches taller. He hugged her for a few extra seconds. Her cheek pressed against his chest. She heard him sniffle as she smelled his unique, musky scent.

"I'll miss you terribly, Heniek," she whispered.

He whispered, "Me too."

She walked toward the window, her fingers drifted over the quilt *Safta* D'Vora, Mama's mama, had created just for her. She rested her palm on the warm wood of the art déco wardrobe full of her dresses, skirts, and blouses. She pushed the lace curtains aside and pulled the window open just a bit.

Vegetable and flower gardens surrounded the Lipka family's warm, welcoming home, bounded by their lumber mill. From her window she heard the stamping of hooves as horse teams hauled in fresh-cut logs and the foreman stored them in the yard according to type and size. She watched a construction crew working to prefabricate a barn in the enormous courtyard. Later, the workmen would load the parts onto a long, wide wagon and reassemble the barn on the customer's site.

The chicken coop stood next to a haystack and the cowshed, and bright white domestic ducks waddled nearby. Her everyday chores included gathering eggs and milking the cow. It was Yutka's task to reach under the broody, red hens, avoid their sharp beaks, and retrieve the brown eggs. Yutka also helped Mama churn butter and slowly pasteurize the milk. *I don't mind milking and churning,* she thought, *but I won't miss those nasty hens.*

When she leaned her forehead on the cold glass, her breath fogged the window and masked the world she knew while she imagined her new life.

> *In the garden at her uncle's vineyard in* Eretz Israel, *her gloved hands work the sandy soil, coaxing young vines to produce grapes.... On her hands and knees, she plants seeds in the warm, composted soil. Soon the seeds will grow into melon, squash, strawberries, peppers, and tomatoes... In the orchard, the scent of citrus wafts in the air as she climbs a ladder and reaches beyond the waxy leaves to pick a firm, dimpled sphere. Sinking her thumbnails into the peel, she watches sparks of citrus oil burst into the sunlight and inhales the citrusy fragrance. Sweet orange juice drips from her fingers as she pulls the segments apart and puts one in her mouth. Her eyes close, delicious.*

With her palm, Yutka wiped her condensed breath from the cold glass, revealing Mama in her garden below. She had finished pulling weeds in the flower beds, already full of yellow forsythia, white and orange jonquils, and dense clusters of purple, pink, lavender, and white hyacinths. The sweetly intoxicating aroma wafted through Yutka's window mixed with the smell of lumber and hay. Mama, wearing a heavy blue hand-knit sweater, vigorously hoed the black dirt in the awakening vegetable patch. Yutka watched for several minutes, noticing Mama's strokes were far more aggressive than the soil demanded.

Yutka returned to her packing. She folded the clothes she had placed on the bed and pushed them into her knapsack. Butterflies fluttered in her stomach as she thought about traveling on a boat crowded with people from countries across Europe; Jewish strangers whose customs, rituals, and language might differ from her own. In Dobrzyń, she rarely met new people. Since her childhood, the weekly routine had been the same. Papa went to work and to *shul*, Mama cooked, cleaned, worked in her kitchen garden, and volunteered at the library.

On Fridays they ate Sabbath dinner, usually with her sister Rozka, brother-in-law Zigi, Heniek, and his wife Sonya. Uncle Srulik and Aunt Zipporah had joined them for Sabbath dinners until they emigrated. She missed those family gatherings when Papa and Uncle Srulik told stories of her grandfather Fiebush Lipka's adventures when Papa and Srulik were children.

Fiebush Lipka had been good friends with Dobrzyń's Catholic Priest, Father Maximilian, who preached benevolence to all people, but Father Maximilian died in 1934, when Yutka was thirteen. The new priest assigned to the Dobrzyń parish was Father Jarzębski, an active member of the anti-Semitic movement known as *Endecja*. Jarzębski's anti-Semitic sermons quickly changed Dobrzyń's companionable complexion. Soon, Jews were likely to be harassed and assaulted, especially if they walked the streets at night. The Polish authorities no longer provided facilities for the Jewish population of Dobrzyń so the Lipka's property became the refuge for both children and adults.

During the daylight house, the property teemed with horse-drawn carts but after closing time, the nature of the traffic changed. Their home and adjacent lumber yard became inhabited by youngsters of all ages. They enjoyed physical activities like soccer, volleyball, running sprints, hurdles, and distance jumping into pits of sawdust. In the barn, Yutka's papa rigged swings and a net above a pit of sawdust so they could try trapeze. The younger children were content with their *Policemen and Thieves* game.

Members of youth movements from various Jewish political affiliations met to enjoy the freedom of good-natured political debates, arguing the logic behind the variations of the Zionist movement. Whether Revolutionary, Labor or Revisionist they argued the process but they all agreed that someday, there should be a Free State of Israel.

Chapter 9

Marseille, France, March 1939

While Yutka and her friends waited for a telegram, Betar Agents found an appropriate vessel owned by the Greek shipping magnate, Mr. Minakoulis.

Minakoulis had chartered the ship to transport alcoholic liquors to the United States during Prohibition and had no qualms about smuggling Jews instead. Mr. Minakoulis assured Betar Officials the *Parita's* crew of fifteen seasoned maritime smugglers were well-qualified to crew the voyage to *Eretz* Israel and, he promised, seven days after leaving the port of Constanța, smaller boats would meet them off the coast of Cyprus to smuggle them safely through the British blockade while keeping his ship far away from British waters.

The barely sea-worthy forty-year-old ship slowly cruised from Marseille to the smaller port at Sète, where preparations would be less conspicuous. Once modified, the ship would sail from France to the Rumanian Port of Constanța to board Polish and Rumanian refugees.[5]

Betar hired Herschel Waxman to supply and retrofit the *Parita*. He expected her to arrive that morning. While he waited at the Port of Sète, he watched stars in the deep purple

---

5. Romania became the predominant spelling around 1975.

sky yield to the fingers of magenta, melon, and amber bursting across the horizon, reflecting in the mirror-like surface of the Mediterranean Sea.

He walked the weathered dock beside the moored boats, listening to the water lap against their hulls, smelling coffee, and watching the fishing boats gently sway as the dock began to come to life. A black twill captain's hat covered his bald dome. With a heavy, gray-streaked black beard and broad amicable smile, he introduced himself to fisherman and merchants, while getting a feel for the trustworthy gents among them. He needed to identify loyal merchants who would sell him lumber, coal and other supplies without notifying the authorities. His sixth sense for recognizing virtuous people helped him identify the vendors he could trust.

✡

With his tape measure and note pad, Herschel inspected the *Parita*. He figured the ship could carry a maximum of 750 passengers, no more, but she needed a lot of work. The hull had nearly rusted through in several places, and the engine room needed the help of a skilled mechanic. *We'll need an expert to keep the old girl moving.* He sent a telegram to his Russian friend, Serioja, suggesting Serioja join the Greek crew once the ship reached Constanța.

He notified Betar Officials he expected his workman to complete the repairs, retrofit and supply by June.

During daylight hours, they worked to make the vessel seaworthy. Sparks hissed like fireworks as they reinforced her rusted hull. To avoid the attention of French guards, a barge unloaded lumber and supplies during the night. The smell of fresh-cut pine mingled with the bitter scent of coal as they built compartments with floor to ceiling bunks below deck. They cleaned and upgraded the galley where a cook could prepare meals for the captain and crew and manage the refugees' meals.

They rigged a system to hoist buckets of seawater to fill big barrels to create showers and built hygiene facilities so waste could be washed directly into the sea.

Herschel met with his long-time friend, Adras Alexopoulos, a food merchant. In his Yiddish accented French, Herschel said, "We'll need supplies to feed about 750 people. Do you have suggestions for such a large group?"

"I'll supply all the tinned meals you want. I usually sell them as combat rations for armies all over the world. With the threat of war, my suppliers are pumping them out as fast as they can. I have stock in my warehouse. You can purchase what you need." Entrepreneur that he was, Adras did not offer to discount his supply.

Herschel pulled his small notebook and the tiny stub of a pencil from his shirt pocket. While rubbing his hairy chin, he made a few calculations. "I'll need 16,000 tinned meals, two dozen packages of dehydrated meat and a few crates of onions, turnips, jugs of oil, and bags of flour. The captain and crew will expect more robust meals. We're likely to have extra passengers and there could be delays. It is a fine balance," said Herschel, taking off his hat and rubbing his bald dome, "stocking enough to feed everyone while allowing space for as many refugees as possible. I figure the space required for another day of supplies for 750 passengers means six or seven left behind. I hope this will be enough."

Chapter 10

France 1939

Herschel received a letter from Reuben Hecht, Betar's *Aliyah Bet* leader in Europe. Despite its cryptic wording, Herschel understood he would have fifty more passengers than he planned for.

Hecht organized operations to smuggle Jews from all over Europe, especially Germany and Austria, through Switzerland and across the French border. In Paris, he bribed a hotel owner to hide them until he could arrange for forged documents. Fifty of them would board the *Parita* as soon as she was ready, even before she sailed to the Port of Constanța on the Black Sea, where she would take on the 750 Polish and Rumanian evacuees Herschel had planned for.

When they finished the retrofit in June, and the ship returned to Marseille, Herschel hoped the *Parita* would make many trips and bring thousands of Jews to *Eretz* Israel. He informed the captain regarding the fifty additional passengers waiting in Paris.

"I think it is best to anchor the *Parita* near the island of Château d'If," suggested Captain Vladimir Mikhailovich. "There, Hecht's people can climb aboard unnoticed."

"I agree. I'll find a way to transport them from the train to Château d'If."

Hoisting the Panamanian flag, the captain quietly cast off in the middle of the night to sail the short distance from Marseille to the island of Château d'If. He carried counterfeit papers indicating the *Parita* hauled coal.

Herschel sent a telegram to the little hotel in Paris:

MEET ME IN MARSEILLE STOP
YOUR BROTHER HERSCHEL STOP

This signaled to the refugees the *Parita* was ready for boarding. The Jews from Germany, Austria and France, who had been hiding in a Paris hotel, boarded a train to Marseille on their way to the *Parita*.

In Marseille, Herschel enlisted the support of his friend, the harbormaster. "When the train arrives from Paris, we'll need help transferring the refugees to the *Parita* anchored at Château d'If. The timing must be perfect to avoid alerting the authorities."

"How many refugees?"

"About fifty. Some left their homes months ago," said Herschel. "Their status will be obvious. They will not look like tourists."

"As soon as the train arrives, the refugees can walk from the station to the dock. I'll post a few men at the station to function as guides, the rest of us will be waiting in our boats. We have plenty of fishing boats and manpower," said the harbormaster. "Don't worry Herschel, you have many friends in this port. We will quickly and safely transport the refugees to the *Parita*."

Later that evening, Herschel enjoyed a cold bottle of Kronenbourg beer on the boat of his friend, Adras Alexopoulos, who had sold him the food and supplies he needed for the voyage. "The harbor master is organizing a flotilla of fishermen to take the refugees to the *Parita,* but we still need a strategy for getting them from the train station and onto fishing boats without drawing the attention of the French police. They all have forged papers but in their shabby clothes, they will not look like normal tourists. Any ideas?"

Adras took a big gulp of his beer and wiped the foam from his mustache with his sleeve. "Ah, yes, I have idea! I am leader of my sons' Boy Scout troop here in Marseille," Adras grinned at Herschel, his black eyes sparkling with mischief under his hedgerow of eyebrows. "I have a plan that will distract everyone, including the police, you can count on me and my boys."

On the evening the refugees' train arrived from Paris, Adras gathered the Boy Scout Band and their instruments. "Come along boys, show this port what you've got!" The boys banged their cymbals, beat their drums and blew their horns with abandon while people cheered and small children danced in the street. The loud, discorded little band marched away from the docks, capturing the attention of police, tourists, and residents, leading them away from the evacuees like the Pied Piper of Hamelin.

While the travel-worn refugees scurried through the dark like dry leaves in the wind, a man and his wife, with two little girls, approached Commander Leibovitz. "Commander, I am Mayor Edelman," he said in Yiddish. "As a government official in France, my life and the lives of my wife and daughters are in danger if the Germans invade France. We must immigrate to *Eretz* Israel."

"How old are you and your wife?" asked Leibovitz.

"What do our ages have to…" His wife squeezed his arm and Edelman changed his attitude. "Ah, I am forty, my wife, Joséphine is twenty-eight."

Leibovitz sat on his heels to talk to the little girls, eye to eye. He asked the oldest, "*Quel est votre nom?*"

"Priscilla."

When he asked the younger girl her name, she hid behind her mother's skirt.

"My baby sister is shy," said Priscilla. "Her name is Rochelle."

"How old are you, Priscilla?"

"I am four and Rochelle is three. This is my doll. Her name is Babette."

"Babette has pretty long hair just like yours." Then he looked at Rochelle, peeking out from behind her mother's skirt.

The little girls reminded Leibovitz of dear friends he left behind in Switzerland when he was a boy. Their long black hair, plaited into French braids, fell over their shoulders and their cotton dresses had big, starched bows tied in the back. Leibovitz knew their dark eyes, olive skin and sharp noses would identify them as Jews, and he feared what they would face if the Nazis invaded France. Against his better judgment, Leibovitz charged a hefty fee and gave them a bunk number. "You may board, but you need to understand, most of our passengers will board at the Port of Constanța, and we will be quite crowded. The food will not be tasty or kosher."

"Where do we load our belongings?" asked Edelman, looking over his shoulder toward an open bed truck laden with furniture, steamer trunks and crates.

"I'm sorry, there is only room for a small satchel each."

"Well, what do we do with our belongings?" his voice incredulous.

Leibovitz looked at his manifest, placed his pencil's eraser next to Edelman's name, and without a word, made it clear he was ready to eliminate them from the roster.

"Ah, I see," said Edelman. He turned to his wife, who was still squeezing his arm.

She wiped her tears of gratitude and mumbled to Leibovitz, "*Merci beaucoup.*"

Joséphine Edelman walked to the truck, fumbled with bigger bags, and repacked four small satchels. As she walked back to her family, she turned and gazed at the truckload of furniture and belongings, their possessions, left behind.

Leibovitz understood her pain as she stared at the truck bed piled with treasures she would never see again. No doubt she had spent time deciding on the most important items to bring on the trip, never realizing everything would be left behind on the dock for looters to enjoy.

Leibovitz led them to a fishing boat. As the oars quietly splashed through the water and the fishing boat disappeared into the dark toward Château d'If, Leibovitz thought, *I'm certain Mr. Edelman will not be happy with the accommodations, but I cannot leave those little girls behind.*

Chapter 11

Shabbat Dinner, July 1939

Bluma smiled sadly as her fingers deftly stuffed a goose neck skin with a mixture of flour, finely chopped goose liver, heart, gizzard, and onions caramelized in rendered goose fat, making a *helzel* for the *Shabbat* stew.

She picked up the needle and thread that waited on the counter, sewed the open end of the *helzel* and added it to the enormous pot with the potatoes, beef broth, marrow bones, barley, onions, beans, paprika, turmeric, cumin, and cayenne. Bluma had prepared this favorite dish for Sabbath and holiday dinners since Yutka was a little girl.

Shabbat was a day of rest. *You shall not kindle a fire in any of your dwellings on the Sabbath* (Exodus 35:3). So, all day Friday, Mama worked to assemble the *tshulent*. The pot would simmer overnight on a low flame for Saturday's meal.

Drawn by the wafting aroma of the onions and spices, Yutka came into the kitchen. "Mama, it smells delicious, you're making *tshulent*! My favorite!"

"Every day, I worry today you are leaving…." said Bluma without turning away from the stove. "I hope there is no telegram before we eat *tshulent* tomorrow." Bluma's quiet voice disappeared with the steam as she covered the pot and lowered the flame.

Yutka couldn't resist peeking under the lid, allowing the mouthwatering aromatic steam to waft around her. Normally, Mama would scold Yutka for thieving the aroma. Not today.

While Sonja, her brother's wife, braided two loaves of *challah* and put them in the oven, Yutka helped Bluma prepare chicken soup for *Shabbat* dinner. Usually, Mama made dumplings from matzo, rendered chicken fat and egg, then boiled them in the chicken broth, but today she wrapped goose liver, onion, garlic and cloves into little pockets of dough. "Mama you're making *kreplach*? Today is not a holiday."

Mama turned from the counter and cupped Yutka's round face in her warm, floury hands, "Yes, my Yutka, but *kreplach* are also your favorite and you will..." Mama took a deep breath, shook her head and turned back toward the counter. The rest of the sentence stuck in her heart.

When Mordechai and Heniek came home from synagogue, the family gathered around the dining table. As the sun began to set, Mama lit two candles held in tall, silver candle sticks. Three times she scooped the heat and light toward her face with both hands. Then she covered her face with her warmed hands and sang the blessing.

> *Barukh ata Adonai Eloheinu, Melekh ha'olam, asher kid'shanu b'mitzvotav v'tzivanu l'hadlik ner shel Shabbat.*

> *Blessed are You, Lord our God, King of the universe, Who has sanctified us with His commandments and commanded us to light the Sabbath lamp.*

Before Bluma served the chicken soup and dumplings from the tureen she had placed on the table next to the cloth-covered *challah*, Mordechai started the short ritual by reciting the passage from Genesis describing the creation of the *Shabbat*.[6]

---

6. See Genesis 2:1-4.

Vay'hi erev vay'hi voker
yom hashishi.
Vay'chulu hashamayim v'haaretz v'chol tz'vaam.
Vay'chal Elohim bayom hash'vi-i m'lachto asher asah.
Vayishbot bayom hash'vi-i mikol m'lachto asher asah.
Vay'varech Elohim et yom hash'vi-i vay'kadeish oto,
ki vo shavat mikol m'lachto asher bara Elohim laasot.

And there was evening and there was morning,
    the sixth day.
The heaven and the earth were finished, and all their array.
On the seventh day God finished the work that God had been
    doing, and God ceased on the seventh day from all the
    work that God had done.
And God blessed the seventh day and declared it holy, because
    on it God ceased from all the work of creation that God
    had done.

Everyone sat quietly while Mordechai turned to the sideboard, took the old, patinaed, and dented silver cup decorated with vines, leaves and bunches of grapes into his palm. The *Kiddush* cup had once belong to his papa, Fiebush Lipka, and had been used by generations of Lipka's before him. Mordechai filled it with red wine and chanted *Kiddush*.

Baruch atah, Adonai Eloheinu, Melech haolam, borei p'ri
    hagafen.
Baruch atah, Adonai Eloheinu, Melech haolam, asher kid'shanu
    b'mitzvotav v'ratzah vanu, v'Shabbat kodsho b'ahavah
    uv'ratzon hinchilanu, zikaron l'maaseih v'reishit. Ki hu
    yom t'chilah l'mikra-ei kodesh, zecher litziat Mitzrayim.
    Ki vanu vacharta, v'otanu kidashta, mikol haamim.
    V'Shabbat kodsh'cha b'ahavah uv'ratzon hinchaltanu.
    Baruch atah, Adonai, m'kadeish haShabbat.

> *Blessed are You, Lord our God, Sovereign of all, Creator of the fruit of the vine.*
> *Blessed are You, Lord our God, Sovereign of all, who finding favor with us, sanctified us with commandments. In love and favor, You made the holy Sabbath our heritage as a reminder of the work of Creation. As first among our sacred days, it recalls the Exodus from Egypt. You chose us and set us apart from the peoples. In love and favor You have given us Your holy Shabbat as an inheritance. Blessed are You, Lord, who sanctifies Sabbath.*

The family replied, "Amen." Then Papa lifted the silver tray holding two loaves of *challah*, removed the embroidered cloth, tore off small pieces and passed them to everyone around the table. When everyone had their bread, he recited the blessing:

> *Baruch atah, Adonai*
> *Eloheinu melech haolam,*
> *hamotzi lechem min haaretz.*

> *Blessed are You, Lord our God,*
> *Sovereign of all,*
> *Who brings forth bread from the earth.*

The family said, "Amen," tasted the bread, and said, "*Shabbat Shalom.*"

Shabbat had officially begun.

Mama ladled the chicken soup into bowls, giving Yutka two extra *kreplach.*

Bluma, Mordechai, Heniek, and Sonya bowed their faces toward their soup bowls, hiding their gloomy faces. Everyone knew the telegram would come soon and this would be their last *Shabbat* together before Yutka left for *Eretz* Israel.

✡

On Saturday, Rozka, Zigi, Jerzyk and their new baby, Rebekah, joined Mama, Papa, Heniek, Sonya and Yutka for dinner. "This is the best *tshulent* I have ever tasted! Thank God for our good fortune," said Zigi.

Unusually quiet, little Jerzyk focused on the small bites of potato and beans Rozka put in front of him. He ate with his fingers while his new baby sister, Rebekah, slept in a wooden cradle Bluma's papa had made before Bluma was born.

Bluma gazed around the table at her family as they enjoyed the meal she had lovingly prepared. Her sleeping granddaughter surely warmed her heart, but as Bluma cast her eyes toward the cradle, sorrow and fear darkened her face.

Rozka tried to keep the conversation light, "Mama, your garden is so beautiful this year. The eggplant should be ripe soon."

"Yes," Bluma replied. "The plants enjoy this season's rain and sunshine, and Yutka kept the weeds away."

Although the newspapers reported alarming war activities, they avoided discussing the terrifying topic during dinner. They laughed at little Jerzyk's excitement over feeding himself bits of potato but a gloomy shadow lingered over them like a disagreeable miasma. No one mentioned the telegram Yutka had waited for since April, as if it were a lurking monster about to tear the family apart.

Chapter 12

The Telegram

The next morning, July 9, 1939, there came a knock on the door at the Lipka residence.

Bluma wiped her hands on her apron and answered the door, "*Tak. Co chcesz?*"

A courier dressed in a gray uniform replied in Polish, "Telegram for Miss Yutka Lipka."

"Thank you," whispered Bluma, giving him a *zloty*.

She closed the door and dropped to the bench below the hats, coats and sweaters hanging on pegs by the door. The telegram quivered in her hand.

Yutka came out of her room and down the stairs, "Who was at the…?" She saw the sorrow in her mama's eyes. Bluma pushed the telegram toward Yutka as if it weighed a thousand kilos. Before opening the envelope, Yutka sat on the bench and hugged her mama. "I love you, Mama, but I must do this." For once, she allowed Mama to see her tears.

With trembling hands, Yutka read the telegram aloud:

TAKE MIDNIGHT TRAIN TO WARSAW STOP UNCLE KAROL WILL MEET YOU AT THE STATION STOP

Who is Uncle Karol?" asked Bluma.

"I have no idea. I'm to meet a Betar member and pretend he is family... to avoid suspicion."

Bluma visibly shuddered.

It had been seven months since Yutka paid for her passage on the *Parita*. She thought she was ready, but with her heart in her throat, she gaped at the telegram. Suddenly, it was no longer a plan for her future. Her escape from Poland was imminent. As if her lungs had no air, she held the yellow paper and leaned her head on Mama's shoulder.

After a long hug, Yutka went back to her room.

Filled with an odd mixture of sadness, trepidation and exhilaration, she tipped the contents of her knapsack onto her bed and slowly sorted and repacked everything she would take into her new life, adding a new pair of sandals and the First Aid Kit Heniek had given her. She was sure she had what she needed for the seven-day voyage and the first few days after her arrival. Into a side pocket, she tucked the copy of *Pan Tadeusz* her mama had given her in April, along with a family photo taken in May after Rebekah was born.

Later that Sunday, the family gathered to eat leftover *tshulent* but there was little conversation. The clock on the mantel ticked, cutlery scrapped china. Finally, Yutka broke the silence. "The *tshulent* is even better today, Mama. And look, Jerzyk is so cute." The two-year-old put a bite of potato in his little mouth. "He has discovered his new favorite food."

Everyone laughed and watched him enjoy his potato, but their eyes remained sad.

✡

Yutka stood in the living room, the knapsack on her back. She fiercely hugged her family members one at a time, Mama, Papa, Heniek, Sonya, Rozka, Zigi, and Jerzyk. She held her tiny niece one last time, kissed her downy head, then returned her to Rozka's arms.

Papa grabbed Yutka for another hug and whispered in her ear as he handed her a bundle of US dollars. "Yutka, put this in your money belt, you will need it when you reach *Eretz* Israel."

"I love you, Papa," Yutka whispered as she wiped her tears.

She lifted her chin, looked into the face of each family member, then walked out the front door and turned toward the train station, ignoring her pounding heart.

✡

She began her journey under a dark new moon. The golden glow of oil-burning streetlamps lined the street like a disappearing tunnel leading to the train station. The air was warm and still. At this hour, no one walked the streets, and the houses were mostly dark. She listened to her heels click on the sidewalk, and to her heavy breath.

Certain she would never return to Dobrzyń, she stopped halfway to the station and absorbed the picturesque village where she grew up, etching memories into her heart.

> *The heavy perfume of vivid red corn poppies, and the sweet aroma of purple Iris wafts around her.*
>
> *Youngsters of all ages and various Jewish political affiliations enjoy good-natured political debates, and sport activities at the Lipka property.... The children laugh, play stickball in the summer and throw snowballs in winter.*
>
> *Her voice happy and bright, wearing an apron, Mama calls Yutka, Heniek and Rozka to dinner.*

> *Papa takes Yutka on a tour of the two-hundred-year-old Golub Castle. She is afraid to climb the stone stairs in the cool, dark turret. She reaches for his hand.*

"How old are you miss?" asked the ticket agent.

"Seventeen."

"Why should a girl so young travel alone?"

"My elderly aunt needs my help," she answered softly. She pushed her money through the slot at the base of the window and he gave her the ticket.

As she sat on a wooden bench, waiting for the midnight train from Dobrzyń to Warsaw, she kept an eye out for Tova, Ester, Lala, and Jonas, Betar members who had paid for passage. As if he didn't see her, fellow Betar member, Daniel Pieniek, suddenly appeared at the other end of the bench. He sat down, lit a cigarette, and blew smoke into the night air. "The others, Tova, Ester, Lala, and Jonas, also received telegrams," he said while looking at the train tracks, his elbows resting on his knees, the cigarette pinched between thumb and index finger, "but they were told to wait for the next boat, I came to tell you."

"Are you coming?" she asked softly, gazing down at the ticket in her hand as if she were alone on the bench.

"No, tomorrow I'm going back to school in France." He spoke softly, even though there seemed to be no one else nearby. "Go in peace."

He snuffed his cigarette under his heel on the concrete and disappeared like the smoke. Daniel and his sister, Hania, had been Yutka's dear friends since childhood. Yutka wondered when she would see them again.

At midnight, the incoming train screeched to a halt, breaking the silence. An ugly weightiness hung in the atmosphere as passengers emerged and swiftly disappeared into the damp night. *I am doing the right thing*, she told herself, as she tried to disregard the tug in her heart pulling her toward her family.

She climbed the steps. She found her seat. The whistle blew. Steam blasted around the wheels. The train gained speed.

I hope they will follow. As the train gained speed, the clank of the wheels seemed to repeat, *they must join me—they must join me—they must join me.*

Chapter 13

Train to Constanța

Beyond her reflection in the dark window, rows of streetlights blurred through her tears as the train gained speed and Dobrzyń disappeared. In the preceding days, she hadn't slept well, knowing this day would come soon. She felt as if the telegram had arrived just moments ago. The past twelve hours hadn't been enough time to say her goodbyes.

Yutka leaned her head on the window. The vibration and gentle rock of the train had a calming effect on her jittery nerves, and she fell into a dreamless sleep. She awoke with a jolt when the sun burst over the horizon. She watched as the train passed fields of tall sunflowers with their heavy heads turning in unison toward the morning sun and fields of wheat roiled by the breeze the train created. In the distance, she watched farmers in a row, simultaneously swinging their scythes, beginning an early wheat harvest.

Saba Fiebush must have traveled this same route many times, she thought.

Farming methods in rural Poland hadn't changed since Fiebush Lipka traveled through Europe early in the century. Following the column of scythe-wielding farmers, women and children gathered and bundled the cut wheat, leaving a cloud of dust in their wake. Behind them, a group of peasant women in long skirts, many with babies tied to their backs, gleaned what the harvesters left behind. Their toddlers, too young to work, skittered behind them, gathering what their little hands could manage.

As she disembarked in Warsaw, a stranger made eye contact and nodded ever so slightly. An invisible communication between them confirmed their association. A grin came over his narrow face. His arm lifted in a wide wave, and he hurried toward her. "So glad to see you," he said, hugging and kissing her on both cheeks.

She greeted him with hugs and kisses as if he were a beloved uncle rather than a bearded older man she'd never met before. As they hugged, he slipped forged papers into her hand, along with train tickets for her journey. "Follow me," he whispered. With her arm folded over his, they strolled toward another boarding platform as if they hadn't a care in the world. The old man kissed her on both cheeks and said, "*Leichi l'shalom,* go in peace." As the stranger dissolved into the crowd, she boarded the train that would eventually take her to the Rumanian Port of Constanța.

Yutka settled into a window seat facing the rear of the train.

"Hello, are you going to Constanța?" asked the man in the window seat across from her. His brown leather satchel sat on the luggage rack above him, next to a well-worn wedge-shaped mandolin case with a bowlback and leather chest strap. The man looked very German, with thick blond hair, square jaw, full lips, and eyes as blue as an iceberg lit from within. For a terrifying instant Yutka thought she was on the wrong train.

"Yes," she answered in a crisp voice. She forced herself to relax and breath as others joined them in the passenger coach.

"My name is Yaakov. *Jak masz na imię?*"

Before she could tell him her name, an old woman stumbled into the train car, wobbled and bumped into Yutka's knees as she tried to lift her *walizka* to the rack above the seat next to Yutka.

With a charming smile, the German-looking gentleman quickly stood and helped the old lady with her bag.

"*Sheynem dank*," whispered the breathless old Jewess.

When the old lady had settled into her seat, the man across from Yutka tried again to engage her in conversation, "Where are you from?"

"Dobrzyń," she answered, too uneasy to enjoy a conversation with the stranger. She could focus only on her family and the forged papers she carried.

"I'm from Warsaw. Are you traveling alone?"

"Yes."

"Me too. Would you like a cup of coffee?" he proffered his thermos flask. "It's fresh."

"No, thank you," she said, her voice full of grates and corners, making it clear she was not interested in friendly chit-chat.

Finally, he settled back and leaned his head against the window. As his long dark lashes closed over his beautiful blue eyes, and his breathing slowed, she finally looked at him more closely. *He must be several years older than me*, she thought. She studied his perfectly tailored clothing, flawlessly pressed trousers, and starched shirt. As her gaze fell to his full lips, his knee twitched and accidentally bumped hers. Her heart leaped. This handsome and debonair gentleman made her uneasy.

Yutka stared out the train window, facing the past. Tall church steeples announced quaint villages that looked like toys beyond the rolling fields. Ancient, decrepit castles occasionally dotted the landscape while lazy summer rivers flowed into sparkling clear blue lakes. Fields of oil-rich rapeseed flowers glowed in the bright yellow sunshine and a gentle breeze danced over the waving golden wheat fields.

At the border town of Shniatim, officials boarded the train to check tickets and travel documents. Yutka put on her most convivial smile, handed him her ticket and documents. With a stern expression, he paused for a moment, looking at her face as if he could hear the wild beat of her heart. He examined her documents. She held her breath. Finally, he nodded and handed the papers back to her. She tried to keep her face neutral and not show her relief as sweat trickled between her breasts.

The old lady sitting next to Yutka was not so fortunate, "These papers are counterfeit," snarled the official. "Come with me."

As if she held an anvil in her lap, Yutka forced herself to stay in her seat. The air in their train car became deathly still as the passengers tried not to watch the official man-handle the old woman. Yutka turned her face toward the window as if the train zooming past held her interest. The gentleman across from Yutka, Yaakov, began to rise from his seat to help the old lady, but Yutka surprised both herself and Yaakov when she pressed her foot to his shin. Their eyes met. He nodded slightly and settled back into his seat.

Their fellow passengers sat like stone, staring at nothing. At the last moment, before the official hauled the frail old woman down the passageway, Yutka looked over and the old lady made eye contact, as if to say, "Help me."

Yutka's heart pounded, *I wish I could...*, she thought, then glanced away. She knew helping the old Jewess would end her escape to *Eretz* Israel. *I am a refugee, too*, she thought. Silently thanking God and the Betar operatives for her skillfully forged papers, she lifted her chin, looked out the window and watched the interlocking maze of tracks as the whistle blew and the train began to move. Silent tension in the hot, humid train car felt like a single withheld breath.

She noticed all of the passengers were close to her age, except for Yaakov. *How many are headed for the Parita?* she wondered. She suspected everyone in the train car carried forged documents.

The conductor came by, peered inside the coach, slammed the door closed and locked it. Yaakov leaned forward and whispered to Yutka, "Why are we locked in?" The tone of his voice had changed from beguiling to alarmed. She saw that his anxiety matched her own.

"If you were a Betar member, you would know. They told us that authorities would seal the train cars during the trip from Shniatim to Constanța. The Romanian government doesn't want Jews getting off the train and staying in their country." Her voice sounded confident, but her stomach twisted.

Chapter 14

Constanţa, Rumania, July 12, 1939

When the train screeched to a halt in Constanţa, Yaakov stood and turned to retrieve his satchel and mandolin. Pausing for just a moment, he noticed the old lady's *walizka* isolated on the luggage rack. Wondering what had become of the old woman, he shivered as if a sudden arctic breeze blew through the hot railway carriage.

Although he didn't know her name, Yaakov sensed Yutka's strength and determination as she stood to leave the train. He followed her as they joined the jostling crowd on the humming platform. He had known her for less than twenty-four hours, but he already knew she would be his wife. Young and petite, she had a round face and dark eyes like pools of ink that snapped with intelligence and drew him closer despite her efforts to dissuade him.

He followed her, wondering where she planned to spend the night, but there were hundreds of refugees leaving the platform, all of them trying to weave their way through traffic to find food and overnight accommodation.

Cyclists and horse-drawn wagons filled the streets. When Yaakov tried to cross, a bus horn blared, *aah-ooh-gah, aah-ooh-gah*. He lost sight of Yutka in the mayhem.

✡

Yutka walked through the narrow streets and dark cobblestoned alleys. Finally, she stopped a friendly-looking young woman who carried a toddler on her hip, "*Kannst du mir bitte helfen?*" she asked, showing the woman the slip of paper with the address of the youth hostel where she would stay the night.

The blonde, blue-eyed woman, much taller than Yutka, pointed, "Just two streets over," she said in German, then hurried on her way as if talking to a Jew frightened her.

"*Danke*," nodded Yutka.

When she found the address, Yutka paused for a few moments. The little cottage had probably been an elegant vicarage many years before. Weathered bricks arched above the diamond-shaped muntin windows. Even from across the street, she could smell the dense honeysuckle that nearly covered the peeling blue shutters and climbed over the bricks and onto the low-pitched gray slate roof. Her shoes clicked on the cobbled street. She breathed the hearty scent of celery, parsley, thyme and lovage mixed with the smoke from wood stoves.

When she knocked, a wrinkled and bent white-haired woman opened the heavy, ornately carved door. Even shorter than Yutka and quite stout, the woman's welcoming smile revealed few remaining teeth. Her eyes looked like restless beads behind thick glasses as she looked in both directions. "*Willkommen.*" Her voice quivered with age.

As Yutka offered her hand, "Hallo, I'm Yutka…," the old woman pulled her into the cottage with unexpected strength and closed the wooden door.

The creases around the old woman's smile grew deeper, "*Ja, Ja. Willkommen*, Yootka." She spoke an unfamiliar German dialect but communicated well enough. Yutka relaxed a little, knowing she was in the right place.

The old woman's small hands with swollen joints proffered a chipped blue plate holding a slice of dark bread and a sprinkle of salt, the traditional Rumanian welcome.

"*Danke*," whispered Yutka as a fresh sea breeze through the open window fluffed the lace curtains and freshened the cottage. She looked around for a place to sit among the other Jewish refugees seated on mismatched furniture. She found a spot among the others on the floor. As she slid her back down the wall, Yutka noticed that the red, blue and yellow Persian rug had once been exotic and expensive, but with years of sunshine and traffic, it was now faded and threadbare.

With her back against the wall, she spoke to the redheaded young woman next to her. "*Hallo*, I'm Yutka. I come from Poland."

"*Hallo*, I am Oshrah, I come from Cluj, a village northwest of Constanța.

"Are you taking the boat to *Eretz* Israel?" asked Yutka.

"*Ja*," said Oshrah, with a distant voice. "Are you frightened?"

"*Ja!*" said Yutka. "I've never been away from my family for more than a day."

"Same!" said Oshrah.

Later, as yellow and orange light through the leaded glass cast diamond pattern shadows onto the wall above Yutka and Oshrah, the old lady served each of her guests a mug of chicken soup and a slice of *schwarzbrot*.

Curling up on the cottage floor to sleep next to Oshrah and other girls their age, it seemed Yutka had just closed her eyes when the old woman woke them offering a small breakfast of hard-boiled eggs and more dark bread.

Yutka, Oshrah and the other girls thanked the old woman for her hospitality, then found their way through the alleys to join the mass of strangely quiet refugees surging toward the harbor. Their faces were somber as they clutched a *walizka* or knapsack filled with their worldly belongings. As the crowd moved toward the *Parita*, Yutka watched the heavily armed police shoulder their weapons. Their animosity charge the air like a thunderstorm. She knew they would just as soon mow them down like wheat as allow them to leave the country.

At one point, the crowd parted enough for Yutka to see the boat tied to the pier and the dappled spots of rust on the faded red hull. She was astonished at the vessel's small size. *How can there be room for all of these people?*

Chapter 15

Boarding the *Parita*

Commander of the *Parita*, Erwin Leibovitz, stood on the dock next to the ship as the rusty old vessel bobbed against the fenders at the Port of Constanța. He was the tallest man on the dock. His short curly brown hair merged with his beard around close-set penetrating hazel eyes and long narrow nose. His soft furry face looked even younger than his twenty years.

Betar officials had persuaded port authorities to grant permission to dock the *Parita* and board the fleeing Jews at Constanța. The Polish and Rumanian governments were eager to rid their countries of Jews.

As the morning mist drifted up from the sea, Leibovitz noticed a bow-legged older gentleman wearing a mariner's cap. Apparently, the old man and his stained and scratched leather sailor's duffel had been around the world many times. The sailor's weathered, jovial, square face, with a bulbous nose and bushy salt-bleached eyebrows, beamed with confidence and warmth. His cheerful gray eyes locked onto Leibovitz.

"*Guten Morgen*, you must be Commander Leibovitz. I'm Serioja," he said in a raspy voice with a heavy Russian accent. "Herschel Waxman asked me to meet the *Parita* here. I'm to be the second engineer." The friendly Russian shook hands with Leibovitz.

"Ah yes, happy to meet you Serioja. Herschel told us that if anyone can keep this old girl running, it's you. Welcome to the *Parita*. You'll find the captain in the wheelhouse."

Most of the refugees were between fifteen and twenty-five years old and members of Betar Youth groups. As the ship's roster grew however, Betar officials had made a few exceptions, allowing strong, healthy non-members to join the voyage. Non-members, including Yaakov, paid much higher fares to help cover the expenses of members who could not afford the trip.

In the end, 850 Jews crowded into the space built for 750. The bunks, more like pine shelves, stacked from floor to ceiling, one meter tall. Between two aisles, the bunks were four meters across to accommodate six passengers, making it necessary for passengers to climb over one another to get to and from their own bunks.

Yutka watched the Polish and Rumanian girls she'd met at the cottage descend into the women's compartment, but Yutka was assigned to the family compartment. Climbing down the companionway into the dimly lit space toward her assigned bunk, she noticed the scent of fresh cut pine so much like the lumber yard behind the Lipka home in Dobrzyń. The scent of pine would always remind her of home, even now, mixed with the unpleasant human tang.

She liked the location of her top bunk next to the hull. Because of the curve of the hull, a single column of narrower bunks nestled against the outside wall. Her bunk, a little over a half-meter wide and less than a meter to the ceiling above, suited Yutka's petite frame. She could sit up. A taller person would have been quite uncomfortable. The top bunk offered her a small amount of privacy; no one would bang her with a *walizka* as they walked by, nor climb over her to get to their bunk.

The commander made Yutka the platoon leader in the family compartment. She would assist the children and other passengers. She also had responsibility to take roll call every day. It was especially important on this, the first day of the voyage.

The air in her compartment throbbed with excitement and trepidation as emotional passengers found their numbered bunks. She heard a man shouting in French and hurried to intervene.

"What is the problem?" asked Yutka, looking up at what seemed like a disembodied bald head looking over the edge of a bunk. A couple stood nearby, clutching each other, holding the slip of paper with their assigned bunk number.

The bald head spoke. "We have occupied this bunk since we left France. Now, these two, who don't even speak French, are trying to join us. It is unthinkable to share our bed!"

"I understand, it is highly unusual for two families to share a sleeping space," Yutka said to the indignant passenger as he climbed down from the top bunk. She wondered why the commander had allowed this plump older man to join the group of fit Betar youth. She guessed he must be at least forty. Grateful for her mastery of French, she said, "However, these are unique circumstances. In order to accommodate as many refugees as possible, the bunks must accommodate six people. Passengers are required to share the space, as necessary."

"Do you realize, *petite fille*, I am Mayor Edelman the Mayor of Gignac-la-Nerthe?" He looked down on Yutka in every way. She was a female. She was young. She was inches shorter and half his girth.

"I'm sure that you were an important figure in Gignac-la-Nerthe but, sir, on the *Parita* you have the same privileges as any other passenger. You're required to share your bunk with Mr. and Mrs. Dornbusch." She nodded toward the intimidated couple huddled next to her.

"*Feh*! I will discuss this with the commander."

"Mr. Edelman, as platoon leader, it's my responsibility to

take all complaints in this compartment to the commander."

"*Feh!*" Ignoring Yutka, Mr. Edelman stomped to the end of the aisle, climbed the companionway to join a few other disgruntled men huddled around the commander.

While her husband marched up to the deck, Mrs. Edelman climbed down from the bunk and, in French, introduced herself to Yutka. "I am Joséphine Edelman. Please excuse my husband, he worries about our safety. I'd like you to meet our daughters." Yutka looked up to see two little girls looking wide-eyed over the edge of their bunk. "This is Priscilla, and this is Rochelle. Girls this is *Mademoiselle* Yutka."

"*Enchante, Mademoiselle* Yutka," said Priscilla, while Rochelle hid behind her older sister.

"*Enchante*, Priscilla, how old are you?"

Priscilla held up four fingers. "And this is my doll, Babette."

"Nice to meet you too, Babette. Rochelle, how old are you?"

Three little fingers appeared from behind Priscilla. "My baby sister is shy," Priscilla offered.

Yutka introduced Joséphine, Priscilla, and Rochelle Edelman to the newlywed couple. "This is Mr. and Mrs. Dornbusch. They will be sharing this space until we arrive in *Eretz* Israel."

Mrs. Dornbusch reached up to shake hands with Priscilla and Babette. Rochelle wouldn't shake her hand, but she giggled when Mrs. Dornbusch said, "Hallo, Babette."

Yutka was sure they would get along fine, *If Mr. Edelman can behave himself*, she thought.

Yutka translated for Mrs. Edelman as she spoke to the Dornbusch couple. "I apologize for my husband. He is a kind man once you know him."

Mr. and Mrs. Dornbusch climbed into the bunk, both with smiles that didn't reach their worried eyes.

Mrs. Dornbusch looked down at Yutka with a soft smile, "*Vielen dank, Fräulein* Yutka."

✡

Commander Leibovitz shouted above the clamor, "Gentleman, please! I will consider requests and complaints from platoon leaders only. Please return to your compartment and talk to your platoon leader. That is all!" The commander turned, but Mr. Edelman tapped him on the shoulder.

"*Le commandant*, I need to discuss my family's shared bunk." Mr. Edelman was an opportunist. Not a Zionist. Not a Betar member. He spoke French and enough Yiddish. He didn't understand what the commander had just said in German to the other men.

The commander looked down at stocky Mr. Edelman. Although the commander didn't speak French, he understood Edelman's complaint. "Did you discuss your sleeping arrangements with your platoon leader?"

Edelman switched to Yiddish. "That little girl? *Feh*! What does she know of authority? As you know, I am the Mayor of Gignac-la-Nerthe," said Mr. Edelman, as if Leibovitz would understand the former mayor's importance and override Yutka's decision.

Leibovitz had no patience for this self-righteous passenger. He took a deep breath, ready to dismiss Mr. Edelman outright, but he wanted to make a point about Yutka's position as platoon leader. "Mr. Edelman, Betar is in charge of this mission, and you are not a member. Be glad I allowed you and your family to board. Yutka has been a member of Betar for almost five years, and she is well versed on the rules of this voyage," his voice grew louder as he spoke. "Miss Lipka is absolutely right. You are a refugee like the rest of us. Go back to your bunk and be satisfied with the space I assigned to you."

✡

Leibovitz stood at the bow, facing the warm salty breeze, doubting his decision to allow the Edelmans on board. He remembered another last-minute decision he'd made earlier that day in Constanța.

"*Excuse me sir,*" *a Betar operative interrupts* Erwin's thoughts. "*These people would like to speak to you.*"

Leibovitz looks at a bent old couple. The woman leans heavily on a cane. Dark blotches over a road map of blue veins cover her hands. Her knuckles are swollen with arthritis. As a pious Jew, she covers her white hair using a faded rose-print sheitel *tied at the back of her head. The sea breeze flutters curly wisps escaping the headscarf around her deeply wrinkled round face. She has a wide, kind smile, with recessed lips due to missing teeth. Shadows of deep laugh lines surround her cloudy brown eyes, remnants of her hard but happy life.*

Her husband, wearing a long black coat, limps toward Leibovitz while leading a swayback, brown mare with protruding hip bones and ribs. The mare pulls a rickety wooden wagon that is stacked with a small table, two chairs, a caned rocking chair, a lamp with a dented shade, and a few burlap bundles. "*Please take us to* Eretz Israel? *Soldiers, they destroy our village and kill our son, his wife and our grandchildren.*" *Tears spill from the old man's eyes and run over his sunken cheeks into his long, white, frizzled beard. He wears a yarmulke under his dusty flat-brimmed hat.*

The woman's thin smile turns to despair. "*We travel long. We have no home.*"

The old people speak Yiddish, but Leibovitz hears the harsh consonants of Russian or Bulgarian. Indeed, they have come a long way. Leibovitz looks at his roster as if he doesn't already know that the ship is one hundred passengers over her limit.

Leibovitz looks up from his manifest and notices other refugees wandering near the dock. He takes a deep breath, then another, steeling his heart.

"I'm sorry. The Parita can carry no more passengers." He closes his eyes and justifies his decision in his own mind. He knows if he allows this old couple to board, they will not be able to descend the companionway to their compartment or climb into their bunk. The sanitary facilities will be impossible for them to navigate. Worst of all, they might not be healthy enough to survive the harsh conditions of the seven-day journey. And, beyond all that, other refugees milling about the port will also ask to board. I must draw a line at 850 passengers.

"This is the most difficult decision I have ever made," he whispers to the old couple. With his eyes burning, Leibovitz finds strength. "There is no more room on this ship. There will be other ships coming soon. Perhaps you can board the next one. I am so sorry."

The old people hang their heads, mumble, "Благодарю вас," and lead the old horse away from the dock. Leibovitz's mind wonders to the nasty and entitled Mr. Edelman. Not a fair trade, Leibovitz thinks, but the Edelman's little girls will grow up in the free state of Israel.

As the crowd jostled toward the *Parita,* Yaakov watched in vain for the girl with the beautiful round face and intelligent black eyes, but without success. On the boat, he found his assigned bunk in the men's compartment and crawled over two teenage brothers who clearly hadn't bathed for some time. He hugged his cherished mandolin to his chest like an infant, used his satchel for a pillow and asked in German, "Where are you from?"

"Munich," responded the older boy with wispy chin whiskers the color of sand on his drawn, pale face. "We've been on the boat already seven days."

"Are you with your family?"

"*Nein*," said the younger boy with sad eyes. "Papa was trying to emigrate, but he was arrested last year."

"Why was your papa arrested?" asked Yaakov.

The boys looked at each other and shrugged, "The Nazis, do they need a reason? Papa is Jewish physics professor. In Germany, it is reason enough. One day the Nazis, they announce Jews could not go to school. My name is Klaus, and my brother is Reiner, but they change our names to Israel and stamp a J on our passports. We had to do as they said. My sister and her husband took us in but one night we come home, and our mama, sister, and brother-in-law are gone. Neighbors, the Muellers, said the Nazis rounded up all the Jews in the neighborhood and put them on a train. The Muellers were kind people and hid us in their attic, but they were afraid other neighbors would report them. Mr. Mueller knew a man who was helping smuggle Jews out of Germany, Dr. Hecht. His network helped us cross the border into France. We hid in a hotel in Paris until a train brought us to *Parita*."

Yaakov laid on his bunk focusing on the knotty pine board above him, trying to think of anything but his reeling stomach. On his left, three young Betar members moaned softly, trying to avoid being sick. On his right, the young brothers slept soundly, acclimated to the sea after their seven-day voyage from France.

Finally, as perspiration soaked his shirt, he rolled over the sleeping teens leaving his mandolin in his place and started up the aisle. Suddenly, he heard a loud retching sound. A young man in a top bunk vomited down Yaakov's back. With his hand over his mouth, Yaakov ran up the companionway to the stern and violently vomited over the side. He took off his shirt and dropped it into the sea.

✡

Yutka completed roll call, and all passengers in the family compartment settled into their bunks. As the boat gained speed, her stomach filled with butterflies of anticipation. *We're on our way*, she thought, *just seven more days and we'll be in* Eretz *Israel.* The hull vibrated as the *Parita* cruised through the deep swells of the Black Sea.

Rolling onto her side on the hard, pine board with her elbow under her head, she focused on the rust spotted interior of the hull. Like clouds in the sky, the rust spots morphed into familiar shapes, a bird's wings, the face of a kitten, a tulip. In the dim light, the rusty shadows blended together as the butterflies of anticipation swirled into something more sinister. Her head spun with every side-to-side roll and every up and down swell, as if she rode a watery carnival ride. Up down, side to side, up down, side to side. Her stomach roiled. She sweat profusely and swallowed excess saliva. Tossing her legs over the edge of her bunk, she leapt to the aisle. Holding her hand over her mouth, she raced up to the bow, hung over the railing and vomited into the sea that looked strangely calm, considering its effect on her stomach. She closed her eyes, but the boat reeled even more. The sound of other passengers retching overboard started her heaving again. Finally, satisfied that there was nothing left in her stomach, she found a bucket of sea water and a tin cup the crew had placed on deck. She took a mouthful and spit over the side. The salt water helped reduce the taste of bile left in her mouth.

Yutka slowly trudged back to her bunk. Others had also been seasick but hadn't made it to the deck in time. As she entered the family compartment, the vile smell of vomit sent her rushing back to the bow. Finally, she sat curled on the deck, hugging her shins, resting her forehead on her knees, trying to calm the nausea.

She noticed a crew member carrying buckets of salt water and a mop below deck. When he emerged, Yutka looked up,

"*Danke,* the smell is overwhelming." She quickly returned her forehead to her knees. Just looking up at him made the deck spin around her.

"In a day or two your queasiness will subside," he replied in Russian accented German.

"Ah, but this is no way to spend my birthday. I am eighteen today," said Yutka, with her forehead on her knees.

"What is your name?"

"I am Yutka," she said, trying to be cordial.

"Nice to meet you, Yutka. I am Serioja. Have a happy birthday in spite of the sea," he patted her dark wavy hair. "Soon you will feel better."

"I hope it doesn't take days," moaned Yutka. She sat with her forehead on her knees, breathing deeply until Serioja returned with a pail of hot ginger tea. Just the smell of it made her feel a little better.

"Take a dram of this," he poured tea into a tin mug. "I make ginger tea for you and your compartment. It will help ease queasiness. Also, look at the horizon when you can and when you walk, keep your knees slightly bent."

Serioja had been a bachelor, married to the sea all his life. His face, weathered by salt and wind, looked as hard as stone, but he had a heart of wax. "You rest here." Again, he patted Yutka's curly head. To the old man, she was a child; they were all children. "Focus on how happy you will be to arrive in *Eretz* Israel in a few days. Now, I take tea to everyone in your compartment."

The sun shone into her eyes as she watched Serioja's ethereal silhouette. With stooped shoulders and bowed legs he slowly shuffled toward the hatch. He carried the pail of tea and a stack of shiny, dented tin cups, their handles looped over his gnarled fingers.

Keeping her knees bent, staring at the horizon, as Serioja suggested, instead of thinking about her roiling stomach, Yutka thought about her Betar friends.

"I want to become a dentist, but Jews cannot go to dental school in Poland, so I have decided go to France and apply to university," says Yutka's friend Hania, Daniel's sister.

"Do you speak French?" asks Yutka.

"Not yet. Daniel and I signed up for lessons. You should join us. Who knows what languages we will need in the future!"

They begin their French lessons the following week and practice speaking to each other.

"Bonjour Daniel, comment vas-tu aujourd'hui?"

"Très bien Yutka, et toi?"

"Très bien."

Especially after the row with Mr. Edelman, Yutka was happy Hania had suggested studying French. She was also glad she had studied the map pinned to the wall of Betar's meeting room. When the ship slowed, she knew they were passing through Turkish waters. The Turks had closed the Bosphorus Strait to ships of war and the refugees could be in danger if the Turks inspected the coal carrier's cargo. Yutka feared the Turks would sink the *Parita* and drown them all.

As their old iron ship slowly chugged her way through the nineteen-mile strait, the smell of land and the pungent aroma of cinnamon, sumac, mint and roasting lamb mixed with the rank smell of vomit and unwashed humans on board.

When the hull vibrated again, she knew the increase in speed would be short-lived as they sailed through the Sea of Marmara. After passing through the Dardanelles Strait, the boat gained speed again. An involuntary sign of relief escaped Yutka's lungs as the boat left unfriendly Turkish waters and sailed into the Aegean Sea.

Chapter 16

Elsa's Story

Yutka noticed a pretty young woman, with wildly curly blonde hair, occupying the top bunk at Yutka's feet. She leaned on her elbow, "*Witam*, I'm Yutka," she said in Polish.

"*Parlez-vous français?*" the girl asked in French, rolling onto her belly and propping her chin on her knuckles. Long pale lashes framed deep blue eyes, and her flawless pale skin and rosy cheeks gave her the look of a French actress.

"*Oui*," replied Yutka.

"I'm Elsa. I'm born in France, but we are living in Vienna for Papa's work," Elsa replied in French.

"You came aboard in Marseille?"

"*Oui*, actually Château d'If. We have been at sea for already seven days."

"How did you learn about the boat?" asked Yutka.

"I've been a member of Betar Youth since Papa moved us to Vienna. I told him what I learned at meetings, but Papa says Gentiles who owned his company will keep us safe. He says *Aliyah Bet* is bad idea." Frustration and sadness deepened Elsa's voice.

"My Papa too," said Yutka as she crawled to the end of her bunk and sat up cross-legged, facing Elsa. "I told him Germans will arrest him, but he wouldn't listen. I paid for passage and hope they will follow. How did you make the long trip from Austria alone?"

Elsa twisted a lock of her blonde curly hair around her finger. "With Dr. Hecht and Betar's help, a small group of us fled Austria in early March. We traveled from Vienna to Liechtenstein.

>Dr. Hecht, traveling on a Swiss passport, is a tall, thin Jew with narrow set dark eyes. He combs his hair dramatically back from his forehead and sports a pencil mustache and goatee. He keeps the collar of his long black coat turned up around his ears in all weather.
>
>Known as a dynamo for his shrewd ability to negotiate and his no-nonsense decisions, he's well known among government officials across Europe.
>
>Hecht makes arrangements to smuggle refugees, including Elsa, across Austria hidden in a truck full of cabbage. Then they hike through muddy wooded trails, sinking into the mud up to their shins. Elsa falls behind when she stops to dig out her shoe sucked off by the mud. While trying to wipe the sticky mud from her clothing and out from under her fingernails, she struggles to catch up with the others.
>
>Trekking through Switzerland to France, a guide leads a small group of women and children up steep mountain trails. Sometimes the snow is so deep it feels like swimming in ice. One woman struggles to carry her two small children so Elsa offers to help. She climbs most of the way with a three-year-old boy clinging to her back. The trail becomes steep and her legs are numb from cold and exhaustion. She slips on the ice and falls flat with the little boy hugging her neck. Her fingernails dig into the snow and ice to prevent them from sliding off the trail and down the mountain side.
>
>Finally, the little group crosses into France. Hecht has arranged to smuggle them to safe houses scattered around the French countryside.

Elsa hides in the back of an old truck as it bumps over back roads to a farmhouse in a village near the border. Out of the cold, Elsa feels like she's on fire when her skin starts to warm by the roaring fire. The inn keeper serves soup that warms her insides and tastes better that any soup she's ever eaten. Her heart swells with gratitude as she uses a dry chunk of bread to soak up every drop of broth.

They must stay indoors, out of sight, but they are well-fed, enjoying bread, goat cheese and soup. A few weeks later, operatives smuggle them to a small hotel in Paris where Dr. Hecht has bribed the owner to hide German and Austrian Jews until further arrangements can be made.

The French police are diligently checking documents, so they must stay indoors. Elsa shares a tiny hotel room, meant for a romantic couple, with ten strangers. One hundred refugees share two bathrooms.

Sometimes the hotel owners stand guard so the little children can play in the hallway. Elsa crawls on her hands and knees, playing horsey to entertain the surprisingly well-behaved children. They understand their predicament better than some of the adults. The owners bring the refugees hearty pot au feu, *bread and sometimes cheese, which Elsa is grateful for. Two older women, however, cause trouble. They complain about the unvarying menu and lack of privacy, and they argue about going outside, they want to see Paris.*

One night, the screams of a woman in labor pull Elsa from a light sleep. Then, through the wall, she hears the faint broken wail of a newborn. She worries about the mother and baby in these difficult times.

Hecht arranges for some of the refugees to go to Brazil and a few to the United States. Fifty of the them, including

Elsa, will take a train to Marseille where they will board the Parita once her refit is complete.

After hiding in the hotel for four weeks, they cheer when the inn keeper reads the telegram:

MEET ME IN MARSEILLE STOP YOUR BROTHER HERSCHEL STOP

Before they leave the hotel, Hecht's operatives provide them with forged travel documents and train tickets to Marseille. Because it is illegal for Jews to travel to Eretz Israel, Elsa's papers list Brazil as her destination.

Terrified that the French police will stop them before they reach the train, they hide in lorries under tarps between crates of empty wine bottles. In fashionable Paris, no matter what her papers say, Elsa knows no one will believe she's a tourist. Her clothes are dirty and her hair is wild and disheveled.

On the train, the conductor comes by to check tickets and travel documents, then locks the doors so the Jews can't leave the train until they reach Marseille.

"*Oui*, we were also locked into the train carriage," said Yutka. "And my documents list my destination as Ecuador!" Her tone became low and serious. "So few countries will have us. When I walked to the boat, it felt as if the Rumanian police might shoot at any moment."

"At the doc in Marseille," Elsa leaned closer to Yutka, enjoying a bit of gossip. "Mr. Edelman begged the commander to let his family come. The commander sat on his heels to talk with the little girls eye to eye while a group of little boys beat drums and blew their horns. The girls were shy but very polite and absolutely adorable. I couldn't hear what the girls said, but he agreed to let them board. He sure had a soft spot for those cute little girls. Their father is much older than the rest of us. And," Elsa whispered, "he's fat and ungrateful!"

"That explains why the commander allowed him on board."

"In the Marseille train station, fishermen directed us through the dark toward the fishing boats. The crates of sweet-smelling fruit we passed reminded me of the treats Maman made during Rosh Hashanah."

Half listening to Elsa's story, Yutka became distracted by her own memories of Rosh Hashanah.

> On a brisk day in mid-September, the day before Rosh Hashanah, four-year-old Yutka and her mama walk to the market carrying baskets. Mama's basket is much bigger than Yutka's. Heniek and Rozka stay at home with Papa, but Yutka, the youngest by seven years, wants to come along.
>
> Yutka face turns back and forth from the pile of apples above her head to her mama. "Mama, why do you smell each apple?"
>
> "Because I want to buy the sweetest apples for Rosh Hashanah." One by one Mama puts apples in Yutka's basket. "Be careful you should drop and bruise the apples."
>
> Later, Mama will slice the apples and serve them with the golden honey she buys from the honey vendor.
>
> Before leaving the market, Mama selects eggs, inspecting each one by holding it up to the sunlight.
>
> "Why do you look at the egg in the sunshine?"
>
> "To be certain the egg is fresh and kosher."
>
> "But how can you tell?" wondered little Yutka.
>
> "If there is a speck inside I know it is not kosher and if it has a big air pocket, it is too old." Mama gently places each well-inspected fresh egg, one by one in her own big basket.
>
> As friends and family arrive for the holiday, they

greet each other with, "L'shana tovah tikatevu, *May you be inscribed for a good year.*"

Uncle Srulik, Aunt Zipporah and friends respond, "L'shana tovah, L'chaim!"

For dinner Mama serves the foods that represent positive wishes, followed by the delicacies that symbolize a sweet new year.

The next day, they all walk to the Dreventz River to perform the Tashlich ceremony. They say prayers then, using the challah left from dinner, they each toss small pieces of bread into the moving water.

"Papa, why are we feeding the ducks the challah Aunt Zipporah made?"

"We are not feeding the ducks," laughs Papa. "We are symbolically casting away our sins. The ducks are happy for the Tashlich ceremony."[7]

"What does sim-ball-lick-lee mean?"

"We pretend that the pieces of bread are our sins."

Yutka looks confused and Papa says, "Don't worry Yutka, someday you will understand symbolism."

Next to the apples and honey this is little Yutka's favorite part of Rosh Hashanah, feeding the ducks.

Ignoring her aching heart, Yutka tried to swing her focus back to Elsa.

"I watched the stars reflect on the dark sea as the kind Greek fisherman rowed to the island of Château d'If," Elsa continued. "I couldn't understand a word he said, but he had kind eyes and a happy, reassuring grin behind his thick black beard.

"At dawn, the boat finally headed toward the sea. I wanted to go on deck to see the Mediterranean at sunrise. I had never seen a body of water bigger than the Seine River, but we had to

---

7. Micha 7:19

stay below deck until we were far from shore. Some people were seasick and the commander let them go on deck. I felt better lying still in my bunk listening to the water and feeling the vibration of the boat."

"Ugh, let's not talk of sea sickness—my stomach has not recovered," said Yutka.

"When the commander finally allowed us to come on deck, we watched the lights of Marseilles fade..." Elsa couldn't explain the excruciating pain and exaltation that had boiled in her belly like a river overflowing its banks. She had hugged herself as if hugging her parents, and tugged childhood memories as close as she could, wondering if she would ever see France again. "My maman and papa would love to see the beautiful sea...." Elsa became quiet. "I think I will nap now," she whispered as she scooted down and put her head on her knapsack.

Yutka was grateful that during the months it took Betar to find and retrofit a suitable ship, she had waited at home in Dobrzyń, with her own family, sleeping in her own bed, while Elsa and the others made the difficult and dangerous trek through cold mud and snow, over steep mountains to France. And while Elsa and the others boarded the *Parita* for the seven-day voyage from Château d'If to Constanța, Yutka still waited for the telegram and then made the two-day train trip from Dobrzyń to Port of Constanța.

Chapter 17

The first few days at sea, July 1939

Tolerating the uncomfortable accommodations, constant motion of the boat, seasickness and terrible food seemed a modest price to pay to reach the land where they thought diaspora Jews would no longer fear persecution. During the first week, despite the dire conditions, morale on the ship was high. In the family compartment, where Yutka was a platoon leader, immigrants huddled along the passageway, playing with the children and talking about their plans once they arrived in *Eretz* Israel. "My sister immigrated five years ago, I can't wait to see her again," said one young woman. The burley father of four youngsters beamed, "My brother immigrated a few years ago. He lives at *Kibbutz Matsuda*. There my children will learn to be Jews without the threat of violence around every corner—especially in their school."

When it was their turn to go on deck, they sang *Hava Nagila* and other folk songs from their own regions. Betar boys scampered up the masts, making room for others to dance the *horah*.

✡

"Shalom. I am Yutka," she introduced herself to the woman in the bottom bunk below hers.

Dark eyes surrounded by bruise-like circles looked up at Yutka, speaking silent words. Yutka shivered as if those sunken eyes told the story of the unimaginable horrors the woman had witnessed. "My name is Zosia, and this is Channah," the young mother's voice was reedy, a hoarse whisper.

"If you like, I'll hold the baby while you eat?" Yutka softly offered in Yiddish.

"*A sheynem dank.*"

Yutka whispered, "*Nisht do kein farvos,*" denying the need for thanks, "My niece is a few months older. I miss her terribly." Her arms curled around the tiny infant as she hummed a lullaby and thought of her own childhood in Dobrzyń.

> *On Simchat Torah, the last day of Sukkot, Yutka (6), Heniek (14), and Rozka (13), are with Mama and Papa spending the evening dancing, singing and rejoicing with other members of their synagogue in Dobrzyń.*
>
> *Dinner smells so good, Yutka can hardly wait for Mama to light the candles and say the blessing.*
>
> *Barukh ata Adonai Eloheinu, Melekh ha'olam, asher kid'shanu b'mitzvotav v'tzivanu l'hadlik ner shel yom tov.*
>
> *Blessed are You, Lord our God, Ruler of the Universe, who has sanctified us with commandments, and commanded us to light festival candles.*
>
> *Yutka's eyes water as she leans in to smell the pungent spicy fragrance of homemade horseradish that Mama serves with gefilte fish.*

> *Her head leans back, and she sniffs the air filled with the aroma of chicken soup, goose liver* kreplach, *and beef brisket roasted with potatoes and carrots. She breathes ginger, cinnamon, cloves, and lemon as Mama serves the noodle* kugel. *Mama surprises everyone when she serves* marak perot *with apricots, dried plums, and lemon juice.*

On the third day at sea, half awake on her dark bunk, as the boat rolled with the sea, she thought she heard her sister Rozka whispering to her new baby, Rebekah, but it was Zosia's voice softly soothing her nursing infant. She thought she heard Papa snoring, but it was Mr. Edelman's thunder-like snore. She thought she heard Mama softly crying, but it was Elsa in the bunk next to hers.

Keeping her eyes closed, she heard the hollow sound of water rushing by the bow and the groan of the vibrating iron vessel. Yutka's back ached against the bare pine shelf, reminding her she was not in her own bed in Dobrzyń. In the absolute darkness, she tried to go back to sleep but the bitter smell of coal, vomit, and body odor destroyed the pleasure of her dream.

It was Yutka's turn for a saltwater shower. Opening her knapsack, she gazed at the family photo on top of her clean underwear. As if holding her baby niece, she removed the photo from the pocket of her knapsack and gently placed it on the bare wood of her bunk. Then she gathered a clean skirt, blouse, and underwear, along with a towel and soap. Bringing the bar to her face, she breathed in the smell of sunshine, lavender and cleanliness. For a moment, she lingered in her bunk with her legs crossed, holding the soap with both hands, remembering the first time she helped Mama make soap....

Seven-year-old Yutka watches Mama pour big jars of honey into a pot of boiling water, getting ready to make a batch of soap. Standing on a wooden stool, Yutka stirs the pot until the honey dissolves. Her face sweats as the sweet vapor condenses on her face.

As Yutka steps down from her stool, Mama says, "While the mixture cools, you can help shell the peas from the garden and I will peel potatoes for dinner."

Later Mama says, "Now let's add the yeast," Yutka steps back onto the stool and sprinkles the dry yeast over the warm amber broth and stirs with the long handled wooden spoon until the yeast dissolves.

"Yutka, will you hold the funnel steady while I pour? That funnel and this jug are very old. My mama used them when she made mead."

"Mead! I thought we were making soap?" Yutka looked at her mama with a crinkled forehead.

"We are making soap, but first we must brew the mead."

"It smells so sweet," breathed Yutka, "not like soap." She picks up an odd-shaped glass device. Rolling it round in her hands, she asks, "Why do you need this curly thing?"

"That is a bubble airlock, be careful, it's made of glass." Yutka's little fingers hand her mama the device. "I'll use it to stopper the jug so this mixture can ferment safely."

"What is ferment?"

"When the yeast eats the sweet honey, it creates air bubbles and alcohol. The airlock allows the bubbles to escape. If we corked the jug with no way to let the bubbles out, the jug would blow up and we should have a terrible mess!"

"Don't you use yeast when you make bread?"

"That's right! When I put yeast in flour and water, the bubbles created by the yeast make the bread rise."

"Does bread have alcohol in it?"

"No, the alcohol evaporates."

"What does evaporate mean?"

"Oy vey! So many questions! Maybe later you should ask your Papa about evaporation, tak?"

Every day, Yutka sits by the jug, watching the bubbles rise through the water in the airlock. "Is it ready yet?"

"Is it ready yet?"

"Now is it ready?"

"Not yet. We need to wait until the yeast stops eating. Then the air bubbles stop rising."

The next day Yutka runs to her mama in the backyard, "Mama, Mama, there are no bubbles in that curly glass thing. Is it ready now?"

Mama finishes hanging the laundry, the line still too high for Yutka's help.

"Looks like we're ready to bottle the mead. We'll fill a few wine bottles for drinking and put the rest in jugs."

Yutka looks at her mama with wide eyes, "Wine bottles! You can drink this? I thought we were making soap!"

Mama laughs, "Mead is sweet wine. When the yeast eats the honey, it makes alcohol. It won't taste like soap until we get to the end of the process. You want I should pour you a taste of the mead?"

"No, thank you," Yutka shakes her head and wrinkles her nose.

They place the bottles and jugs of mead on a shelf in the pantry.

A few days later, Yutka asks, "When are we going to finish making soap?"

"How about after breakfast?" says Mama. "You can measure and add the oils, but I'll add the lye. Lye can burn your skin."

"Won't that make the soap burn our skin?"

"No, the lye causes a chemical reaction."

"What's a chemical reaction?"

"Oy vey! I knew you would ask. You should ask your Papa about chemical reactions, tak?

Yutka measures vegetable oil, tallow, sunflower oil, and rendered goose fat into a big pot of mead according to her mama's direction. Mama lights the burner. When the mixture is hot, Mama adds the lye and salt.

Yutka eyes open wide, "Mama! Why are you adding salt, we aren't going to eat this are we?"

"Salt will make the soap harder and last longer."

Yutka looks at her mama with doubt in her eyes, then realizes, "Is that a chemical reaction?"

Mama laughs, "Yes, I suppose it is."

"Now what do we do?" asks Yutka.

"The oils, lye and mead need to cook for several hours."

"Hours!" Yutka lets out a big sigh and folds her arms over her chest. She can see that her mama is growing impatient with all the questions.

"Are you losing interest in making soap?" asks Mama.

"Oh no Mama, I'd rather make soap than bread or soup. It's a lot more fun, but soap takes a long time."

After they finish the dinner dishes, Mama asks Yutka, "You want I should let you ladle the liquid into the molds?"

"Sure!" Yutka climbs back onto the wooden stool.

"There's one more step," says Bluma.

"More?" Yutka rolls her eyes as Bluma hands her

a small bottle. "Pour a few drops of this into the soap mixture. Careful! Just a few drops."

Yutka twists the eyedropper from the vial. "Oh Mama, lavender oil! I love the smell of lavender." She inhales the fragrance as she allows tiny drops to fall into the mixture.

"That is plenty," says Mama.

Yutka puts the eye dropper back into the vile and hands it to Mama. Then she brings her little fingers to her nose.

"I also love the smell of lavender." Mama smiles and breathes deeply as she makes sure the cap is on tight. "Lavender reminds me of my mama, your Safta D'Vora."

Mama hands Yutka the ladle, and Yutka slowly transfers the warm liquid soap from the pot to the brick-shaped molds.

"Good job, you hardly spilled any. I remember helping my mama make soap with these same tin molds."

"They are as big as bricks, aren't they too big for bars of soap?"

"Once the bricks are dry enough, we'll slice them into bars and let them dry even more. The dryer they are the longer the soap will last."

Finally, the day comes to cut the bricks into bars. Yutka watches Mama push the big knife into the first brick of translucent soap. Again, the room fills with the scent of lavender. They wrap the bars in soft paper. Mama hands Yutka three wrapped bars of soap. "Put these in your dresser drawers. Your clothes will smell fresh."

"I love making soap with you Mama, and lavender smells so good!" Yutka hugs Mama around the waist and Bluma pats Yutka's head.

Sitting on her bunk, Yutka touched the top of her head as if she should feel Mama's hand resting there.

She climbed to the sunny deck, clutching her clean clothes, towel and soap, ready for her first sea-water shower. The sun beat down on her head and a warm breeze ruffled her oily hair. The shower door creaked on its hinges. Although no one could see her in the wooden stall, showering outdoors in the sunshine made her uneasy and, she realized, there was no lock on the door. *I have no choice,* she thought. She hung her clothes on a nail, then closed her eyes and put her head back. Feeling a little unsteady as the boat rolled over swells, she gently pulled the cord to wet her hair and skin. Her breath sucked deeply into her lungs as the cold seawater splashed onto her head and shoulders. Despite vigorous rubbing, the wet bar of soap created no lather. She rubbed the soap on her skin and pulled the rope again to rinse away the scum. When the barrel with her ration of bath water was empty, her skin felt rough from the soap and salt, not smooth and clean like a bath at home in her parent's house.

Yutka tossed her dirty clothes onto her bunk, then climbed up and shimmied into her space. She rolled the dirty garments together and tucked them under the clean clothes that still smelled slightly of lavender. She looked at the family photo. Her family members seemed to watch her hang the towel to dry on the side of her bunk and stow the paper-wrapped soap in a pocket of her knapsack. She kissed her salty finger and touched the face of each family member then gently put the photo back into its pocket.

She tried to comb her stiff, wet hair. "Elsa, have you tried the saltwater shower? My soap wouldn't make a lather."

"*Oui,*" said Elsa. "I'm not sure the shower was worth the effort. My skin feels itchy, and my hair must look a fright!"

She tugged long, curly blonde clumps like wings on the sides of her head. "My hair is unruly even in fresh water. Now I can't even get a comb through it!"

"My skin is itchy too, and it feels like my hair will never be the same. I'll be so glad when we reach *Eretz* Israel, and I can wash my clothes and take a proper bath!"

"Just a few more days," smiled Elsa.

Chapter 18

Day 6 at Sea, July 19, 1939

Tossing and turning on the hard pine board, unable to fall asleep, Yutka silently shimmied off the bunk, carefully found footholds on the lower bunks, and stepped down past refugees sleeping below. She was especially careful not to disturb Zosia and Channah in the bottom bunk, just centimeters from the floor.

She felt her way along the aisle until she came to the companionway and climbed toward the deck. Drawn by the sound of water slapping the iron bow, she slipped into the dark as she smelled salt, seaweed, and citrus wafting from an orange grove on Cyprus. For a few moments, she leaned over the bulwark, watching the ship cut through the black water, creating white bow waves. She heard their breath spew before she saw the dolphins break the surface, sparkling like sequins in the dim moonlight, escorting the ship as if keeping the Jewish refugees safe from sea monsters and other predators.

Using a coil of heavy rope for a pillow, she stretched out on the damp deck and crossed her arms over her midriff, holding herself together. She thought she heard a melancholy melody float in the warm, salty air, *Just my imagination*, she decided. *Tomorrow night, we will be in* Eretz Israel *where I will kiss the ground.*

She had never seen a sky so black or the smear of milky stars so bright. How could her family live under the same stars? It seemed like years since she said goodbye to them. She wondered when she would see them again, her mama, Bluma, her papa, Mordechai, her brother, Heniek, her sister, Rozka, her niece, Rebekah, nephew, Jerzyk, and many aunts, uncles, and cousins. It never crossed her mind that they might never join her in *Eretz Israel*.

The deck pulsed beneath her as she gazed at the stars. Her mind twisted with suspense, fear, and hope. She knew tomorrow would be the most dangerous leg of the seven-day journey. After dark, they would climb aboard the transfer boats. The smaller, faster, more nimble crafts would secretly break the British blockade and dock at a pier, probably in Haifa. If discovered, British warships could sink the boats, turn them away, or arrest the refugees or send them back to Europe. That they would go ashore without immigration certificates was the least of her worries.

The next night, a loud, reverberating bang, as if the boat had split apart, woke Yutka at midnight. When her heart slowed and her wits returned, she realized it was the earsplitting roar of the anchor chain uncoiling and dropping into the deep water north of Cyprus. It meant that they were only hours from their destination. She put her hand on her chest and took a deep breath as her heart pounding wildly.

In the pitch dark, she rolled up her blanket, stowed her few belongings in her knapsack, and made sure her money belt was secure. As refugees in the bunks below rubbed their eyes and stretched, she climbed down from her bunk and secured the knapsack straps over her shoulders.

On deck, in the dim moonlight and warm, still air, her anxiety grew as the silence continued. "Shouldn't we be hearing the transfer boats?" she whispered to Elsa, who had joined.

"Maybe they are a little late?"

As if holding their collective breath, packed shoulder to shoulder, the refugees remained still, listening for the transfer boats. They waited on deck until the apricot glow of morning cast their shadows across the deck. The commander ordered all refugees to return to their compartments, out of sight on what was, supposedly, a Panamanian coal carrier. The crew pulled anchor, and the *Parita* avoided suspicion by zigzagging through the waters near the north shore of Cyprus. Neither the transfer boats nor the *Parita* had radio communication.

The next night, when Yutka and her new friend Elsa walked around the deck, Yutka heard music, clearly this time. She saw the silhouette of a man sitting on an orange crate, hunched over his mandolin. As they came closer, his eyes and rapt grin caught the moonlight. He nodded toward Yutka and kept playing.

Yutka nodded slightly, lifted her chin a tad, and kept walking.

"He's gorgeous, do you know him?" Elsa whispered as she tripped over her own toes turning to look at him.

"We met on the train. He's a flirt and he looks younger in the dark."

"Nonsense! I saw how you looked at him," teased Elsa. "And how his eyes sparkled when he recognized you."

"That was just moonlight." As they walked around the deck, and the half-moon reflected off the water, Yutka asked, "Where will you stay when we land?"

"I have directions to *Beth Hachalutzot* on King George Street. I didn't write to them since I'm illegal; who knows who might have read the mail, but I'm sure they will have a bed for me. There are probably others on board who will probably stay there."

"Yes, they told us about Beth Hachalutzot during a Betar meeting. A place for single woman immigrants, they call us pioneers," she laughed. "They will teach you Hebrew and a trade, if you want. If I can't find my uncle and aunt, I'll join you."

They continued to walk around the deck while waiting for the transfer boats. Yutka asked, "Smell the scent of Jerusalem pine trees wafting on the breeze?"

"Sort of bitter?"

"It's warm and woody. Soon, that aroma will be the scent of home." Yutka's eyes closed, her head tilted back, and she filled her lungs with salty air and the perfume of Jerusalem pine. "Home," she whispered.

"*Oui*," Elsa said softly, "but I will always miss of the flowers, wild thyme, and herbs of Provence."

Chapter 19

Yutka and Yaakov meet on the *Parita*

To conserve coal, the captain anchored north of Cyprus again the next night. When Yutka and Elsa walked the deck, the mandolin player stopped playing and introduced himself. "Hello, I'm Yaakov, didn't we meet on the train from Warsaw?"

"Yes, we did," Yutka responded in Polish.

"I was hoping you came aboard safely," said Yaakov with a captivating smile.

"*Bonjour*, I'm Elsa, you play beautifully," gushed eighteen-year-old Elsa in French.

"*Merci beaucoup.* I am, that is, I was a member of the Ger Mandolin Orchestra." Yaakov replied in perfect French, as he strummed a tremolo. "We often performed concerts on the banks of the Vistula River. I love how the water enhances the sound."

"You said you were from Warsaw," said Yutka, as if he had lied to her on the train. *Why am I being so rude to this man?* she wondered.

"I've been living in Warsaw for twelve years, but I grew up in Góra Kalwaria." Yaakov stood, his mandolin suspended by the strap around his shoulder. He looked out over the dark sea. In a low, calm voice of deep longing, he said, "We practiced with tireless diligence. I recall beautiful evenings when the orchestra would promenade, even in wintery cold, and misty autumn. We brought a great deal of joy to the *shtetl*…"

"And you bring joy to the *Parita* as well," said Elsa, looking around at the refugees on deck. "We have so little to bring us joy."

"*Oui*, like everyone on board, I miss my family.… My papa is a rabbi.…"

"Didn't your papa want you to follow in his footsteps?" Yutka asked, realizing again that her tone sounded harsh.

"Yes, of course, my family planned my life, they even selected a wife for me.… I'm a Jew but not Orthodox, I did not fit their plan for me. When I refused to become a rabbi, Papa and Mama were disappointed."

"What did *you* want to study," asked Elsa.

"I hoped to become a medical doctor, but medical schools in Poland did not admit Jews. I left Góra Kalwaria, joined the Polish army and became a medic. That's where I earned the nickname, Doctor Polo."

"Polo?" asked Elsa.

"My name is Yaakov Polonecki."

"How did you learn to speak French?" asked Yutka. Her voice still sounding accusatory. It was unusual for both of them to speak French so fluently.

"As a boy, one of my best friends came to Góra Kalwaria from France. Then, when I was considering studying medicine in France, I took a course in Warsaw."

"How did you hear about the *Parita*?" Yutka continued her interrogation.

"My friend read an article by Ze'ev Jabotinsky in the *Inser Welt* about Jews emigrating from Poland. The article was very vague, but I began asking questions around Warsaw and learned about the *Parita*. I made my decision to immigrate and returned to Góra Kalwaria to say goodbye to Mama and Papa. I tried to persuade them to come with me, but Papa was certain God would protect them. They were sad I was leaving, but proud…

and relieved," he laughed. "I had finally made a decision about my life. Our neighbors and friends called me *halutz* for making the *Aliyah Bet* to *Eretz* Israel. The entire *shtetl* escorted me to the edge of Góra Kalwaria, shouting '*L'Shana Haba'ah B'Yerushalayim, Next year in Jerusalem.*'[8] The farewell greeting has a new meaning for me now."

Yutka realized she had judged him harshly based on his dapper wardrobe, handsome face, and of course, he wasn't a member of Betar. But she and Yaakov had more in common than she had guessed. He defied his papa and, like her he was a rebel.

---

8. *The Hebrew farewell greeting means* Next year in Jerusalem

Chapter 20

Yaakov

When Yaakov was born in 1907, his parents assumed he would become a rabbi like his papa and generations of Polonecki men before him. But, even as a little boy, Yaakov envisioned a God different from his papa's God. He did not believe it was God's will that he should become a rabbi. He believed his talent for sports and music were God given. *If God wants me to be a rabbi, He should make me* illui, thought Yaakov.

For his eighth birthday, Yaakov's uncle gave him a tear-shaped Embergher mandolin, with a bowlback and four pairs of gut strings.

"Yaakov, listen while I tune the strings. The pairs must match exactly."

His uncle was surprised when Yaakov didn't need the piano or a tuning fork to hear the correct tone. "Excellent, Yaakov!"

His uncle included several extra packets of string in a pocket of the case.

"Why do I need the extra strings?" asked Yaakov.

"You never know when a string might break. With a pocket of spare strings, you are always prepared. Watch, I will show you how to install a new string."

Over the next few years Yaakov taught himself to read music, and he learned to play by watching his uncle. Yaakov fell in love with music. It was not long before his family members and friends began asking him to perform during Rosh Hashanah, *Hanukkah*, and at weddings. Sharing his music became his biggest joy.

One afternoon when Yaakov was twelve, his mama walked into his room, "Yaakov, put the mandolin away, you should study for your bar mitzvah. Papa will expect perfection."

"Yes, Mama." Yaakov leaned his mandolin against the wall in the corner and opened the *Torah*, but as soon as he heard his mama in the kitchen, he resumed his mandolin practice. He planned to play with the Ger Mandolin Orchestra on Sunday at the I.L. Peretz Library, God willing.

Yaakov had little interest in the courses his papa expected him to study, Talmud, Halacha, rituals, rabbinical thought, ethics, pastoral counseling and homiletics. As often as possible, he played soccer and became quite good at it. Of course, he never told them about the professional soccer team he joined, or that he dated *shiksas*.

His parents arranged a marriage for him. "The matchmaker assures us," his mama gushed. "She is a beautiful princess who will obey Jewish laws and keep you very happy."

"But I don't love her, I don't know her. I have never even met her!"

"My Yaakov, we do not marry the woman we love, we come to love the woman we marry. Your friends have all married and given their parents grandchildren," said his papa.

"Heaven forbid you should never give us grandchildren," moaned Yaakov's mama with her hand on her heart.

Yaakov respected his papa and in his younger days had studied the *Torah* every day and attended *yeshiva*. He had tried many times to subtly reject his papa's efforts to make him a rabbi, but his papa always brushed Yaakov's doubts aside. "My Yaakov, of course you will become a rabbi, what else should you be?"

This time Yaakov answered in an unrelenting voice. "Papa, I am twenty-two years old, and I can decide for myself. Please hear me Papa, I will not become a rabbi."

Yaakov watched his papa's cheeks become pale above his bristly white beard. "We have been rabbis for six generations, it is your obligation to God, your destiny."

"I am truly sorry, Papa. All my life, I have tried to study and follow in your footsteps, but I am not like you, Papa, I cannot, I will not, become a rabbi. Tomorrow I will leave to join the Polish army and become a medic."

Yaakov's papa sat in his well-worn chair, and put his face in his hands, "Yaakov... My Yaakov..."

Chapter 21

July 23, 1939

*P*arita's Greek cook, Nikos, wiped the sweat from his brow with a dirty red bandanna. He had little cooking experience, however he'd been working on ships since he was a child. His parents both worked for a shipping company, and he was born on a ship halfway between Mykonos and Rhodes. Nikos learned to walk on sea legs before he walked on land. His grandmother taught him to cook while his parents worked at the Port of Rhodes. When he was older, he learned about the sea from his father. He had a limited range in the galley, but Nikos understood what it took to manage a kitchen that rocked and swayed at the wishes of the sea.

He stood in the galley of the *Parita*, taking stock of the remaining food supply. The *Parita* had been at anchor overnight, near the Kyrenia coast of Cyprus conserving coal while waiting for the transfer boats. No longer freshened by the slight breeze the cruising ship created, the air was sweltering below deck. The stink of unwashed humans, vomit, and bilge water caught in his throat. He coughed as he climbed through the bowels of the ship, listening to the groan of her metal hull.

He found his way to the wheelhouse. "Captain," he said in Greek, "we have enough tinned food to feed the refugees one more meal. I have only a few packages of dehydrated meat, a half-crate of onions, even fewer turnips, a bit of macaroni and a little flour and oil. What will we do?"

"We can no longer afford to make special meals for the crew. You should make soup instead of distributing the tins. Stretch the remaining supply over the next few days. Surely by then the transfer boats will come."

"Aye aye, Captain."

Nikos descended to the galley and started boiling big vats of water. He opened a package of dehydrated meat, usually used to feed the captain and crew, and tipped it into the boiling water. He added two hundred tins of rations, a few chopped onions and turnips, making thin soup to feed 850 passengers and the crew.

As Nikos chopped turnips into tiny cubes, he thought of the pretty red-headed girl in the woman's compartment. He didn't know her name, but she was the most beautiful girl he had ever met, even now, with her greasy red hair and dirty fingernails. During the first few days, when she came to get her ration of tinned food, he'd handed it to her personally, but felt too shy to speak to her.

When it was her platoon's turn on deck, he heard someone call her by name, Oshrah. Even her name sounded like a goddess. He took his break when she was on deck, hoping she would notice him. With the sun at her back, her red hair, long-since free of its pins, glowed like flaming scribbles around her head as the warm breeze tossed it across her face. Still, he was sure she hadn't noticed him.

Finally, he gathered his nerve and spoke to her, "Γεια σας, με λένε Nikos."

She looked at him curiously but seemed to understand enough. "I am Oshrah," she said in her native Romanian dialect.

They stood looking at each other, then she said, "Nice to meet you, Nikos," and returned to her compartment.

Of course, all he understood was his own name, Nikos. It sounded like honey on her tongue.

The next day when she came to collect her ration of thin soup, he said, "*Sprichst du Deutsch?*" then held his breath.

"*Ja*," she grinned, "thanks for the soup," she said in rough German with a heavy dialect.

"*Gerne geschehen*," he replied in terrible German.

Their romance had begun.

Chapter 22

July 25, 1939

Yutka contemplated the tiny bits of meat floating on top of her thin soup and thought of the chores she disliked so much in Dobrzyń. *I am so hungry,* she thought. *I would happily reach into a broody hen's nest to retrieve a warm, fresh egg. And, oh, for a glass of sweet milk straight from our old cow.*

She heard the pale, broken cry of the starving newborn. Zosia, hunching over the purplish-red infant, tried to nurse, but her naked breasts hung as flat as empty pockets; the baby was too frail to suckle. Yutka noticed Zosia's spine poking through her thin cotton dress. Her hands were red and chapped and her long, dark hair hung in a felted mat down her back. A few clumps of black fuzz spread over the baby's bald head.

Yutka put her own serving on the table, then reached to hold the infant while Zosia drank her soup. "You're very brave to travel alone with a newborn baby."

"I should be so brave," tears rolled from Zosia's sunken eyes, as she spoke in Yiddish, finally able to speak of the horror she had experienced. "They give me no choice. The Germans, they kill my husband, my baby boy, and my mama and papa. I run to hide in woods. Resistance woman, she find me, take me to safe-house. Channah born in Paris hotel while we wait for boat." Zosia brought the soup to her lips.

Yutka cuddled the nearly weightless bundle to her chest. Accompanied by the drone of the ship's engine and vibration of the hull, she crooned an ancient Sephardic lullaby, inviting the baby to sleep peacefully.

Durme, durme ermozo ijiko,
Durme, durme sin ansia i dolor,
Serra tus lindos ojikos,
Durme kon savor

Sleep, sleep, my beautiful little girl,
Sleep, sleep with no worry or pain,
Close your nice little eyes,
Sleep delightfully.

The infant stopped her fragile wailing and frantically twisted her tiny, twig-like fingers around her mouth, her head turning side to side as if her gaping bird-like mouth might find food. Yutka remembered her sister Rozka singing the lullaby to Jerzyk and Rebekah.

Zosia whispered, "You have lovely voice and a way with babies."

"Please have my soup too," said Yutka, pointing to the tin she used as a soup bowl. "You need energy to nurse your baby."

"*A sheynem dank*, God bless."

When Yutka gently returned Channah to her mother's skeletal arms, Yutka realized tears had spilled from own her eyes. She longed to sing to her nephew and new niece.

Later that day, Yutka climbed to the wheelhouse, "Captain, may I have a word?" she asked in German, looking up at the tall Russian.

"What is it, Miss?"

"There is a woman on board who is nursing a three-week-old baby. The mother is so undernourished and dehydrated, the baby will not survive. Is it possible for the woman to get extra rations of soup and water?"

Captain Mikhailovich stroked his bearded chin with the back of his fingers while his sad dark eyes looked out to sea, "What is your name?"

"I am Yutka Lipka from Dobrzyń, Poland," she said as she raised her chin.

"Have you discussed this with your platoon leader?"

"I am the leader of my platoon sir. I'm sorry, but I came straight to you instead of going to Commander Leibovitz. The baby will die if the mother doesn't get food soon."

When the captain turned his face toward her, she looked into his sad black eyes. In a stern, deep voice, he spoke German with a heavy Greek accent, "It is courageous of you to ask, Miss Lipka, but sadly, if the transfer boats don't come tonight, we will have thin soup for only one more day. Everyone on board is starving, not just the young mother and her baby. If nothing changes, I will be forced to return the ship to France. Perhaps tonight the rendezvous boats will come. Otherwise, tomorrow we sail to Alexandretta and try to buy bread and water. If we succeed, I will see that the mother gets extra rations."

Chapter 23

Bread and Water

At daybreak on the fourth day of waiting for the transfer boats, the captain cruised to the Port at Alexandretta, but the Turkish authorities refused to sell the Jews bread and water and demanded the ship leave immediately or they would shoot to kill.

Captain Mikhailovich cruised back to the waters off Cyprus, but the overnight wait for the transfer boats proved futile again. He set sail for Rhodes, hoping he could buy bread and water even though Italian fascists occupied Rhodes.

Yutka held her breath as Italian officers in the Port of Rhodes, with guns pointed at his back, escorted Captain Mikhailovich back to *Parita*.

When the captain was safely on board, Commander Leibovitz shouted, "We will protest!"

The starving and dehydrated refugees who had survived on thin soup for over a week roared in agreement.

"What if they shoot at us?" shrieked Elsa.

"Then we should die from bullets!" said Commander Leibovitz. "All of us will die of starvation if we fail. What do we have to lose?"

Just then, about fifty meters away, a ferry passed, carrying passengers from one end of Rhodes to the other. "Here's our opportunity," shouted Jacob Ariel. "If we annoy them enough, perhaps they will relent and sell us bread and water so we will leave."

Like a flock of frenzied gulls, they shouted in their native tongues. More refugees joined the protest, some so feeble their voices hoarsely chirped the words.

Yutka saw the crowd gathering on shore and clearly heard them shouting, "*Hessun ebreo!*" She didn't speak Italian, but their angry faces made their message clear.

When the ferry passed them every two hours, they repeated their chant for bread and water.

As they shouted, the shadow of a plane cast over the refugees on deck. Yutka held her breath, closed her eyes, and prayed, too frightened to move. She waited for the thump of fiery bombs. The crack-crack-crack of gunfire. Any second, she and her comrades would fall into a heap of bleeding bodies. The *Parita* would sink. The terrifying moment, actually milliseconds, ended when she heard the seaplane's pontoons splash onto the water. She opened her eyes to watch saltwater spray over the plane as the flying boat broke the lustrous surface of the turquoise sea and coasted to the dock.

Yutka found her breath when a young man opened the plane's door and waved his arms over his head toward them. She had seen photos of Eri Jabotinsky, Ze'ev Jabotinsky's son. The refugees cheered. The Italian port guard met Eri and two other Betarim and escorted them into the maritime office at gunpoint.

For over an hour, while negotiations continued, Yutka, Elsa, Yaakov and the others chanted in their native tongues creating an explosion of sound. Their disheveled appearance told the story more clearly than their words.

Chapter 24

The *Marco Polo*

A shockingly gigantic luxury liner, the *Marco Polo*, with its eight decks, cinema, lounges, library, swimming pool, and gym, moored in the waters near the port of Rhodes just 183 meters from the *Parita*. Each of her passengers enjoyed a cabin with clean linens on a comfortable mattress, with a private bathroom in every cabin. Over fifteen hundred vacationers enjoyed all they could eat and drink in a variety of formal dining rooms and casual cafés.

The new Mrs. Goldfarb, a sophisticated American wearing a vibrant blue silk blouse with a calf-length pencil skirt and a matching hat snuggled into her wavy blonde hair, sat with her husband in the formal dining room of the luxury liner. Mrs. Goldfarb ate only half of her serving of filet mignon cooked with rosemary, butter, olive oil, and black pepper, then put her knife and fork at 5:00 and 7:00 and placed her hands in her lap waiting for the server to remove her half-full plate. Another waiter served her French vanilla ice cream covered with sliced fresh peaches.

Mr. Goldfarb had finished all of his salmon with *mousseline* sauce and fresh cucumber when the waiter brought his peaches in chartreuse jelly. Mr. Goldfarb leaned over his dessert, breathed the cinnamon and cloves, "Ah, it smells as good as it looks."

She rested her hand with her sparkling diamond ring on the white tablecloth next to his plate. He lifted her hand and kissed her palm.

After finishing their desserts, Mr. and Mrs. Goldfarb climbed the grand staircase to the promenade deck where a waiter served them Quinta Das Carvalhas tawny port wine in Royal Scot Crystal glasses. Mr. Goldfarb sniffed the fine port, his eyes sparkling toward his beautiful wife, then took a sip. "Marvelous! It has notes of walnut and hazelnut followed by racy orange zest, dates, and ginger."

Mrs. Goldfarb giggled at her husband's pretentious analysis. "Darling, you're just showing off!"

He grinned and took another sip, "It's lovely. Tell me I'm wrong."

She sniffed and took a sip, "You're right, darling. The port is lovely and smooth." She relaxed after their decadent meal with her white stockings and wide-toed blue shoes propped on the lounge chair. "But I don't smell walnuts and ginger," she laughed.

The Goldfarbs heard chanting, but they could not decipher the blur of languages.

לחם ומים (Hebrew)
עסן און וואסער (Yiddish)
Mâncare și apă (Rumanian)
Jedzenie i woda (Polish)
Nahrung und wasser (German)
Еда и вода (Russian)
Nourriture et eau (French)

"What's the ruckus?" Mr. Goldfarb asked a passing waiter.

"Seems to be some sort of protest," he said, skittering by in his crisp white uniform, unwilling to discuss the unsavory matter.

Another server came by with the bottle of port, offering to refill their glass. "It's lovely port, but no, thank you," said Mr. Goldfarb. They put their empty crystal glasses on the waiter's silver tray and walked to the stern of the luxury liner.

Mrs. Goldfarb put her monogrammed linen hankie to her nose. "What is that wretched smell?" From high above the shabby *Parita*, they saw refugees waving toward the passing ferry. They listened to them chant and realized they were demanding bread and water. Mrs. Goldfarb turned to her husband. "That little boat appears to be bursting with Jewish refugees," she said. "This is a lovely honeymoon darling but suddenly I feel pampered and foolish on this magnificent ship." They hugged, and he kissed her forehead.

"It appears that the unrest in Europe is escalating," he said. "From the looks of it, Hitler is intensifying his push for *judenrein*. Bloody bastard."

The Goldfarbs listened to the growing crowd on shore shouting, "*No Jews!*"

"I'm questioning our safety, darling. We should return to New York as soon as possible. This is not a suitable time to cruise the Mediterranean.

"I'll have a word with the captain."

While her husband went to the wheelhouse, Mrs. Goldfarb found the purser and arranged for supplies to be sent to the *Parita*. Within an hour, the *Marco Polo* crew lowered two sparkling white dinghies into the blue water. When they pulled alongside carrying crates of oranges and kegs of beer, Yutka, Elsa, Yaakov and some of the other refugees waved thank you to the tourist high above them on the aft deck of the gigantic ship moored next to them. Mrs. Goldfarb couldn't have known that hundreds of refugees huddled below deck, some too afraid and others too sick to join the protest.

Yutka watched the crew hoist the first crates of oranges onto the deck. The sweet citrus scent made Yutka's stomach twist. Commander Leibovitz and the crew quickly took charge and rationed the oranges as the refugees swarmed around the crates.

"Return to your compartments," shouted the commander. "Platoon leaders will distribute the oranges and beer."

As the ship rocked at its moorage, Yutka and Yaakov moved from bunk to bunk, rationing the orange sections among the hungry refugees. Too soon, the fruit was gone. Less than a section of orange and a dram of beer was a poor alternative for bread and water.

Yutka licked her fingers, her only ration.

✡

Even Eri Jabotinsky could not persuade the Italian fascists to sell the Jews water, food, and coal.

After the *Parita* had moored in the port at Rhodes for three days, six Italian soldiers boarded the vessel. With rifles and machine guns, they demanded that the *Parita* leave port. The refugees huddled in their bunks in their putrid, infernal compartments, wondering if the soldiers would sink the boat and drown them all. Finally, in international waters, the soldiers disembarked to their own ship, promising to shoot to kill if the *Parita* returned to Rhodes.

Chapter 25

Entertaining the children

As the sea roiled beneath the *Parita* and the days dragged on, Elsa noticed Mrs. Edelman on deck doing her best to occupy four-year-old Priscilla and three-year-old Rochelle, while Mr. Edelman languished in their bunk with spells of seasickness. "Hello Mrs. Edelman, will you introduce me to your daughters?"

"This is Priscilla, and this is Rochelle, girls this is *Mademoiselle* Elsa." Both girls had long dark hair pulled back into thick plaits, with curly wisps escaping around their round faces. Elsa was sad to see the dark circles under their eyes. Rochelle remained entirely serious, but even as hungry as she was, Priscilla danced with mischief. "*Enchanté, Mademoiselle* Elsa," replied Priscilla, while Rochelle lowered her chin and stared up at Elsa through her long, dark eyelashes.

Elsa sat on the deck leaning against the bow and crossed her legs like a yogi. "Can I tell you a story?" she asked the girls.

Priscilla jumped and clapped, "*Oui, Oui,* tell us a story." She ran to sit next to Elsa, with her doll, Babette, in her lap. Her sister Rochelle peeked from behind their maman's skirt.

"Do you want to hear a story about a little rabbit?"

Rochelle nodded yes but stayed close to her maman. Her eyelashes cast shadows on her pale cheeks.

"Once upon a time," began Elsa, "there was a little rabbit who lived in a hollow tree with his maman, brothers and sisters. His name was Pierre." As Elsa told the story, Rochelle slowly sat down beside her sister with her little legs straight out in front of her and her back against the droopy bow at the back of her dress. Elsa told them the story of the mischievous rabbit who was so hungry, he disobeyed his maman and crept into the farmer's garden to pilfer a carrot."

A tear rolled down Priscilla's check.

"Are you afraid for the little bunny?" asked Elsa.

"*Non*, I am hungry too."

"Oh sweetie." Her heart aching, Elsa hugged Priscilla's bony shoulders. "We are all hungry but as soon as the boat arrives in *Eretz* Israel you and Rochelle will have all the food you want."

The second engineer, Serioja, was nearby. As Elsa told the story about the hungry rabbit, Serioja went below deck and returned just as she finished. Serioja introduced himself in German, "*Hallo, Ich bin Serioja,*" he said, pointing to himself. "*Ich habe brot für dich.*"

The little French girls didn't know what he said, but his meaning was clear. He tore a chunk of bread in two and offered it to Rochelle and Priscilla. At first, they gazed wide-eyed at the bread, then turned to their maman, "*Oui, dis merci.*"

Both girls whispered, "*Merci beaucoup, Monsieur* Serioja," and he put the bread into their outstretched little hands.

Then he turned to Elsa, "It is a terrible thing that children should be so hungry." Yutka, standing nearby, translated his German to French for Elsa and the girls.

✡

Elsa held a daily story time for Rochelle and Priscilla in the family compartment. When possible, they sat in the shade of the wheelhouse, out of the oppressive heat and vile milieu below deck. Sometimes the boys joined them. The boys spoke only German, so Yutka translated.

One morning, as they sat in their story circle, Serioja brought a loaf of bread and pulled off chunks for each child.

"*Jetzt werde ich dir eine geschichte erzählen.*" Serioja offered to tell a story.

"Serioja, since the girls do not speak German, I will translate your story for them, yes?"

"*Sehr gut.*"

Yutka sat down with the children and Elsa. "Serioja will tell you a story and I will translate so everyone will understand, *oui*?"

Sometimes Yutka's translation was superfluous, as Serioja told the story with his animated face and lively gestures.

"When I was no more than a child, I worked on ships out in the Atlantic Ocean where the water was deep, cold, and dark green, nothing like the Mediterranean Sea where the water is the color of blue and much warmer. My first job was on a ship called the *Preussen*. She had an iron hull like the *Parita*, but she had five tall masts and huge square sails. She used the wind for energy instead of these loud smelly steam engines, and there was no smoke from the stacks."

As their faces turned up to see the smear of dark smoke staining the clear blue sky, Yutka translated.

"The *Preussen* could cruise at twenty knots, the fastest windjammer ever built. And she was so quiet," Yutka whispered. "The only sound was the water lapping onto her prow, the wind whistling through the rigging and the flap of the sails."

Serioja put his hands next to his mouth and made the sound of whistling wind with his breath. "A ship that size would never travel on a sea as small as this." His arms swept around, indicating the surrounding sea.

"Bigger than this? We can't even see land!" gasped one boy.

"That's right, just imagine! The oceans are much bigger than the Mediterranean Sea. My job on the *Preussen* was to help rig the sails. I was a little tyke for my age, so it was easy for me to climb hand over foot way up to the top of those tall masts."

Serioja mimes climbing the mast.

"Weren't you afraid?"

"Aye, sometimes," Serioja nodded his head, then pointed to the duck-egg-blue sky above the *Parita*. "Sometimes I sat in the crow's nest on the main mast high above the deck and I was too afraid to climb back down."

Their little faces turned toward the sky. "What's a crow's nest?" asked Priscilla.

"A crow's nest is like a basket at the top of the tallest mast on a ship propelled by the wind. Sailors can see far into the distance and watch out for obstacles like shallow water or other ships. When I was in the crow's nest and the wind was strong, I had to hold on tight because the mast whipped from side to side, as though she tried to throw me into the sea." Serioja made sounds like the wind and pretended to hold on as he swayed from side to side.

"One calm day, I was in the crow's nest, enjoying the view of the vast deep green ocean. Suddenly, I saw a sea monster." Serioja's mouth flew open, and his eyes grew big with fear, and so did the children's. His arms flew out to his sides. "It was long like a serpent, but it had fins like a fish. From the crow's nest I could see in the water that it was longer than our ship!" His volume increasing, he said, "The creature came straight up out of the deep green water with his mouth wide open, wide enough to swallow the whole ship. Afraid or not, I scrambled down the mast as fast as I could and ran to tell the captain what I saw. Now, mind you, I was no more than a child. The captain laughed at me." Serioja used a deep voice, to sound like the captain, "'There is no creature in the ocean so big as to swallow this ship.'" Serioja pushed his head back, laughed in a low voice as if he were the captain. "'Ha, ha, ha. Perhaps, little boy, you need to take a rest.' Just then the creature came alongside the ship and the grownup sailors saw the monster open its mouth. They shouted and came running to the captain's bridge, but before the captain could react, huge, purple storm clouds materialized out of the west. Suddenly, the wind blew hard, and the ship rocked on the waves." Serioja rolled side to side and spoke faster. "We hurried to man the sails and forgot all about the giant sea serpent. The sky was as dark as night. Lightning flashed around us brighter than the sun. The thunder was so loud my ears hurt." He put his hands over his ears and squeezed his eyes shut while Yutka translated.

"The swells grew. Our ship seemed so tiny on those mountainous crests. The wind tossed us high onto the top of one crest, then we fell into the deep trough. A wave tossed us so high, the ship became airborne and rolled onto her side. We held on tight, and the cold rain and sea water poured over us. We thought we'd roll over overboard into the deep trough at the bottom of the giant waves."

"*Tu as survécu?*" whispered four-year-old Priscilla, her black diamond eyes as big as dumplings.

Elsa noticed Priscilla used the word *survived,* a word that, sadly, even a four-year-old on the *Parita* was familiar with.

"For sure I did survive and so did the rest of the crew. That giant sea serpent curled around our ship." The children sucked in their breath. "But instead of crushing the iron hull in its mighty grip, which we all expected, of course," Serioja looked around and nodded to the children as Yutka translated. "He gently set us upright in the high winds and lurching waves. He coiled around the hull, keeping us from capsizing until the storm passed. When the sun came out and the swells disappeared, the monster slithered through the sea and disappeared into the dark green water."

"Are there sea monsters like that here?" asked Priscilla, looking anxiously toward the water.

"Like I said, the Mediterranean Sea is far too warm for such creatures."

Elsa asked the children, "Do you think Serioja's story is true?"

The oldest boy, Emmanuel, smiled. "No, it's just a story, like in books. In school our teacher told us about the book, *Moby Dick*. It was just a story. The big whale wasn't real."

Elsa noticed that Priscilla and the younger boys relaxed when they learned Serioja had invented his tale. With Yutka's translations, the story lasted longer than usual. Rochelle had fallen asleep in her mother's lap long before the monster materialized in Serioja's story.

"Thank you for the bread," said Priscilla, looking at Serioja with her black diamond eyes surrounded with purple shadows. "And thank you for telling us a story."

Serioja often shared food and stories with the children. He became known on the *Parita* as *The Angel*.

Chapter 26

Levivots

The Greek cook, Nikos, was in the galley cleaning when the Rumanian redhead and a few other Rumanian women approached him. In her halting German she asked, "My friends will like to make *levivot* for people. You have flour and oil?"

Beside himself that this beauty actually spoke to him, Nikos eagerly replied, "Let's look in the larder," even though he knew their request was unauthorized.

"There is enough flour and oil," said Nikos, "but it will take the entire night to make 850 pancakes."

"*Da. Da,*" the young women bobbed their heads with excitement.

While Nikos and Oshrah found an alcove where they could be alone, the women went to work.

They added boiling water to flour and kneaded the dough until it became soft and slightly sticky. They toiled throughout the night frying batches of *levivot*, making enough for every refugee to have just one small pancake.

It was the French group's turn to eat first, then the Polish group. They were all delighted with the surprise *levivots* accompanying their runny soup. Although warned to take only one pancake, some refugees were too hungry to resist.

When the Rumanian's turn came, they saw Mr. Edelman and a few others, standing around smiling, chewing, with a pancake in each hand. The platters were empty. "*You ganefs!*" screamed a fifteen-year-old Rumanian. "The women spent the night cooking for all of us, and you ate our *levivot*! For days we have nothing but thin soup! They are making something special, and you eat our portion! *Ganefs!*

Commander Leibovitz remained unaware of the trespass on the kitchen and the resulting situation until the angry mob spilled onto the deck. The fifteen-year-old Rumanian, balanced on his friend's shoulders, was shouting above his angry countrymen, "We smelled the warm, fresh food all night, and the *ganefs* ate our *levivots*! We demand justice!"

Commander Leibovitz intervened, "Stop the shouting and come with me." He led the small group to the stern of the ship. "Listen to me. I will see that you receive a double ration of soup."

"Ha! You offer us more lousy soup! We won't stand for it!"

"The women made the *levivot* without permission," said Leibovitz. "Nonetheless, if you calm down and quit causing trouble, I'll discuss the situation with the cook. Stay here and I'll be back in a few minutes."

The commander returned to the grumbling crowd, "I have arranged for the group who did not get a *levivot* to have macaroni in their soup."

By now, the Rumanian teens were so irate, not to mention hungry, they continued to demand retribution. "We will see for ourselves what food is left," yelled one young Rumanian. "We'll find something in the storeroom."

"I will take two of you on a tour of the storeroom, and you can report to the others, but believe me, the shelves are bare." Commander Leibovitz feared he would have a mutiny on his hands if he didn't satisfy the cheated Rumanians, even if the *levivots* were unauthorized.

After convincing the boys that the larder was truly bare, he gathered the group on deck. "Sit and listen to me," he said in a soft voice.

When they quieted and sat on the deck next to him, he continued, "The best I can do is offer all of you is macaroni in a double portion of soup. It is all I have to offer. You have seen the situation for yourselves. The larder is empty."

They grumbled but agreed.

Then quietly, almost to himself, the commander added, "Let us hope we can buy food in Izmir tomorrow."

Just when Leibovitz thought he had satisfied the passengers, Mr. Edelman began making trouble again, leading a group of men from the family compartment, "Our commander is just a boy!" shouted Mr. Edelman, a pest throughout the trip. "What can he know about commanding a ship!"

Another man shouted, "He's the reason we are starving!" A few others gathered around.

Flanked by two Betar operatives, Jacob Ariel and Elijaha Even, Commander Leibovitz used an orange crate as a podium on the stern of the boat. The small group booed loudly but Leibovitz raised his hands to speak. "Betar leaders put this ship under my command. I have the responsibility to bring you to *Eretz* Israel. You have my commitment to carry out my mission, fulfill this promise and complete the *Parita's* mission. If you doubt me, throw me off the deck into the sea."

The refugees were silent, except for Edelman. He knew nothing of *Erwin* Leibovitz's background. He based his discontent solely on his own hunger and "Erwin's" youthful face rather than on the young man's credentials. As Edelman continued to complain, Jacob Ariel and Eliyaha Even stood on either side of him. Eliyaha announced to the mob, "Leibovitz has more knowledge and experience in his twenty years than you can ever hope to achieve. Now, Mr. Edelman, you're causing trouble again, a punishable offence. The commander warned you of additional disciplinary measures. If you cause trouble again, we will strap you to that post near the bow of the boat for twelve hours, no questions asked. Do you understand?" They released his arms, and he scurried back to his bunk.

Chapter 27

Ekmek ve su, Izmir, August 8th

The captain cruised to Izmir, hoping that the Turks would be more accommodating. Yutka, Elsa, Yaakov, and others, stood at the bow watching a crew member row Captain Mikhailvich ashore. While the crew member waited in the dinghy, the captain climbed onto the dock and saluted a Turkish guard who wore a black-tasseled red *tarboosh*, which Yutka thought looked strangely out of place above his khaki German-looking uniform.

While the captain disappeared into port headquarters, Commander Leibovitz rallied the refugees again. "Let's tell them what we need so they'll understand."

"*Ekmek ve su* is Turkish for bread and water," said Yaakov.

Yutka looked at Yaakov, "You also speak Turkish?"

"Enough," one eyebrow went up as he lifted his shoulders and laughed, then admitted, "I asked the cook."

Yutka and the other platoon leaders taught everyone on deck the Turkish phrase. Soon, they all chanted in unison. "*Ekmek ve su! Ekmek ve su! Ekmek ve su!*"

They watched Captain Mikhailvich step into the dinghy, at gunpoint, and row back to the *Parita*. The port authorities had refused to sell provisions to the Jews, however, they had agreed to supply water.

The spiteful Turks rowed alongside the *Parita,* laughing with their bare feet dangling in the buckets of fresh water. The dehydrated immigrants didn't notice or care. Yutka, and other platoon leaders took buckets of water to their compartments, but there was scarcely enough for each passenger to have a small drink, not nearly enough to recover from their severe dehydration.

They cruised back to Cyprus, hoping the transfer boats would come to take the immigrants aboard, maneuver through the British blockade and deliver them to their new homeland. Night after night, the boats failed to appear. With nothing to do, they languished in their uncomfortable bunks, staring at the rusty hull or the pine boards above them.

Serioja noticed the children were becoming more and more snippy and irritable as hunger and boredom settled over them. He used a carpenter's flat yellow pencil to divide a piece of cardboard into one hundred two-inch squares, creating a board game to entertain them. After numbering the squares 1-100, he drew ladders and slides and cut out cardboard pawns for each child and made a spinner numbered from 1 to 5.

He demonstrated the rules of the game. "If a player lands on the first rung of a ladder, the player's pawn skips over squares, but if the player's pawn lands on a slide the player falls back. The first player to reach the 100th square is the winner." The board game was especially entertaining for three-year-old Rochelle and her sister Priscilla who were learning to count, and even the older boy, Emmanuel, enjoyed playing the game with the little girls, all of them learning Hebrew with Yutka's help.

✡

Yutka and Elsa strolled the deck as the light sea breeze tossed their matted hair and sunrise lit their dirty faces. After so many days on the *Parita*, their sea legs no longer noticed the motion of the boat and the vibration of the metal hull.

Elsa shrieked, pointing at the horizon, "Is that a submarine?"

Yutka, standing beside Elsa, tented her hand over her eyes. They watched the long dark underwater shadow come closer. "If it is a submarine, it's likely to torpedo the ship." They put their arms around each other and stood dead still, expecting to see a torpedo hiss through the water as they watched the dark figure move closer.

"It's not a submarine, it's a whale!" shouted Yutka, finally taking a breath. "See the spout! What else could it be? Look! There's more than one!"

The dark gray backs of the gigantic creatures crested, clearly not submarines. Their blunt shaped snouts surfaced, and with a soft *fwissshhhh* sound, water sprayed from their blowholes, before their fins disappeared one by one below the turquoise surface.

One creature came closer, curious about the boat. Its large watery eye looked straight up at Yutka and Elsa leaning over the railing as if over a backyard fence. Waving at the curious creature, Yutka said, "They're sperm whales. I saw pictures in a book at school but never dreamed I'd actually see real ones! So far I've counted at least seven or eight. And look! There's a baby staying close to its mama."

Other refugees from their platoon joined them at the side of the boat. "They are living their lives as if there is no war," said a woman behind Yutka.

"They look so happy and well-fed in their crystal clean home," said another.

The group of fifty refugees solemnly watched as the pod of whales, sovereign and self-reliant, swam away.

Chapter 28

Zosia and Channah

Again, the *Parita* zigzagged off the coast of Cyprus. The days seemed long, the nights even longer as they waited for the transfer boats that never came.

One morning at dawn, Yutka climbed from her bunk to do the needful, used a page from her notebook for toilet paper and a ladle of sea water to wash. The salt stung her chapped hands as she shook them dry.

Rather than going back to her bunk, to mitigate the boredom, she absentmindedly descended the stairs below the galley exploring the ship. Perspiration trickled down her back. The heat was oppressive. The hull groaned even louder. The engine's roar was deafening. She passed pipes that supplied steam and noticed a tiny, sizzling leak. She cupped her hands over the steam and hot water condensed on her palms. It took only a few seconds for her to collect enough vapor to wash her hands. Repeating the process, she rubbed warm water on her face. "Thank you for this tiny pleasure," she whispered aloud, although she wondered if God was listening.

She groped her way down the companion way through the quiet compartment toward her bunk. Before climbing up, she stood in the aisle focusing on Zosia and the baby. Something didn't feel right. Waiting for her eyes to adjust to the dim light Yutka gazed at the skeletal infant, asleep in her mother's bony arms. Yutka suddenly realized, the baby's lips were deep blue. "Zosia," she screamed. "Channah isn't breathing!" As Zosia opened her sunken eyes, Yutka yelled, "Elsa, find the medic!"

Immediately awake, Elsa jumped from her top bunk without touching the bunks in between. She scaled the companionway to the deck ran to the aft compartment hatchway jumped below deck in the men's compartment scarcely touching the steps and at the top of her lungs she shouted, "Yaakov! Yaakov! We need a medic! Yaakov!"

When she saw Yaakov climb over his two bunkmates, she screamed, "Hurry! The baby isn't breathing!"

Yaakov raced across the deck and crashed down the steps into the family compartment. He found Yutka in the aisle. She closed her eyes as she bowed her head. "I'm afraid we're losing Zosia too," she whispered.

Yaakov knelt next to the bottom bunk, the knees of his once-pristine trousers soaked up the rancid muck of vomit and sludge. He checked Zosia's pulse and whispered to her gently, "My name is Yaakov. I am a medic. I'm here to help you."

Unaware of Yaakov's presence, Zosia hugged her dead baby while descending into a feverish stupor.

Zosia, five months pregnant, her husband, and their son, flee their home near Munich, trying to escape to France. Hiding in ditches and forests, they have nearly reached the Liechtenstein border when Nazi soldiers spot them. As if in target practice, the Nazis soldiers shoulder their rifles and take aim at the escaping Jews. A friend and member of the resistance pushes Zosia out of sight. Zosia hears the loud crack-crack-crack. She watches as her husband's chest turns bright red and he falls to the ground, clutching their two-year-old son whose head flops back when a bullet rips through his tiny neck. The loud sound reverberates all around while she crouches behind a pile of debris. Her friend holds her tight. A silent wail rises from Zosia's gaping mouth. She fights to run to her child and husband. "You must save yourself and your baby," whispers her friend, resting her red, chapped hand on Zosia's slightly swollen belly.

The Nazis march on, leaving the bleeding bodies in the dust that rises from beneath their gleaming black boots. They laugh as if they have eliminated a pack of pesky rodents.

When the Nazis are out of sight, her friend leads Zosia into the dense forest where they wander among the oak, spruce, and Scots pine, trying to stay safe. They meet up with other Jews who are escaping across Liechtenstein to France. Hiding beneath a stinking pile of rubbish in the bed of a garbage truck, the operatives smuggle Zosia across the border to a safe house in the French countryside. "You will hide here until our ship is ready to transfer refugees to Eretz Israel."

"I have no money to pay for such a trip."

"Don't worry, you and your husband were members of Betar, you will have a place on the ship when it is time."

Three months later, the operatives move Zosia to the hotel in Paris where Dr. Reuben Hecht has arranged for a group of German and Austrian Jews to hide from the authorities. In the small hotel room with ten other refugees, Zosia's contractions begin. One of the Jewish mothers helps during the short labor. The woman cleans the tiny, malnourished newborn, not even two kilos. Then she takes off her dirty, tattered shawl, so faded its original color is a mystery. She swaddles the tiny infant.

"What is her name?" asks the de facto midwife.
"After my mama, Channah...

Finally, Zosia's eyes fluttered open and she hears Yaakov. "No medic can help us now," she said in a raspy whisper. "My husband, my baby boy, and now my Channah are all dead."

Feeling helpless, Yutka, Yaakov, and Elsa whispered a blessing for the baby, "*Yehi zichra baruch.*"

In the midst of her sorrow and fear, Yutka shivered with a flicker of gratitude, *This could have been my newborn niece, dead in Rozka's arms.*

Elsa stood behind Yaakov; the terror of the past few months reflected in her deep blue eyes.

"Elsa, please find water for Zosia," directed Yaakov.

"No bother, I am going to my family now," whispered Zosia, but Elsa had already leapt onto the deck.

Yutka knelt down on the edge of Zosia's bunk, next to Yaakov. Even in the repressive heat, she could feel the fire of Zosia's fever, "Zosia, we will help you survive. Life will be better when we reach *Eretz* Israel."

Elsa hurried down the companionway, trying not to spill the tin of precious water. Yaakov gently slid his hand behind Zosia's head and tried to help her drink.

"No. I must stay with my Channah," she rasped. She closed her eyes as her head rolled in Yaakov's hand.

Yaakov passed the tin of water back to Elsa and pressed his fingers to Zosia's neck. "She is also gone." He slowly lowered her head to the hard pine board.

Yutka heard whispered blessings throughout the sweltering family compartment, "*Yehi zichra baruch.*"

Yaakov slowly backed away and climbed onto the deck.

✡

Yutka was not an orthodox Jew however, she felt compelled to perform the *Tahara* for Zosia and Channah.

"We have no seven pitchers of warm water and sponge to cleanse the bodies," Yutka looked at Elsa. "We have only this small tin of water, but I will do the *Tahara* ceremony as best I can."

Yutka climbed to her bunk, dug to the bottom of her knapsack, and retrieved a rag. The rags were the only clean items left in her knapsack, but they had lost the scent of lavender and sunshine.

She crouched next to Zosia's bunk, ignoring the muck on her own knees and the stench in her nostrils. As she lightly sprinkled the precious water over the bodies, the tension and despair lifted from her shoulders, as if she had stepped outside of herself. A profound connection to her faith consumed her. *The* Tahara *will provide comfort to their souls. God will understand.*

As she whispered prayers, she wiped the drops of water away from Zosia's face, neck, and shoulders. Yutka distinctly sensed the two souls hovering, ready for their transition.

Then, without moving Channah, still clutched in her mother's arms, Yutka gently eased the damp cloth over the baby's microscopic eyelashes closed against her skeletal cheeks. Yutka cleaned the fisted hands, no bigger than olives. For a few moments, Yutka held the diminutive, unnaturally dark-skinned feet, smaller than her thumb, cupped in her palm. *Jerzyk and Rebekah were never this small,* she thought as she swabbed the tiny, wrinkled soles. Those perfect toes, like apple seeds, would never touch the red dirt of *Eretz* Israel.

Yaakov appeared beside her.

"Where did you find a white sheet?" she asked.

"The captain will not miss it," he softly answered with a tight, wry smile.

Without a word, Elsa helped Yutka gently wrap Zosia and the baby in the shroud, then said a prayer, "May you be a messenger for all of Israel. Zosia and Channah, go in peace, rest in peace, and arise in your turn at the end of days."

On such a small ship, they could not isolate the children from the tragedy. Three-year-old Rochelle, four-year-old Priscilla, and the others sat quietly in their bunks.

"What is wrong with the baby," Priscilla whispered to her maman. "She looks purple."

Joséphine Edelman couldn't hide her tears. "Her maman was too hungry and weak to produce milk for her." She paused, deciding the truth was the best answer. "The baby has died."

"Because she was so hungry?"

Joséphine could see where the questioning would go, "Yes, my sweet girl, they died because the baby and the mother were both too hungry. A brand new baby must have its mother's milk but Zosia was to hungry to make it."

Priscilla's innocent, dark, sunken eyes, looked at her maman, asking the inevitable question, "I am hungry. Will I die too?"

Mrs. Edelman squeezed her daughter to her, "No my sweet, you are old enough to eat soup and bread."

Nearly four hundred nautical miles from *Eretz* Israel, there would be no opportunity for burial in the red earth. After dark, when they could safely go on deck without passing ships noticing them, they carried the shroud-wrapped bodies, feet first, into the warm night air. As word spread through the bowels of the ship, refugees and Greek crew members joined them.

Nikos, the cook, comforted Oshrah while she wept.

The brothers from Yaakov's bunk, Klaus and Reiner, wiped their tears.

Mr. and Mrs. Edelman stood among the crowd, grim-faced, clinging to their daughters.

Water pinged against the iron hull. The keel softly vibrated as the engine idled in honor of Zosia and Channah.

"Look!" pointed Yutka. "The water has blue light in it. What's happening?" She looked around to see if the light came from another ship or a submarine.

"It's called bioluminescence," said Serioja. "Amazing, yes?"

"How does it happen?"

"I don't understand how they do it but tiny organism, like jelly fish and squid, create light, just like fireflies, yes?"

"It's as if God lit candles in the sea," whispered Yutka.

The Jews on board represented many nationalities, many languages, and many branches of Judaism. Shoulder to shoulder, they bowed their heads and prayed together.

"Zosia must have been the woman who had a baby in the Paris hotel. I saw her carrying the baby to a fishing boat when we left the train in Marseille." Elsa wiped her eyes with her fists as if she were a child. She looked around. "So many have come on deck to honor her. Zosia thought she was alone in the world.... I wish this gathering could have been her welcome to a new life in a new land, not her funeral."

Yaakov led them as they prayed the Mourner's *Kaddish*.

> *May the great Name of God be exalted and sanctified, throughout the world, which He has created according to his will. May His Kingship be established in your lifetime and in your days, and in the lifetime of the entire household of Israel, swiftly and in the near future; and say, Amen.*
>
> *May His great name be blessed, forever and ever. Blessed, praised, glorified, exalted, extolled, honored, elevated and lauded be the Name of the holy one, Blessed is He, above and beyond any blessings and hymns, Praises and consolations which are uttered in the world.* Everyone chanted, "Amen."

> *May there be abundant peace from Heaven, and life, upon us and upon all Israel; and say, Amen.*
> *He who makes peace in his high holy places, may he bring peace upon us, and upon all Israel.*

Again everyone chanted, "Amen."

The bright white shroud seemed to glow in the starlight as the crew gently lowered Zosia and the baby into the blue bioluminescence, even though Jewish law forbid internment at sea.

"God will understand," Yaakov whispered.

He looked around at weeping passengers. They wept not only for Zosia and the baby but for the families they left behind. And they wept with fear of their unknown future.

Yaakov couldn't stop thoughts of his sister Mala and his niece, Halina, in Warsaw, and his mama and papa in Góra Kalwaria. He sat on an orange crate and played his favorite Yiddish lullaby. Yutka stood next to him. Her contralto voice punctuated the warm night air as if the melody sprang from the depths of her soul.

Yaakov couldn't control the tears that rolled into his beard. His heart ached. He knew he would never again hear this lullaby without thinking of Yutka's voice floating toward the starlight over the dark Mediterranean Sea.

> *Unter Channah's vigele*
> *Shteyt a klor vayse tzigele*
> *Dos tzigele is geforn handlen*
> *Dos vet zayn dayn baruf,*
> *Rozhinkes mit mandlen*
> *Shlof zhe Channah, shlof*
> *Shlof zhe Channah, shlof!*

Under Channah's cradle,
there stands a snow-white kid
that has been to market.
It will be your calling, too–
Trading in raisins and almonds,
And now sleep, Channah, sleep.

    As Yaakov continued to play, the starving, dehydrated refugees stayed on deck, each quietly praying in his/her own way. Some sat on deck, rocking with their arms wrapped around bent knees, others stood leaning with their forearms on the bulwark, watching the undulating bioluminescent swells.
    The last song Yaakov played was the favorite of every Jewish woman he had ever known, *My Yiddish Môme*.
    Yutka began to sing.

My yiddishe momme I need her more then ever now
My yiddishe momme I'd like to kiss that wrinkled brow
I long to hold her hands once more as in days gone by.....

    Overcome, Yutka's voice diminished like unraveling twine. She turned her back and faced out to sea.
    Yaakov finished playing the song as the sky turned from black to deep purple, and the stars faded into apricot light.
    The refugees slowly ambled back to their rancid bunks, as the balmy breeze wafted with the scent of seaweed, salt, and hope.

Chapter 29

Serioja's dreidel game

The day after Zosia and Channah died, Serioja decided the children needed a distraction to take their minds off their fear, hunger and boredom. He sorted through a pile of scrap lumber the carpenters had left after building the bunks and selected a block of pine the size of a small child's fist. He carved a *dreidel*.

Certain that the children would remember the game traditionally played during *Hanukkah*, he stepped down the companionway into the sweltering family compartment. In German, he said to Yutka, "I have created another game for the children."

When Yutka translated, Priscilla, Rochelle, and the other children, all part of the group who boarded in France, followed Serioja onto the sun-drenched deck, curious about the game Serioja had created. In the shadow of the wheelhouse, Serioja guided the children to sit in a circle. The old man groaned as he lowered to one knee and made the *dreidel* spin.

"A *dreidel*!" four-year-old Priscilla clapped, her sparkling eyes dulled by hunger and bordered by dark circles.

"And here are your tokens," Yutka translated as Serioja dropped four rose-gold coins with holes in the center into each child's outstretched palm. "Because we have no chocolate coins we will use these for tokens."

As if to smell foil-wrapped chocolate, Priscilla brought the tokens to her nose.

Serioja handed the *dreidel* to fifteen-year-old Emmanuel, the stowaway. Emmanuel had climbed aboard during the night in Constanța and concealed himself under a tarp in the sweltering engine room until heat and hunger forced him out of hiding. His body and clothes were filthy, but his eyes shone brightly from deep in his gaunt face.

"You have played spin the *dreidel* during *Hanukkah, ja?*" asked Serioja in German. "Could you remind the children how to play even if it is months until *Hanukkah?*"

"I have played many times," said Emmanuel, happily taking charge of the younger children. Yutka translated as he pointed to each Hebrew symbol on the four sides of the dreidel, *"Ness (miracle/*miracle*), Gadol (est super/*great*), Haya (est passé/*happened*), Sham (et est là/*over there*)."*

"What miracle happened?" asked a little boy, just old enough to understand that there was meaning behind these words.

Yutka translated as Emmanuel told the story. "One day, in ancient times, brave Machabee warriors took back the Holy Temple in Jerusalem from the Greeks and a miracle happened. There was only a small vat of olive oil in the Holy Temple, enough to light the *menorah* for just one day, but God made the oil last for eight days, giving them enough time to prepare kosher olive oil to use in the *menorah*. That is the miracle we celebrate during the eight days of *Hanukkah.*"

"Oui," said Yutka. She looked around the circle of children and realized that they hadn't known the ancient story of the oil.

"Here's how we play spin the *dreidel.*" Emmanuel held up one of his coins. "We put a token in the middle of the circle."

Each child placed one of their coins in the center.

He held up the *dreidel* and showed the children the four sides. "The first player spins the *dreidel*. If it lands with the NESS (miracle) side up, the player should do nothing and the next player spins the *dreidel*. When the top falls with the HAYA (happened) side up, the player gets to take half of the coins in the middle, and if the *dreidel* lands on GADOL (great), the player takes all the tokens in the middle. If it lands with the SHAM (over there) side up, the player must add a token to the middle. When you are out of tokens, you are out of the game. We spin the *dreidel* until the winner has all the tokens."

Serioja, Elsa, Yutka, and Joséphine stood outside the circle and watched the children play the game, occasionally reminding them how to play. When it was three-year-old Rochelle's turn, her little fingers fumbled with the top. She couldn't make it spin, so Elsa sat on the deck to help her. Overcoming her shyness, Rochelle snuggled into Elsa's lap. When the *dreidel* landed on *GADOL,* Elsa asked Rochelle, "Do you know what this letter is?"

Rochelle sat quietly, holding the *dreidel* in her tiny hands, then she sprang to her feet and jumped up and down, shouting, "*Gadol, ça veut dire super!*"

Priscilla clapped and squealed, "Rochelle, you win all the coins!"

Elsa's deep blue eyes looked up at Joséphine, "I'm surprised Rochelle recognizes the Hebrew letter."

"I have been teaching the girls the Hebrew alphabet," said Rochelle's mama, Joséphine. She kissed the top of her three-year-old daughter's head. "*Brava*, Rochelle, *brava!*" Then she looked back at Elsa, "They should begin reading Hebrew not French, *oui?*"

A few days later, as the *Parita* continued zigzagging through the Mediterranean, Serioja interrupted their game, handing each child their very own *dreidel* to play with their new friends once they arrived in Israel. He'd made one for Elsa and Yutka as well.

On the four sides he had carved Hebrew letters.

"Can any of you tell the difference between your own *dreidel* and the one you've been playing with?" Yutka translated.

Emmanuel rolled the new toy in his palms, carefully inspecting each side. Then a big smile of recognition glowed on his hallow face.

"What's the difference Emmanuel?" asked Yutka.

"When I played spin the *dreidel* in Germany, the meaning of the four sides read, "a great, miracle, happened, OVER THERE," just like the one we've been playing with here on the ship. But when I play the game in *Eretz* Israel with this new *dreidel*," he held it up for Yutka to see, "the meaning will be different. This *dreidel* reads, NESS, GADOL, HAYA, PO, a great miracle happened HERE!"

Everyone sat in the circle, each holding their new *dreidel* while the magnitude of this message seized Elsa, Yutka, Joséphine, and the children.

"Serioja is truly an angel," whispered Joséphine Edelman.

Chapter 30

Mama's Books

Before going to sleep, Yutka opened the side pocket of her knapsack and gently tugged out the family photo along with the copy of *Pan Tadeusz* her mother had given her. Dim light in her bunk made it impossible to see the picture or to read the book. She touched the photo as if her fingertip could see the face of each family member smiling at her. She held the book's worn leather cover between her palms and opened to the middle of the volume. Bringing the pages to her face, she breathed in the faint scent of home, if only imagined, and remembered the day Mama gave her the book....

> *Mama walks into Yutka's room, wearing her heavy blue sweater, wafting the fragrance of turned soil, fertile leaf mold, and the fresh green scent of early spring.*
>
> *She hugs a book to her chest. Polish letters embossed in gold spell the title and author, it has a well-worn leather cover, and the pages are soft from many readings.* "Do you have room in your knapsack for this?" *asks Mama.*
>
> "Oh Mama, Pan Tadeusz *is your favorite, how could I take it?"*

"It is also your favorite. Someday, when we see each other again, you will return it to me," says Mama. "I have many more lovely poetry books to read. Let me tell you how I came to have so many books written in German." Mama sits on Yutka's bed and tells the family legend. Yutka has heard it many times before, but she loves the sound of her mother's voice celebrating each word.

"Late one night, not long after your papa and I marry, Oberleutnant Schmidt's horse draws up to Doctor Dawidowicz's house. His pounding on the door echoes throughout the shtetl. When the old Jewish doctor answers, there stands Schmidt with a comatose soldier drooping over his shoulder. Still wearing his dressing gown and house shoes, the doctor leads Schmidt into the surgery. Schmidt dumps the soldier onto the exam table as the room fills with the stink of stale liquor and urine. The old Jewish doctor does what he can, but the soldier dies.

"'Old man, you are under arrest for killing a German soldier, you could have saved him!' shouts Oberleutnant Schmidt. Out of respect, Schmidt does not bind the old man's hands and feet, or throw him over the back of the horse, the customary procedure in case of murder. Instead, he hoists the diminutive old doctor onto the horse in front of him, and they trot off to the jail, the old doctor still in his night clothes. A red house shoe falls from the doctor's right foot and settles on the dark, dusty street.

Mrs. Dawidowicz hears the commotion. She runs out the front door just in time to see the horse disappear into the night. She picks up her husband's house shoe and returns to the cottage in despair.

"My new father-in-law, Fiebush Lipka, your saba, he is an important businessman. When Mrs. Dawidowicz tells him that Schmidt has arrested Doctor Dawidowicz because the drunken German soldier died in the surgery Fiebush devises a plan.

"Fiebush is friends with the local priest, Father Maximilian, and often shares a glass of wine with him. Fiebush arranges a meeting with Father Maximilian and Oberleutnant Schmidt, who he knows is also Catholic. The meeting goes well. The three men enjoy fine wine and share stories of their adventures as young men. Before they say goodnight, the priest convinces Oberleutnant Schmidt that Doctor Dawidowicz is an excellent doctor. 'He is a kind man and holds hostility toward no one, German, Catholic or otherwise. The doctor could not reverse the soldier's alcohol poisoning. You should not blame the his death on the doctor.'

"In those days Germans, Catholics, and Jews could be friends. Schmidt releases the doctor with an apology and returns the doctor to his cottage to reunite with his grateful wife and his red house shoe.

"Weeks later Oberleutnant Schmidt summons Fiebush Lipka to his office. Fiebush assumes another anti-Semitic crisis has developed. 'How can I help, Herr Schmidt?'

"'I understand your new daughter-in-law is a lover of poetry,' said Oberleutnant Schmidt with a grin on his square face, his blue eyes sparkling. He lifts the lid of a wooden crate filled with leather bound books with gold lettering and gilded edges. 'She should read German poetry by Goethe. Please deliver these books to her with my best regards.' To this day no one knows how Oberleutnant Schmidt knew I loved poetry."

✡

Unable to sleep, Yutka spent most of the next night on deck, her head resting on the rope pillow, contemplating the veil of stars. The ever-present vibration of the moving ship and the smell of sea air blended with the bright woody tones of Yaakov's mandolin. The aria from Mozart's "Don Giovanni" hovered over the dark water, but she resisted the tug that drew her to join him. When the sun peeked over the horizon, she slowly unfolded from the rusty deck, feeling far older than her eighteen years. Her back felt stiff, her shoulders throbbed, her joints ached. She was dizzy and weak, but hunger pangs had eased.

As her early morning shadow crawled across the deck, she raised her knee, put her arms out beside her and watched her shadow change shape. As she moved her arms slowly and switched legs, the shadow suddenly had four legs and four arms.

"Good morning," Yaakov whispered from behind her. She turned to find his bright grin surrounded by the uncivilized ginger-colored beard that had grown during the voyage. His cheeks were hollow and dark circles surrounded his iceberg-blue eyes, as if he'd lost a fistfight.

"Good morning, Yaakov," she said quietly. Yutka turned back toward her shadow, exhaling a poignant sigh. "In Dobrzyń, I shadow danced with my little nephew, Jerzyk...." Her chin lowered regardless of her efforts to keep it high.

"My sister's daughter, Halina," said Yaakov in a low rumbling voice, "loved for me to put her on my shoulders and dance around the park. We made shadow creatures with many arms and legs in the pink evening light. Sometimes before bedtime I removed a lamp shade and created shadow animals on the wall with my hands... A bunny, a bird, a fish..."

"How old is Halina?"

"Three. I'm completely smitten. It was difficult to say goodbye.... I was living with my sister Mala and her husband, Simi, in Warsaw, so I spent a lot of time with Halina over the past two years...."

"Do you have other siblings?"

"Yes, I have a older brother, Arie, who immigrated to *Eretz* Israel a few years ago with his wife. Sadly, they still have no children."

"It's good you have a home to go when we arrive in *Eretz* Israel."

"They have not responded to my letter. I hope the address I have for them is correct...." He looked at the clear turquoise sea with his forearms folded on the bulwark, then turned back to Yutka, "How old is your nephew Jerzyk?"

"His second birthday was in February, and my niece Rebekah was born in April."

"I know how much you miss them...." his voice sounded strained and breathy.

She looked up to see his eyes fill with tears.

"I just hope they *all* catch the next boat," he whispered. His eyes closed as if in prayer.

As the sun warmed their backs, they watched the fingers of sunrise streak over their heads. Jagged Cypriot rocks reflected the rosy glow of sunrise. Crystal-clear turquoise water lapped against the sparkling beach as if the calming breath of the sea flowed in and out.

The *Parita* glided past a castle built on a bank of rocks jutting into the sea. Knowing it had to be hundreds of years old, Yutka thought of the Greeks who had built the vast structure so close to the sea. The screeching gulls gave pitch to her hunger as thoughts of food seized her daydreams. She imagined Greeks, both men and women in their long togas, sitting at wooden tables, eating delicious traditional Cypriot foods, grilled meat kebabs, fried *halloumi* cheese, olives, *kolokasi*, lamb, artichokes, chickpeas, and *stifado* while listening to gulls overhead, screaming for their share. She took a deep breath, smelling only the sea.

As the ship moved beyond the gray-brown abandoned battlement, battered by time and the sea, Yaakov softly broke the silence. "I think I'll head back to my nice hard bunk."

His words wrenched Yutka back to the reality of their

circumstances.

As he turned to walk away, she said, "Yaakov. What's that on your neck?"

His hand reached toward the back of his head, "It's an ugly boil. Sorry you noticed it."

"Don't touch it," she scolded. "Your hands can't be clean. I have an idea, wait here, I'll be right back."

She quietly returned to her bunk, collected her First Aid Kit and a clean rag. Back on deck, she whispered, "Follow me."

Yaakov followed Yutka past the galley, into the bowels of the ship to the leaking pipe she had discovered under the stairs. He watched her hold the clean cloth over the steam until it was wet and hot, "Place this on the boil. The heat will help it drain.... And don't tell anyone about this pipe. If everyone on board finds this hot water, no doubt the captain will have the leak fixed in a hurry."

Astonished by her willingness to help him and to share her secret discovery, he laughed. "I'm supposed to be Doctor Polo! Thank you, Yutka."

"I didn't even ask if you brought medical supplies with you?"

He lowered his square jaw, "Sadly, that never occurred to me."

Yutka laughed. "I didn't think of it either. My brother gave me his Boy Scout kit.... Here's ointment for that boil so it doesn't get infected. Stay here and keep the cloth hot for a while. If you can sneak down here a few times and hold a hot compress over the boil, it should heal. But be careful, don't let anyone follow you!"

As he watched her climb the ladder back toward her compartment, he felt reassured. His love for her grew; he glowed with her willingness to help him.

Chapter 31

Back to Constantinople

Captain Vladimir Mikhailovich directed the refugees to go below deck as the ship cruised through the hostile waters of the Sea of Marmara toward Constantinople.

Frightened the first time they passed Constantinople, Yutka knew if the authorities discovered the ship carried Jews instead of coal, the refugees could be in grave danger. This time however, the captain would go ashore hoping the Turks would sell them food and water. They were out of options. If he was unsuccessful, he would cruise back to France.

The refugees huddled in their sweltering compartment, more frightened than at any other time since they left home.

When he went ashore, to his astonishment, as if ordained, the captain discovered that Ze'ev Jabotinsky had sent a Betar official, Ben Horin, to Constantinople to negotiate with port officials regarding future sailings. Eri Jabotinsky had briefed his father after his failed negotiations in Rhodes, but because the *Parita* had no radio, Jabotinsky remained unaware that, three weeks later, passengers on the *Parita* were in crisis because the transfer boats had never turned up. With Ben Horin's negotiations and funds, Captain Mikhailovich restocked the *Parita* with water, food, coal and medical supplies. By then, many of the refugees, especially the families in Yutka's compartment, were severely dehydrated and starving. Like Zosia and Elsa, most of them were part of the group who had survived a grueling ordeal even before boarding the *Parita* in France.

✡

From her bunk, Yutka heard water splashing into the storage tanks. She heard boats coming alongside. Finally, a crew member came down the companionway. "Good news, everyone!" he said in Greek. "They have agreed to sell us bread and water!"

The only words Yutka understood were *ekmek ve su*.

Yutka approached the Greek and tried to talk to him in German. "Are you saying we're loading food?" Then she switched to French. Everyone in her compartment remained in their bunks as ordered, listening to the commotion above them.

Finally, the crew member said, "*Ja! Ja!* Food!" in clear enough German that she understood. She hugged him. When she turned, she saw hopeful faces protruding from bunks up and down the aisle.

Yutka announced to her platoon in German, then again in French, "They are loading food and water! *Ekmek ve su!*"

Everyone cheered, "*Ekmek ve su!*"

"We must stay below, but we will soon have our turn!" she shouted above the cheering. "I'll be back with food," she shouted as she climbed to the deck.

✡

Thanks to Ben Horin's efforts, dock workers at the port of Constantinople filled *Parita's* water tanks and hoisted crates of oranges, cartons of bread, meat, vegetables and other supplies onto her deck.

Erwin Leibovitz tried to maintain order. He ordered platoon leaders and crew members to carry loaves of bread to each compartment. "Nikos you should prepare rich broth; many are too week for solid food."

Nikos hurried to the galley with crew members helping him carry supplies.

Yaakov carried a crate of oranges to the family compartment to help Yutka feed the refugees who were too weak to help themselves. The fresh citrus scent did little to dilute the rancid miasma below deck.

Yutka knelt next to a lower bunk, gently lifted a boy's head and squeezed orange juice into the dehydrated child's mouth. His bird-like lips trembled, eager for more. She placed a peeled orange section on the mother's tongue, "Slowly," she cautioned, pushing the woman's sweaty hair away from her forehead. Tears trickled from the woman's eyes onto Yutka's fingers as the young mother sucked the juice from the sweet pulp. Her dark, sunken eyes conveyed her gratitude.

Yaakov helped Yutka tear off chunks of bread for passengers in the family compartment. They gave everyone a tin of water and suggested they dip bits of bread in it and eat slowly. "If you eat too fast, you will be sick," Yaakov warned. Fifteen-year-old Emmanuel was so hungry he wolfed down the bread and gulped the water then ran to the deck to vomit overboard.

Once the refugees had eaten a meal and gone to sleep, Commander *Erwin* Leibovitz leaned against the railing, listening to Yaakov play his mandolin. The rapid, cheerful melody changed to a quiet, slow, more thoughtful rhythm, then back to the fast, cheerful melody.

"That's incredible. I've never heard music like that played on a mandolin. What was it?"

"*Vivaldi's Concerto in C Major*," said Yaakov as he continued to strum his beloved mandolin.

Erwin opened a tin of cigarettes and offered one to Yaakov. "Thanks, I haven't had a smoke since I left Warsaw," said Yaakov. Then he noticed the tin. "Balkan Sobranie cigarettes. This is an expensive brand in Poland. Are you sure you want to share?"

"Help yourself. I picked up quite a few tins the last time I was in Cyprus. They are good to have on hand when I need a bribe."

Yaakov blocked the breeze with his cupped hand while *Erwin* held a match. Yaakov took a deep drag and blew the smoke over his shoulder. "There's something so soothing about smoking." He took another drag, "Ah, I never smoked a Balkan Sobranie. Now I know what the fuss is about… So smooth and complex." The woody, sweet smoke wafted around them.

"Do you mind if I ask you a question?" asked Yaakov.

"Not at all."

"How did someone so young come to be the commander of a ship carrying 850 illegal immigrants to *Eretz* Israel?"

Erwin laughed and choked on the smoke. Coughing, he said, "You're one of the oldest passengers on the boat." Regaining his breath, he added, "It does not surprise me you ask this question. My parents were active Zionists when they lived in Switzerland. I was born there. We immigrated to *Eretz* Israel ten years ago.

"They enrolled me in a school called Gymnasia Herzliya named after Theodor Herzl. From there I went to boarding school at *Mikve Yisrael* Youth Village where I studied agriculture firsthand. That's where I became a member of *Haganah* and learned about combat and munitions. We met and trained in secret, underground chambers, originally dug for the wine production process at the school. Those chambers became a *slik* where we hid our guns and ammunition from the British. We had a secret exit so *Haganah* soldiers could escape if the British discovered the caves."

"You must have maritime experience?" asked Yaakov.

"All through school I was an active member of *Zebulon*, an organization that taught us how to operate large sailing ships and how to navigate in open water." "*Zebulon will live by the seashore and be a haven for ships*," quoted Yaakov.[9]

---

9. *Genesis 49:13*

Leibovitz looked at Yaakov with raised eyebrows.

"I studied to be a rabbi," Yaakov shrugged.

"Yes, the school was named for the *Zebulon* tribe because the sea will become an important part of growing the new state of Israel. We should all know our way around a ship and the sea."

"Why did you leave Tel Aviv? The rest of us are struggling to get there."

"Like I said, my parents were active Zionists and I've been a member of Betar since I was thirteen. I wanted to help my fellow Jews escape persecution and colonize Israel. In Tel Aviv, I met Dr. Reuben Hecht who was friends with my parents. After dinner one night, he asked me to fly to Europe with him and help with *Aliyah Bet*. Then he assigned me to this command… What about your training, Yaakov?" asked *Erwin*. "I know you're a medic."

"My schooling has been mostly vocational. At first Papa tried to make me a rabbi and I studied rabbinical law until my parents found a wife for me. I didn't want to be a rabbi and I didn't want to marry someone I didn't know. I left home, joined the Polish army and became a medic. After my discharge, I went to barber school, and I also have an international, commercial drivers' license."

"You should have no trouble finding a job in Tel Aviv," said *Erwin*. "Another cigarette?"

"No thanks. I think I'll try to get some sleep, but first, I have another question."

Erwin nodded, "Of course."

"How much longer do we wait?"

Erwin unfolded his long legs and got to his feet. "Tomorrow." He looked around to be certain no Greek crew members were listening. "If the transfer boats don't show up, the captain plans to return to France. Instead, Betar will take control of the *Parita* and head straight to Tel Aviv."

Chapter 32

Mutiny, August 20, 1939

The next day, while the refugees enjoyed hearty broth, bread, and fresh fruit, the captain zigzagged the *Parita* near the northern coast of Cyprus, but again, the transfer boats were nowhere in sight. The refugees below deck had no idea how close they were to returning to France.

Commander Leibovitz, along with two of his operatives, climbed to the wheelhouse and barked, "Enough waiting! We will reach *Eretz* Israel, peacefully or not! Captain, set course for Tel Aviv!"

In the dead of night, as they neared waters patrolled by British warships, the captain turned off the engines and ordered his crew to drop anchor. As they bobbed in the light of a nearly full moon, the captain asserted, "I refuse to breach the British blockade. They will arrest the crew and seize the ship. My orders are to return the *Parita* to France."

"We understand your dilemma," said Leibovitz. "You and your crew have treated us kindly, however we have no more choices. It is clear the transfer boats will not be coming and we refuse to return to France. We are taking control of the ship." Leibovitz turned to his lieutenant, "Jacob, lock the crew in their quarters."

Without protest, as the *Parita* silently drifted at anchor in the moonlight, the captain and the crew followed Jacob below deck.

Before going below, Serioja asked, "Who will steer the ship?"

"Avraham Bash is on board. He has navigation experience," said Leibovitz.

"There is no dock, how will passengers disembark if you go straight to Tel Aviv?" Serioja worried.

"We will climb down rope ladders or jump into the sea and swim. The British expect illegal ships to zigzag through the night toward a port. They will never expect us to slam full speed onto the beach in bright daylight. By the time they realize we have arrived, the refugees will be safely ashore."

On August 22, 1939, as the sky turned from purple to apricot, and water gently lapped against the anchored ship, the Betar operatives took down the Panamanian flag and raised the white flag with the blue Star of David between two blue stripes. They gazed up at the gleaming flag, then erupted in a cheer.

"Will you have any problems navigating to Tel Aviv?" Leibovitz asked Avraham Bash.

"No sir, however, we will probably hit a sandbar before we reach the beach."

"So be it!" shouted Leibovitz as Bash climbed to the wheelhouse.

Leibovitz turned to his operatives, "Gather sledgehammers or any tool you can find. When we reach the beach, destroy the engine."

Once they were ready to proceed to Tel Aviv, Leibovitz released the captain and his crew and escorted them to the deck. "Take the lifeboats. The British can't arrest you for smuggling Jews if you're not on board when we enter British waters."

As the sun broke over the horizon, the captain and crew gathered on deck to climb into two lifeboats. Joséphine Edelman, clinging to Rochelle and holding Priscilla's hand, pushed through the crowd, shouting, "Serioja! Serioja! Wait!"

With one foot over the railing, Serioja turned to face them with a kind smile.

Rochelle lifted her tiny, stick-like arms to hug Serioja and kissed him on both cheeks, while Priscilla hugged his leg and shouted, "*Merci beaucoup, Monsieur* Serioja."

Joséphine asked, "Serioja, are you going back to Russia?"

"I plan to stay here," he said. "I am too old for another such adventure."

"You made this voyage bearable for the children and all of us. I hope we will soon meet again."

The captain urged him to board the lifeboat. Serioja tipped his briny hat and shouted above the chaos, "*L'Shana Haba'ah B'Yerushalayim*. Next year in Jerusalem!"

Then the captain shouted at Nikos, "*Gib zich a shukl*."

Nikos stood with his arm over Oshrah's shoulders. "Captain, sir, with all due respect, I'd like to stay on board."

"Ah, I understand," grinned the captain as he threw his leg over the railing. He saluted the group huddled near him, "*Leichu l'shalom!*"[10]

As the lifeboats with the captain and his crew pulled away from the *Parita*, Commander Leibovitz shouted, "Weigh anchor!" Then he dashed to the wheelhouse to join Avraham Bash. "Full speed ahead!"

In her bunk below deck, Yutka heard the anchor grinding up from the depths and the ship shuddered violently. A strange noise erupted from the engine room way below. With her heart pounding, she climbed onto the deck. "What's happening? It sounds like the boat will explode!"

"We're going as fast as this old bucket of bolts will carry us," laughed the Betar operative, Eliyahu. "We're headed straight for Tel Aviv."

---

10. *Leichu l'shalom*, Hebrew for go in peace

A few hours later, Leibovitz announced over the PA system, "Attention all passengers! The ship will soon reach Tel Aviv. Be ready to disembark. Also we may hit a sand bar before we reach the beach. Be prepared."

Betar operatives hurried to the engine room with crowbars and hammers ready to smash the engine beyond repair as soon as the ship stopped moving. The *Parita* would be incapable of returning to France.

Shoulder to shoulder, pressed together like tinned sardines, smelling even worse, the refugees crowded the deck. As the *Parita* shuttered through the crystal-clear Mediterranean Sea, they sang *Hatikvah*.

Kol od ba'le'vav p'nima,
Nefesh yehudi ho'miyah.
U'lefa-atei mizrach kadimah,
Ayin le'Tziyyon tzofiyah.
Od lo avda tikva-teinu,
Ha'tikvah bat sh'not al-payim
Lih-yot am chofshi b'ar-tzeinu
the land of Tziyyon v'Yerushalayim.

As long as within our hearts
The Jewish soul sings,
As long as forward to the East
To Zion, looks the eye –
Our hope is not yet lost,
It is two thousand years old,
To be a free people in our land
The land of Zion and Jerusalem

Elsa, Yutka and Yaakov stood near the bow as Tel Aviv materialized on the horizon. The White City glowed like a bright, heavenly mirage. Low white-caped waves swept toward the shimmering sand like cerulean silk.

"The city doesn't look real," whispered Elsa. "It is so beautiful."

As they drew closer, the de facto captain announced over the loudspeaker, "Attention all passengers! Brace for impact!"

Crowded together on deck, they heard the grinding noise and felt the shudder as the hull scraped bottom. When the *Parita* jolted to a stop on the sandbar, they rocked like empty wine bottles tightly packed in a crate.

Cheers on shore welcomed them as people raced toward the ship. For a split second, Yaakov looked down into Yutka's eyes. Then the crowd on deck surged toward the rope ladders, and they lost sight of each other.

Chapter 33

Tel Aviv Beach, August 22, 1939

In the early morning hours of August 22, 1939, forty-five days after Yutka left her family behind in Dobrzyń, Avraham Bash purposefully lodged the *Parita* on the sandbar hidden beneath the gently rhythmic waves, less than fifty meters from the Tel Aviv beach.

When Commander Leibovitz sounded the loud sirens announcing their arrival, a huge crowd swarmed the beach, ready to welcome the immigrants to *Eretz* Israel. Before the British even knew the illegal ship had landed, men in rocking surfboats materialized next to the listing *Parita*, ready to row passengers to shore.

Thin and weak but propelled by adrenalin, passengers spilled over the railing onto rope ladders and climbed into the boats. Some of the younger refugees jumped into the water and swam the last fifty meters.

Yaakov pushed an orange crate next to the railing, quickly unrolled a rope ladder and began helping them climb down. "Hurry, hurry, don't be afraid, they will help you at the bottom of the ladder, "*Leichu l'shalom*. Go in Peace."

Among the first of the male passengers to climb onto the rope ladder were Yaakov's bunk mates, Reiner and Klaus.

"Where will you go?" shouted Yaakov as they climbed onto the rope ladder.

"We hope to find our father's brother," said Klaus, his face covered with fine sandy whiskers. "He was an architect in Germany and emigrated in 1935."

"*Leichu l'shalom*," said Yaakov.

Yaakov noticed the seventeen-year-old Rumanian redhead, Oshrah, and the eighteen-year-old Greek cook, Nikos, climbing onto another rope ladder a few meters away. Neither carried a knapsack. Just like Klaus and Reiner, they arrived in Tel Aviv with only the tattered clothes on their backs and joy painted on their thin, dirty faces. As Nikos swung his leg over, and caged Oshrah between his arms, he gave a big grin and waved to Yaakov.

Mr. and Mrs. Edelman, holding Priscilla and Rochelle, approached. Joséphine climbed onto the swaying rope ladder, and Priscilla gave Yaakov a kiss on both cheeks as he lifted her over the railing and set her feet on the rung between her mother's arms. "Hold on tight, little one! *Leichi l'shalom*."

When Yutka appeared by the rope ladder, Yaakov offered his hand. She climbed onto the crate and over the bulwark and shouted above the din of sirens and hollering refugees, "Have you seen Elsa, I lost her in the crowd."

"Yes, she has gone ashore. She said she was walking straight to the Beth Hachalutzot on King George Street."

"Aren't you coming?" Yutka shouted as she found the first rung. "Surely British soldiers are on their way!" She saw the apprehension and exhaustion smothering the glow of his bright blue eyes. Thick ginger whiskers camouflaged his handsome face and matted blond hair reached his collar.

"I'm a medic, I'm needed here." He steadied Yutka's shoulders as her foot found the next rung of the rope ladder. "Please, take my mandolin. If I'm arrested, I'll never see it again." He flung the strap over her head, resting the instrument behind her canvas knapsack. As she disappeared down the ladder into the pandemonium below, she heard his faint words, as if a prayer played only in her head, "I will find you."

Figure 6
Climbing down rope ladders to surfboats

Figure 7
Immigrants arriving at Tel Aviv after 42 days at sea, some too weak to walk, are carried ashore.

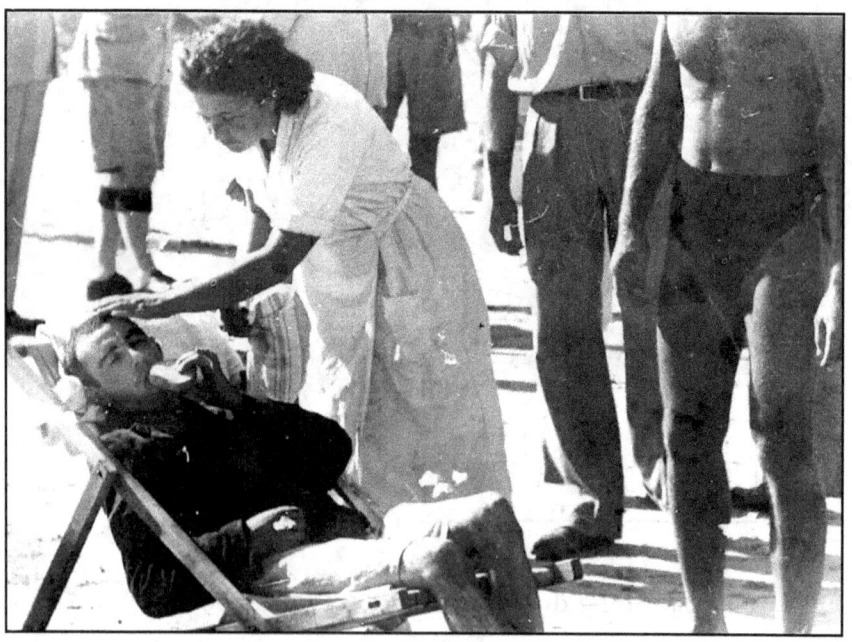

Figure 8
A local woman helping a starving and dehydrated passenger.

Figures 9
Local surfboaters rushed to help the incoming immigrants.

Figure 10
Soon the British cordoned off the beach and arrested the 300 immigrants remaining on the *Parita*, including Yaakov.

PART TWO

Becoming the Free State of Israel

Chapter 34

Tel Aviv, August 21, 1939

"We need to buy supplies for the vineyard," Zipporah said to Srulik. "Let's take the bus to Tel Aviv. My bones tell me there will be a refugee ship coming soon and Yutka will be on it."

Srulik didn't object. His wife's bones were often right about such things.

They checked in at a hotel on Tel Aviv beach. Early the next morning, deafening sirens jarred them from sleep. Zipporah jumped out of bed and to the window in one gigantic leap. She saw the *Parita* lodged on the sandbar and already, locals were running across the beach toward the boat. "Get dressed Srulik, the boat is here!"

Zipporah and Srulik joined the pandemonium. This was not the first boatload of illegal immigrants to land in *Eretz* Israel. There had been many, a few boats landed successfully. However, the British had apprehended some, held them in jail, and took others to concentration camps on Cyprus. Local Jews were always ready to do what they could to help the immigrants. This was the only ship that deliberately wedged itself on a sandbar in bright daylight. Searching the crowd for Yutka, they watched British ships cruising toward the *Parita*.

Zipporah shouted over the din, "Yutka! Yutka! Is that you? Yutka!" They raced across the crowded beach as they watched Yutka leap from a rocking surfboat into knee-deep water and turn to help other passengers jump out before she waded to shore. As they came closer, Yutka stood motionless amid the pandemonium. She looked more eight than eighteen. Her wet clothing hung in tatters on her thin frame; her matted black hair hugged her scalp, her arms and legs looked like frail winter twigs. But, Zipporah noticed, her dirty face glowed with awe and gratitude.

"Yutka, you are here!" screeched Zipporah. "Hallelujah!"

"*Oy vey*! You are so thin!" Srulik put his arms around his diminutive niece, soaking the front of his blue cotton shirt. "It has been five years but even so thin you look even more like your mama!" said Srulik. Zipporah threw a big, clean, white towel over Yutka's shoulders. The trio wrapped in a fierce hug. Uncle Srulik whispered, although he knew the answer, "Were my brother and Bluma on the boat?"

Yutka shook her head, feeling the battle of her emotions split her heart.

Aunt Zipporah shouted, "Quickly now, before the pandemonium subsides, and the British start searching the crowd, we must get you to our hotel room and wash off the *schnootz*."

Safely in the hotel room, Uncle Srulik noticed the instrument hanging behind Yutka's knapsack. "The mandolin must be important for you to bring it on such a journey. I did not know you played," he said as he helped her slip the leather strap over her head.

"It is not mine, Uncle," Yutka said. "A man on the boat played it every day of the journey. As I climbed onto the rope ladder, he threw it over my knapsack and asked me to take care of it. He is a medic and stayed on board to help the sick refugees. I'm sure he was arrested."

"How will he find you?"

"How can he? He knows only that I am Yutka from Dobrzyń, Poland. His name is Yaakov. He is a medic and people on the boat called him Doctor Polo, but I don't remember his last name."

"Did he say where he was from?"

"He boarded the train in Warsaw, but he said he grew up in Góra Kalwaria."

"Did you become *friendly* during the journey?" asked Aunt Zipporah, with a twinkle in her eye.

"No, *Tante* Zipporah! He is much older. We protested and chanted for bread and water.... When a tourist sent us oranges, he helped me feed the starving people in my platoon. No, I did not become *friendly* with Yaakov."

"Israel is a small country," said Aunt Zipporah. "He will find you if it is meant to be."

Chapter 35

Yaakov in Tel Aviv

Yaakov hurried to help the refugees still below deck. Many of them were German and Austrian Jews who had survived horrific circumstances even before they endured weeks of starvation on the *Parita*. When the British boarded the ship, they were in their bunks, too weak or sick to escape.

The British soldiers took Yaakov and the remaining immigrants into custody. "I am a medic, I can help," said Yaakov, but the British soldier didn't understand German. Yaakov tried again in his elementary English. He pointed to himself, "medic, me medic, give help." He bent to gather one end of a stretcher holding an incapacitated refugee, and the soldier understood. They walked to the Ritz Hotel, where the British were setting up a temporary detention center on the balcony, its railing acting as bars of the cell.

As British guards directed the detainees toward a truck bound for Zarafand detention camp, Yaakov stopped them. Speaking German, Yaakov pointed to the people on litters and others leaning against the railing. "These people must be transferred to hospital for proper care," he insisted. "They are severely dehydrated and need IVs immediately." Fortunately, one British guard spoke enough German to understand.

Thanks to Yaakov, they summoned ambulances and gave proper care to the ailing immigrants.

The British confined Yaakov and the remaining immigrants in Zarafand detention camp, near Tel Aviv. The guards distributed soap, and allowed them to shower.

As he stood under the cool flow of clean water, his stomach roiled more than it had throughout the ordeal. Still wet, he collapsed onto his cot.

After Yaakov and his fellow prisoners had showered and found something to wear among the truckloads of clean clothing donated by the *Magen David Adom*, the guards burned their fetid clothing. The foul stench around them dissipated. Conditions in the camp were so much better than conditions on the *Parita*, the immigrants were almost grateful for their incarceration.

The British did not have room to keep all the refugees in the crowded camp, and for ten days they deliberated on what to do with the prisoners. They considered shipping them to a camp in Cyprus or building a camp to house them in Tel Aviv. In the end, the British released the three hundred prisoners and gave them Immigration Certificates that allowed them to legally stay in the country. Of course, they deducted the three hundred certificates from the British Mandate's immigration quota.

Chapter 36

Tel Aviv

On wobbly legs, unsteady after so long at sea, Yutka stood in the shower and feeling the tub heave as if at sea. When she closed her eyes, the world seemed to spin as it had during the first week on the *Parita*.

Gaining her balance, she rubbed a bar of soap between her wet hands and watched the lather develop. *I never thought I could feel so grateful for soap bubbles,* she smiled to herself. As she washed her skin and her hair, her eyes closed with the joy of fresh running warm water and the scent of soap. She pushed the plug down with her toe and watched the seemingly endless flow of warm water fill the tub. She sat down in the chin deep hot water. Using Aunt Zipporah's nail brush, she scrubbed her hands and feet.

Then she added more hot water, leaned back, and let her arms float. For eight months, since hearing Ze'ev Jabotinsky warning, she had carried tension in her back and shoulders. The discomfort had been aggravated by the hard pine bunk. Submerged in clean, warm water, she enjoyed this private, tranquil moment. Worries about her family, the war in Europe, and her future in Israel temporarily subsided. She allowed tears of gratitude.

Finally, as the water cooled, she stepped from the tub and

brought a fresh white towel to her face and inhaled the smell of sunshine, lavender, and liberation. Sliding into a soft hotel bathrobe, she towel-dried her matted head. *Nothing will detangle this mat of hair*, she thought. She unrolled the First Aid Kit Heniek had given her, found the small scissors, and paused, thinking of her brother. *I will write to Heniek and tell him I used these first aid scissors to cut my hair.*

The dull little scissors made a scratchy whine and her breath caught in her throat as chunks of matted black hair fell into the white porcelain sink.

While Yutka took her bath, Aunt Zipporah had ordered soup and bread from room service. Yutka sat next to the little cart and lifted the dome covering the deep bowl of hearty chicken and matzo ball soup. The heavenly scent of dill, parsley and thyme wafted toward her. Yutka looked at the spoon and realized she hadn't seen a real spoon since she left Dobrzyń. On the boat, they used small wooden paddle-like forks to eat their tinned rations. She gathered broth with bites of chicken, onions, carrots, celery, and parsnips and struggled to hold back tears of gratitude as the warm soup slid into her hollow stomach.

"You must eat slowly, Yutka. Your body has had a shock," Aunt Zipporah warned.

Yutka savored every mouthful, then took a small bite of pita bread slathered in olive oil and za'atar. A groan erupted from deep in her throat, "This is the most delicious bread I've ever eaten." Her soup spoon clinked softly against the china bowl. "And the soup…, with real chicken…, and not served in a tin. Thank you…." As she soaked a bite of pita in the chicken broth, she asked, "How did you know I would be on the *Parita* today?"

"We didn't know for sure," said Uncle Srulik. "Your letter led me to believe you were planning to illegally immigrate and this is the first boat that landed since we received your letter." He looked at his wife. "But Zipporah is like you and your mama, she just knows these things. She insisted we should come to Tel Aviv today to buy supplies for the vineyard."

"I *knew* you would be on this boat," said Aunt Zipporah, standing behind her niece hugging Yutka's shoulders while she ate her soup. "We will stay here at the hotel for a few days so you can sleep while Srulik and I buy supplies."

After room service removed the lunch cart, Uncle Srulik and Aunt Zipporah left to go shopping. Yutka put on a nightgown her aunt gave her, and snuggled onto the soft bed, more comfortable than any mattress she could remember. She pulled the clean sheet and soft blanket up to her chin and breathed in soap, sunshine, and normalcy. Feeling safe and satiated, she plunged into a deep sleep.

September 1, 1939

While Yutka recovered, Zipporah and Srulik shopped for supplies. They entered a hardware store and loaded a trolley with things they needed for the vineyard. "Have you heard?" asked the clerk, speaking Hebrew with a Polish accent, "Hitler and Stalin signed a pact promising not to attack each other, then invaded Poland. From what I've heard of Hitler," the old man shook his gray head, "that pact is about as a good as the paper it's written on. When Hitler no longer needs Stalin's support, he'll turn on Russia too." When the clerk looked at Srulik's stricken face, he added, "I hope your family isn't still in Poland?"

Srulik lowered his gaze. "As far as I know, my brothers and their families are still in Dobrzyń. My niece arrived on that refugee ship." His arm waved toward the beach. "But she left home in early July. She's been starving on that boat for over a month."

"May God be with them," muttered the clerk in Yiddish. As always, the clerk arranged to ship their supplies to the vineyard. As Zipporah and Srulik walked to the hotel, Zipporah said, "I hate to tell Yutka that the war has reached Poland. Let's wait until we get home to tell her, give her more time to recover her strength." After peeking into the hotel room where they found Yutka sleeping, they went to a café for dinner, then returned to the room to sleep.

✡

Yutka awoke with sunshine glowing behind the closed curtains. She used the bathroom and chuckled at her delight in the soft toilet paper and the sound of the flushing water. She relished drinking fresh sparkling water from a clean glass, then snuggled back in between the clean sheets on the comfortable mattress.

The next time Yutka awoke, it was nearly dark. Aunt and Uncle were sleeping in the bed next to her. Aunt Zipporah opened her eyes. "You're awake," she whispered.

"What time is it?"

"It's about 5:00 AM. How do you feel?"

Yutka giggled, "Muzzy and hungry," as she snuggled under the light blanket.

"I think you will be hungry for a long time. What should I order for breakfast?"

Yutka folded the blanket away from her face, rolled onto her side, and supported her head on her knuckles and elbow. "Fruit? Vegetables? Pastry? Eggs?" Her eyes sparkled and her head fell back onto the pillow. "Surprise me, Auntie! As long as they don't serve it in a tin!"

On Thursday morning, Zipporah suggested, "Let's take a bus ride to see Tel Aviv while Srulik discusses our wine with local restaurants and café owners."

Rested and well fed, Yutka stepped onto a bus in front of the hotel and nearly fell backwards onto Zipporah. The driver's hypnotic ice-blue eyes and square jaw looked so familiar, for a moment she thought the driver was Yaakov. Finally, she gathered herself and took a window seat. Zipporah sat beside her. "Are you feeling well, Yutka? Maybe you need more rest before exploring Tel Aviv."

"I'm fine *tante*. The driver looked like someone from the boat but… never mind."

Yutka looked around her in the hot, crowded bus. There were two dark-skinned men in traditional white *dishdashas* and two women in long, black *burqas* that covered even their eyes, clothing she had seen only in books.

The scent of humans, vehicle exhaust, flowers, and food filled the hot, crowded bus. *Still,* she thought, *far more pleasant than any day on the Parita.* The cacophony of languages, Hebrew, Yiddish, Arabic, French, Polish, German and a little English, made her smile, happy that she had studied languages so diligently. She understood all the French, Hebrew, Yiddish, Polish, and German. She understood bits and pieces of the English but none of the Arabic.

Yutka noticed the Tel Aviv architecture. White stucco buildings with thick walls had small windows to keep the heat out. Laundry flapped in the tropical breeze on the flat rooftops. As they drove around Dizengoff Square, Yutka said, "The buildings are so beautiful and different from Poland."

"The Germans accused teachers at Bauhaus School of being communist," said Zipporah. "Many skilled architects came here in the early 1930s and modified the Bauhaus style to accommodate the tropical climate. That's why we call Tel Aviv the White City."

"It is more sophisticated and beautiful than I could have imagined," said Yutka with her nose pressed to the glass.

On Friday, they caught a bus at the end of Ben Gurion Boulevard and turned north along the beach, returning to the vineyard before the start of Sabbath. The Mediterranean Sea looked different from her perspective on shore. Waves more topaz than turquoise, gently folded against the white sand, sparkling in the sunlight. Looking out toward the seemingly endless sea, Yutka enjoyed its beauty without the fear of warships and starvation. She saw people sitting on the beach reading a book or just gazing into the sea. Swimmers dove into the surf and disappeared until their heads popped up like turtles. Some swam around the *Parita* exploring her rusty hull.

As they passed the old Abd al Nabi Muslim Cemetery next to the Tel Aviv beach, close to the listing *Parita*, Yutka noticed a small cluster of shanties that contrasted sharply with the beautiful white Bauhaus buildings in the city center. The shacks next to the beach stood less than a meter apart, built with driftwood, scraps pilfered from constructions sites, and covered with black tar paper to keep the rain out. There were no streets or walkways, and the sea near the shore was discolored due to the absence of waste treatment.

"How could there be such a place in this beautiful city?" asked Yutka.

"During heavy immigration after WWI, people claimed ownership of the undeveloped land left open by Tel Aviv city planners. So far British authorities have done nothing about the squatters. And the housing shortage isn't improving fast enough, so the squatters have no place else to live."

Yutka wondered, *If Saba Lipka hadn't purchased the land in the Jezreel Valley, our family might be forced to live in such a place.* Her heart swelled with gratitude.

About halfway between Tel Aviv and Haifa, they turned inland at Hadera, onto a vast coastal plain where flat land seemed to go on forever. Some parts were dry and desolate, but irrigation greened the crops growing in other parts of the lowland. Soon they gained altitude and the scenery turned rocky. They passed windswept Jerusalem pines that fanned out at the top, looking strangely tropical to Yutka. Long needles grew high above thick, red-orange bark with deep fissures at the base of the bare lower trunk. Breathing deeply, she noticed the woody, bitter scent, different from the healthy, clean, and uplifting scent of the Scots pine forests in Poland. Still, the scent reminded her of home, where the trees reached parallel to the sky, like bristles of a brush.

They passed rolling hills and trees Yutka had never seen, Mediterranean cypress, olive, orange, and Red River gum. The sweet fruity scent of bananas filled the bus as they passed banana groves.

Yutka stepped off the bus onto the red dusty soil. "It smells so good here!" She closed her eyes. "Spice, flowers, and herbs mixed with hot sand. I've never smelled anything like this!"

Zipporah and Srulik began walking up the steep dirt road toward the vineyard, but Yutka stayed behind, took off her sandals and wiggled her toes in the fine red sand.

Zipporah turned, "Yutka, what is it?"

Standing at the base of the Gilboa mountain ridge, Yutka remembered the *Song of Deborah* in the Hebrew Bible, the story of two Jewish women, Deborah, the prophetess and Jael, the warrior, celebrated a military victory when the two women successfully defeated Sisera and his mighty army, *perhaps on this very land,* she thought. She stood taller, lifted her chin, deeply inhaled the hot, dry air and sensed the presence of her *Saba* Fiebush. So much like him, she felt blessed to be part of the *mishpacha* that would continue to fulfill his prophecy.

Yutka looked from her aunt to her uncle, then down at her bare feet, her sandals dangling from her index finger. "I'm here," she said. "I'm here walking on the red dirt of *Eretz* Israel." She turned to face the valley so that her aunt and uncle couldn't see her tears. "That part of my dream has come true!"

Chapter 37

September 1939

Upon release from Zarafand, Yaakov walked to the bus stop carrying his nearly empty satchel that held family photos and books. The shirts and trousers he had worn on the *Parita* were not worth saving. He wore wrinkled mismatched clothing donated by *Magen David Adom*. His ginger-colored beard brushed the top button of his shirt, and his matted blond hair nearly reached his collar.

In Warsaw, his wardrobe had been fashionable, well-tailored and perfectly pressed, his hair always neatly trimmed, and he was clean shaven. At this moment, he was glad no one in Tel Aviv knew him. Then with a chuckle, he realized, *Even if anyone I know saw me, they would not recognize me.*

He took a bus to Zangvill Street where his brother, Arie, and his wife, Sara, lived. They had immigrated to the Land of Israel in 1933. With the money from the sale of their successful grocery store in Warsaw, they had built a beautiful flat-roofed, single-story stucco dwelling on stilts, surrounded by undeveloped land filled with orange, fig trees, and mulberry bushes.

Sara answered the door. Yaakov stood there looking nothing like her dapper brother-in-law. She inhaled sharply and nearly slammed the door before he could say, "Sara, it's me, Yaakov!"

She finally noticed his stunning iceberg-blue eyes and his dashing grin lost in the storm of facial hair. "Yaakov? Oh Yaakov! You are here!" squealed Sara as her tears gathered. "We prayed you would come."

Arie heard the commotion and came to Sara's side, ready to throw the bum into the street, but then he hesitated, "Yaakov? Brother! Is it really you?"

"Did you get my letter? I know it was vague but…"

"No letter from you has come," said Arie. "No matter, you are here! Come in! Come in!"

After a long hug, Sara made tea, and they settled into the sitting room. "Tell us, how did you get here? From the looks of you, it was not an easy journey."

"I paid for passage on a ship called the *Parita*, chartered by the Betar Youth Movement; the boat lodged on the sandbar. But the seven-day trip I paid dearly for took forty-two days."

"We saw the ship listing near the beach."

"Fishing boats were supposed take smaller groups of us to shore in the middle of the night, but they never came. We ran out of food and water. It's a miracle we survived. The Betar commander finally gave up on the transfer boats, led a mutiny, and we plowed full speed ahead into the sandbar in bright daylight."

"Couldn't you get to shore before the British came?"

"Hundreds came ashore before the British even knew we'd landed, and I could have joined them, but I'm a medic so I stayed to help evacuate the sick refugees on board. Some of them had been traveling for weeks even before boarding the boat. Some were still extremely dehydrated. The British took the sick to hospital and the rest of us to Zarafand for ten days. I was released and I'm a legal resident." He pulled his new ID from his wrinkled shirt pocket and proudly waved it in the air. Then he looked out the wide windows facing the turquoise Mediterranean, smelling the sweet scent of mulberry, citrus and the sea. "Your house is beautiful. Bus driving must pay well in Tel Aviv," he teased, knowing that money they brought from Poland had paid for the land and the house. Then, Yaakov asked, "Have you heard from Mala or Mama and Papa?"

"We have heard nothing. We've written letters…, but nothing…. Where are you staying?'

"I have nowhere… I was hoping…?"

"You are welcome to stay in our guest room for as long as you want. We will love having you here with us," said Sara.

"And I can get a job for you driving a bus with the Dan Transit Cooperative. I'm a member," said Arie. "Didn't you get an official international bus driver's license in Warsaw?"

"Yes, I have the license, but I don't know my way around enough to drive a bus. I'll look for a job as a barber."

"On my route, I pass a barbershop on Dizengoff Street. If you like, I'll drop you there. It's owned by a fellow from Góra Kalwaria. Remember Mr. Bender? He immigrated about the same time we did."

"I remember him! Mr. Bender cut our hair when we were boys."

Mr. Bender gave Yaakov a bear hug when he walked into the shop. "Yaakov! You're here! Your brother said you were hoping to immigrate someday, but the British don't make it easy."

"Hello, Mr. Bender. I was on the *Parita*, the ship lodged on the sand bar," he gestured toward the sea.

"Weren't you arrested?"

"Oh yes, but they took good care of us and only kept us for ten days. Frankly, I needed the rest!" he laughed. "They gave us ID cards and let us go. I am a legal resident!"

"You have good luck. We never know what the British might do. They might have sent to that camp on Cyprus…. Ahh, sit, I will give you nice close shave, and cut your hair for welcome. Your hair I should cut short to take away the mats," he said as he took a cape from its peg.

"Thank you, Mr. Bender." Yaakov sat in the black leather barber chair and Mr. Bender wrapped him in the cape.

As warm water flowed over his head and the clean scent of shampoo rose from the sink, Yaakov asked, "Um, Mr. Bender, I was wondering if maybe you need another barber in your shop? I was a barber for a few years in my sister Mala's salon in Warsaw."

"Mala, a beautiful girl…" Mr. Bender saw Yaakov's sad face. He cleared his throat, "Well, the rheumatism, it is worse, my hands? My hips? To stand all day is painful. How many hours a week can you work?"

"As many hours as you can give me!" Yaakov said with a grin, pulling his arm out from under the cape and shaking Mr. Bender's wet, soapy hand.

As mats of blond hair and ginger-colored whiskers fell to the floor, Yaakov and Mr. Bender laughed about old times in Góra Kalwaria when Yaakov and his brother Arie came to him for haircuts. "Remember the day Arie and I decided to cut each other's hair?" laughed Yaakov.

"*Oy vey*! Only a buzz cut I should give you," chuckled Mr. Bender as his shoulders bounced up and down with mirth.

Just as Mr. Bender pulled the cape from Yaakov's shoulders, the bell on the door jingled, and a customer walked into the shop. Mr. Bender told Yaakov, "Come here tomorrow morning at 9:00 and we will work out the details to again make you a barber."

Yaakov tried to pay Mr. Bender.

"Keep your money, this is welcome gift, see you tomorrow morning."

It didn't take long for Arie and Sara to start searching for a bride for thirty-two-year-old Yaakov. He refused to meet every candidate. Finally, he admitted, "I met a girl from Dobrzyń on the train from Warsaw to Constanța. She was on the *Parita*…

I haven't been able to find her since.... But... this is a small country... I will find her. I gave her my mandolin for safe keeping before the British arrested me."

"She has your precious Embergher mandolin?" exclaimed Arie as his eyebrows raised. "*Oy vey*! Now I understand!"

Sara added, "If it is meant to be you will find her."

Chapter 38

Jezreel Valley, November 1939

One afternoon in November, Aunt Zipporah sat at a table in the back of the meeting hall, watching Yutka teach children from their agricultural community to read and write Hebrew. Zipporah noticed that eighteen-year-old Yutka, thin and petite, looked no older than the children. Zipporah listened to the group recite the alphabet from *Alef* to *Tav* and noticed that the students were completely comfortable and eager to participate. One little girl named Mara could not sit still. She turned on her chair, climbed onto the table, slid down to the floor and back to her chair again, but when Yutka called on her, it was clear she heard and remembered everything Yutka taught them.

Yutka dismissed the class. As the children shrugged into their raincoats, Yutka joined Zipporah for tea.

"You are a natural teacher. And very patient with restless little Mara."

"Thanks, Aunt Zipporah. I remember how much I hated having to sit still and face forward at school. As long as Mara doesn't distract the other children and she continues to learn Hebrew, what difference should fidgeting make? It is not that I'm a good teacher, they're bright children. They learn so fast!"

"Do you find that the girls learn faster than the boys?"

Yutka gave a sly smile and said softly, "Yes. At their age this is obvious. But even with the older children, this is true. The girls seem to grasp the language faster than the boys. I'm glad to have both boys and girls in my classes. They motivate one another."

"Yes, it is good that times are changing, and boys and girls can learn together."

✡

Uncle Srulik came into the room and peeled off his raincoat. As he hung it on a peg by the door, the children ran around him, squealing as they ran into the heavy rain. A pool of water beneath his coat turned the stone floor dark as he joined Yutka and Zipporah. He pulled a letter from his pocket. "Yutka, this came for you," he said as he sat down on the bench across from her.

The envelope was creased and stained, as if it had been through a war of its own. "It's from Mama," said Yutka in a breathless whisper.

"I noticed it was postmarked in September from Poland," said Srulik.

<u>After</u> Hitler invaded Poland, they all thought, but no one said it aloud, as if minimizing the consequences.

Yutka held the envelope to her chest and tears came to her eyes. Then she lifted her chin, took a deep breath, and opened the envelope as if it might disintegrate.

> *September 16, 1939*
> *Dearest Yutka,*
>
> *I write quickly. We are safe after German soldiers come to Dobrzyń. From neighbors we learn that they drag Jews and Poles out of homes on night of Rosh Hashanah. They led them all to Dobrzyń market square, guarded by heavily armed soldiers. Dobrzyń people were arrested, but also from the town of Bolubia. They were searched and money, wrist clocks, pocket-knives, and other valuables were stolen.*

From the assembled people, the Germans formed two marching columns, they led through Golub towards the Toruński woods.

First column, Poles only, were deported to Toruń labor camp.

The fate of the second detainee column (200 Jews and 20 Poles) was different. The detainee column was transported via Wąbdzno and Chełmno to Bydgoszcz and placed in a barracks camp on Gdańska street.

Thank heavens, we avoided roundup. Now, the soldiers are back. They seized Papa's electric plant and confiscated Hirsch's bakeries and other businesses. They are demanding that all Jews must leave Dobrzyń, so we pack all we can on lumberyard wagon pulled by horse team. We cannot bring the old cow, but two red hens and two ducks are in baskets ready to come with us. Daily eggs will be a blessing. After sunset tonight, we flee to Lomzy, a village on Russian border where Sonya grew up. The Hirsch family is part of our caravan including Zigi's parents, Zigi's brother Max and his family. We hope to reach Lomzy without crossing paths with German soldiers. We hear terrible stories of the brutality they inflict on Jews for no reason.

Uncle Moshe is also in our caravan. Moshe is sad to leave Srulik's vineyard but there is no choice for us.

L'hitraot

Mama

"They are safe," whispered Yutka, "but they had to flee Dobrzyń." She read the letter three times then passed it to Uncle Srulik.

Her mind returned to the night she told her Papa about Ze'ev Jabotinsky's forewarning. If she could go back to that day... could she have made a difference? Convinced Papa to leave Poland? She imagined the photos of *Kristallnacht*, imagined German soldiers pointing guns at Papa on his hands and knees. Without another word to Aunt Zipporah and Uncle Srulik, she stood, lifted her chin, took her raincoat from its peg, and stepped into the earthy scent of the stormy afternoon.

As she walked, the wind whistled through the orchard and mixed with heavy rain. She wandered between the rows of grapevines, her arms wrapped around her midriff as she struggled to calm herself. Her hair dripped with rain. Water trickled inside her raincoat. What would happen to the lumber mill? The house where she grew up? She closed her eyes, lifted her chin high and faced the top of the ancient fig tree while rain pounded her closed eyes.

> *In her mind she sees the old, silver Kiddush cup on the sideboard waiting for Shabbat. Her hand brushes the quilt Safta D'Vora made just for her. She smells the lemon oil rubbed into the mahogany bureau full of the clothes she left behind. The aroma of Mama's fresh baked* Challah *wafts around her. She spreads the butter she and her sister churned after milking the cow. Jars of strawberry jam, green beans, pickles and peaches line the cellar shelves.*

Would the Nazis destroy all of Dobrzyń? Would they destroy all of Poland? Her mind tried to block the more unrelenting horrors. The possibility of her family not surviving was unthinkable. She leaned into the wind unconsciously helping their horses pull the wagons faster. Her family must reach Lomzy safely.

Chapter 39

Hanukkah, 1939

Rain tapped at her window as Yutka pushed the curtain aside. Looking out across the garden, she was awed by the abundance of vegetables growing in neat rows. It was December 9, the third day of *Hanukkah*, but broccoli, turnips, cauliflower, cabbage, kohlrabi, and kale looked healthy and robust, along with spinach, beets, carrots, and pea vines.

Yutka opened a drawer in her nightstand to find the *dreidel* Serioja had made for her while the *Parita*, floating in the heat, waited for the transfer boats. She remembered the emptiness and stress caused by starvation, dehydration and anxiety. She sniffed the wooden *dreidel*. A faint scent of pine reminded her of her home in Poland next to the lumberyard, or maybe she imagined the scent of home.

When Yutka thought of Serioja handing out the *dreidels* he'd made, tears gathered. She suddenly realized, *he must have been one of the Lamed Vav Tzadikim*. Jewish mystics believe that there are thirty-six *Righteous People* who emerge out of their concealment and spare Jews from disasters. Once the pending disaster is averted the *Lamed Vav Tzadikim* disappears and becomes anonymous again. Serioja was not a member of the original Greek crew. Herschel Waxman, who managed the retrofit, had hired him to be the second engineer. He joined the crew in Constanța. In the first few days of their voyage, Serioja helped them deal with seasickness. When they ran out of food, Serioja found bread to share with the children, then helped to keep them distracted from their hunger and fear by telling stories and creating games for them to play. She thought, *Perhaps he was one of the thirty-six Righteous People, he certainly was an advocate for children on the Parita.*

Squeezing the primitively carved top in her palms, she peered between her thumbs at the side where Serioja had carved, Po meaning HERE. *How happy Saba Fiebush would be to know that at least some of his clan now celebrate Hanukkah HERE on the property he bought thirty years ago.*

In years past, *Hanukkah* was a happy time for Yutka's family. They made gifts for each other, Mama knitted sweaters, Papa carved toys, and for eight wintry nights, they said their daily blessings and lit a new candle in the *hanukkiah*. They tramped through deep snow to go to *schul*, enjoyed special holiday foods and the company of friends and extended family. It was the festival of lights in the cold, dark Polish winter.

> *After dinner, Papa gives six-year-old Yutka and each of her cousins five chocolate coins wrapped in gold foil. While their parents relax in the living room, the children, dressed in colorful wool sweaters and socks their mamas and aunties knitted for them, sit on the warm wood floor in front of the fireplace. Each child places a token in the center of the circle and they take turns spinning an ancient dreidel that once belonged to their Saba Fiebush. Yutka has the best luck. When she spins the dreidel, it often lands on Gadol which means she takes all the tokens piled in the center. Finally, the game is over when she wins all the tokens.*

Yutka looks at the gold coins scattered in the middle of the circle, while her cousins squeal, "Yutka you won again!" She gathers up the coins into her small hands, and runs to show her papa, "Papa look, I won all the tokens!" Even without his suggestion, Yutka shares her bounty with her cousins. Soon, every child is eating the candy, licking the foil, and smearing their fingers and faces with sweet chocolate.

Hanukkah celebrations in the Land of Israel were the same but different. Although December was much cooler and wetter than the scorching summer months, there were no snowball fights or horse-drawn sleighs, no tying on ice skates to glide over the frozen river, no fur lined boots, knitted scarves, heavy coats and mittens. In Poland she had enjoyed visiting Christian friends' homes filled with the scent of Scots pine Christmas trees decorated with home-made straw-angels, dry fruit and nut garlands, colorful glass balls, tinsel, and strings of red, green and blue lights. In Israel, at least so far, she had no Christian friends.

For eight nights, Uncle Srulik, Aunt Zipporah and workers at the vineyard lit a candle on the *hanukkiah*, said their blessings, danced and sang. Yutka helped Zipporah in the kitchen and practiced making recipes she remembered Mama making during *Hanukkah, kugel, latkes, sufganigot* and brisket. In Poland, Yutka was lucky to have an orange to share with her brother and sister. In Israel, a big wooden bowl of fresh, bright oranges from the orchard waited on the table like a bowl of sweets, ready for all to enjoy at will.

Chapter 40

Tel Aviv, January 1940

Yutka stepped onto a bus for the two-hour ride from the vineyard to Tel Aviv for a visit with her friend Elsa at Beth Hachalutzot. The bus passed pastures of waving wheat, rows of pomegranate trees, banana plantations, and artichokes standing tall with prickly purple thistles at the top of each stem.

"Yutka, *Bienvenue!*" said Elsa.

They kissed each other on both cheeks.

"So happy to see you!"

"Good to see you too, Elsa, I've missed you."

"How do you like living at the vineyard?"

"The garden work is difficult. I have calluses," Yutka raised her rough palms. "But I love putting my hands in the soil, and to know we can grow our own food. Did you realize vegetables grow here, even in winter!? Broccoli, spinach, carrots, peas! Not like the harsh winters in Poland or Austria, where we put up produce at harvest time to survive the winter months. When I'm not in the garden, I teach Hebrew and French to the children in our *Moshav*. How about you Elsa, what have you been doing?"

"I am trying to learn Hebrew," she said, rolling her eyes. "It's so different from French, and I found work in a clothing store."

✡

Yutka and Elsa were walking along Ben Yehuda Street when they heard men's voices shouting from a second-floor apartment balcony, "*Ekmek ve su, Ekmek ve su!*"

They looked up to see two handsome men leaning over the balustrade, frantically waving.

Elsa gasped, "It's the mandolin player, Doctor Polo!"

Yutka knew immediately it was Yaakov, the medic who had stayed on board to help others rather than jumping into a surfboat before the British seized the *Parita*. She knew the sound of Yaakov's voice before she saw his handsome face.

"Wait there!" shouted Yaakov from his friend René's balcony.

Yaakov dashed through René's apartment, not wanting to let Yutka out of his sight. Gripping the handrail, he raced down two flights of stairs several steps at a time, nearly stumbling in his haste. Since that moment on the *Parita* when he threw the strap of his mandolin case over her head and settled it behind her knapsack, he'd watched for her. He often gazed at the street from the barbershop, hoping she would walk by. On two separate occasions, he left a customer in his chair and ran across Dizengoff Street, dodging traffic, horns blasting, to approach a petite dark-haired woman only to discover, to his embarrassment, it wasn't Yutka. They had shared a friendship rarely experienced in the normal world. He was certain that she had grown fond of him. Now that he'd found her, he hoped they could spend time together and she would love him as much as he loved her.

Until that moment, being married and having children entered Yutka's mind only when she refused Aunt Zipporah's references to a possible match. "You are nearly twenty, you should be thinking about getting married!" Zipporah had cautioned.

"I don't need a husband to have a happy life. I love teaching and working in the vineyard," Yutka had protested.

But in those few moments between Yaakov's disappearance into his friend's apartment and his reappearance on the street, her heart shifted. She was so happy to see Yaakov again.

"So nice to see you," said Yaakov, slightly out of breath, René following. He kissed Elsa on both cheeks, then hesitated, looking at Yutka with those startlingly blue eyes and smiling full lips.

She reached for him, and they kissed each other on both cheeks. With him so close, Yutka smelled mint tea on his breath, along with his musky masculine scent that caused strange butterflies in her belly. "It's nice to see you again as well," she said, with no trace of the clipped speech she had used when they first met on the train from Warsaw.

Knowing Elsa spoke only French, Yaakov introduced his friend in French, "Elsa, this is my friend René Goldhacht."

"Nice to meet you René," said Elsa, her face a little flushed.

"And this lovely lady is Yutka," said Yaakov.

"Nice to meet you both. I have heard a lot about you… and your trip on the *Parita*," said René in French.

"How long did the Brits hold you in Zarafend?" Elsa asked Yaakov.

"Only ten days, then they gave us legal ID cards. I think the arrest was worth it. We were so hungry and exhausted, we hardly noticed where we were. They fed us and we slept," replied Yaakov. "Are you two roommates now?"

"Oh no," said Elsa, "I live at Beth Hachalutzot on King George Street, and Yutka lives at a vineyard in the Jezreel Valley."

"How did you decide to live in the Jezreel Valley?"

When Yaakov looked at her, Yutka knew his hypnotic, ice-blue eyes could see into her soul. "My uncle and aunt immigrated here from Poland in 1934 and started the vineyard. I don't know how they found me on the beach that day, but I thank God they did."

"Would you like to join us for lunch? There's a wonderful café just down the street," said René. "My treat."

Yutka hesitated, feeling shy and awkward, but Elsa blurted, "We'd love to," not giving Yutka the chance to decline. "I know the café. They have wonderful *meze*."

Elsa and René walked in-step toward the café, her hand tucked under his arm, as they chatted in French.

"Did my mandolin survive the landing?" Yaakov softly asked in Polish as they walked side by side behind René and Elsa, his hands in his pockets.

"It's in my room at the vineyard, and quite safe," she kept her eyes looking forward, not giving him the opportunity to analyze the sound of her nervous, unbending voice. She was fond of Yaakov, but couldn't overcome her shyness when she was with him.

René held the door, and they found a table by the window. The foursome shared a bottle of *Metzuda* and talked about their lives during the six months since the *Parita*. They munched on carrot and cucumber medallions and triangles of *lavash* dipped in hummus, or *baba ghanoush*, along with a platter of thinly sliced turkey pastrami. The food paired beautifully with the wine. Yutka swirled the wine in the stemmed glass, brought it to her nose and breathed deeply. She closed her eyes and said a silent blessing for the wine and her good fortune.

Yaakov asked Yutka, "How did your aunt and uncle come to have a vineyard in the Jezreel Valley?"

"My grandfather, who was an early Zionist, bought the land in 1909. He believed that Polish Jews should return to *Eretz* Israel to reclaim and cultivate the land. In 1934, Uncle Srulik came to Israel to realize my grandfather's dream, and I guess, so did I. He died the year before I was born but Papa and my uncles often told stories about his adventures and his dedication to Zionism. He hoped the Lipka clan would fulfill the biblical prophesies…"

"*But every man shall sit under his grapevine or fig tree with no one to disturb him. For it was God the lord of hosts who spoke*," quoted Yaakov.

Yutka looked at Yaakov with raised eye brows, surprised and curious.

"I went to *yeshiva*. Sometimes I paid attention?" he shrugged.

✡

While René told them about his life in *Eretz* Israel since he was fifteen years old, Yutka took a deep breath, grateful for these moments of normal life with friends, but then suddenly, she felt sullen and moody. The war raged in Europe. She had read stories of Hitler's advances and brutality, and the letter from Mama in September said they had fled Dobrzyń. She tried, but it was impossible to put them out of her mind. Here she was having wine and fine food with her new friends in Tel Aviv while who knew what horrors her family faced.

Chapter 41

Returning the Mandolin, February 1940

In February, Yutka came to visit Elsa and brought Yaakov's mandolin with her. When she arrived at Beth Hachalutzot, where Elsa lived, she found René waiting for Elsa on a bench across the street in Gan Meir Park, "Shalom René."

"Shalom Yutka. I'm happy you brought Yaakov's mandolin. I look forward to hearing him play."

"He played every day on the *Parita*. He is quite talented." She looked away to hide the blush that came to her cheeks.

When Elsa joined them, René said, "Let's walk to Yaakov's barbershop. He'll close soon."

René opened the door while Elsa and Yutka waved through the window. "I'll be with you soon," Yaakov said softly. He returned his attention to the man relaxed in the barber chair. Yaakov removed the hot towel and used a brush to apply shaving cream.

The bell on the door jingled when the customer left the shop and the three friends entered. "Have a seat while I clean up, it will only be a few minutes."

Elsa sat in the barber chair and spun around while Yaakov cleaned the shampoo sink.

Looking at his mandolin hanging from Yutka's shoulder, Yaakov said, "Thanks for taking care of my old friend."

She noticed his intense sparkling iceberg-blue eyes, perfect white teeth and full sensual lips, but she knew his grin had nothing to do with his mandolin. She lifted her chin, smiled and tried to stop the blush that rose on her round face.

When Yaakov closed the barbershop for the night, they walked back to the park. Yaakov removed the mandolin from its case and took his time tuning pairs of strings until they were perfectly synchronized. First, he played a lively Polish folk song, "*Hej Sokoły!*" They all sang along in French since Elsa did not speak Polish and was just learning Hebrew.

> *Quelque part sous cette eau noire*
> *Un jeune uhlan monte à cheval*
> *Il dit tendrement adieu à sa copine*
> *Encore plus tendrement à l'Ukraine*

> Somewhere from beneath that black water
> A young cavalryman mounts his horse
> He tenderly bids farewell to his girl
> Even more tenderly to Ukraine

"I'd like to invite all of you for Sabbath dinner on Friday," said Yutka. "We have guest rooms where you can sleep. I'll give you a tour of the gardens and vineyard and maybe Yaakov will play his mandolin for us?"

"It will be a pleasure, although as you have heard, it has been months since I played. I will practice in the meantime," promised Yaakov.

✡

On Friday afternoon, René, Elsa, and Yaakov walked from the bus stop, up the hill to the vineyard, and Yutka introduced them to Aunt Zipporah and Uncle Srulik.

"Happy to meet you," said Yaakov as he shook hands with Srulik.

"Ah, you are the mandolin player." Aunt Zipporah's dark eyes quickly scrutinized Yaakov. "Nice to meet you."

"I persuaded Yaakov to bring along his mandolin to play for us," said Yutka.

He held up his mandolin, but Aunt Zipporah noticed Yaakov looked directly at Yutka when he said, "Yes, we are happily reunited." In Yaakov's bright eyes, she saw far more than gratitude for the return of his double stringed instrument. Yutka and Yaakov's affection for each other was obvious to Zipporah, even if Yutka still denied it.

"Come," said Srulik. "I'll show you to your room and then we'll have a glass of wine before dinner."

While René and Yaakov followed Srulik to their sleeping room, Aunt Zipporah led the way to a room only big enough for a single bed, night table, and lamp, where Elsa would sleep. Elsa put her small tote on the bed, and they joined the men for wine on the lawn overlooking the vineyard.

"The vineyard is beautiful. I love the way the trellises climb the hillside like rungs on a ladder," said René. Throughout the evening, René whispered translations to Elsa. She was learning Hebrew but could not keep up with the conversation.

In the dappled shadow of the ancient fig tree, they sat in wooden lawn chairs, their sandaled feet resting in thick green grass.

"This fig tree is so old," said Yutka, looking up into its wide gnarled branches.

"My papa, your *Saba* Fiebush, told me the tree is one reason he chose this land," said Uncle Srulik, sipping his wine. "The tree is more than a thousand years old. I try to imagine how this valley looked when it was a sapling. I doubt it has changed a lot since my papa roamed this land." He patted Yutka's shoulder. "You are a lot like him."

In the distance, mountains crowned with villages rose like islands among the geometric patterned fields of lush green wheat and yellow rapeseed.

"What crop is so blue?" asked Yaakov, pointing toward what looked like flocks of iridescent sunbirds.

"Those are freshwater fishponds where farmers raise carp and tilapia."

"In this land by the sea, farmers raise fish?"

Srulik laughed, "Yes, it seems odd but so many have immigrated from Eastern Europe, there is a huge demand for gefilte fish. There are no other freshwater fish available so enterprising farmers raise carp and tilapia."

"Sounds good to me, gefilte fish is one of my favorites. Mama made it often." Then he added, "How did you know what grape varieties to plant?"

"There had been a lot of trial and error before the wine industry gained ground in the 1800s. In the early days, the Rothschilds brought cuttings from Bordeaux, but a blight killed the vines and they had to start over. They found that Carignan and Cinsault varieties grow well here so that's what I started with. The second year we added Riesling and Chenin Blanc. All the farmers in our *moshav* are observant Jews so the wine we make is kosher."

"Where did you get your vines?" René wanted to know.

"I bought cuttings from the Zichron Ya'akov vineyard, near Haifa. It is the oldest vineyard in *Eretz* Israel, founded in 1882 by the Rothschild family. They own Château Lafite in France.

"Ah yes, I've been there," René said, lifting his glass. "Their wines are *magnifique!*" He gazed at the deep red wine in his stemmed glass and tasted more mindfully, nodding his approval. "It must take a long time for the vines to produce enough fruit."

"We didn't harvest the fruit for three years, giving the vines time to mature."

Yaakov nodded, "*When you enter the land and plant any tree for food, you shall regard its fruit as forbidden. Three years it shall be forbidden for you, not to be eaten.*"[11]

---

11. Leviticus 19:23-25 New International Version (NIV)"

At first, Srulik looked surprised, "Ah yes, Yutka mentioned that you studied to be a rabbi. You're right. That rule made planting the vines our priority. We lived in a tent until we built the trellises and planted. We're just starting to sell our wine in Tel Aviv."

Yutka gazed around her at the white stucco buildings with red tile roofs, lush gardens, and healthy vines. Her aunt and uncle and their *moshav* had worked hard over the past six years since arriving in *Eretz* Israel. She remembered their home filled with the beautiful furniture Srulik and Zipporah had sold before leaving Poland. "It must have been a shock for you to live in a tent in this heat after leaving your beautiful home in Poland."

"Not at all," said Zipporah. "We were so intent on fulfilling your *Saba* Fiebush's dream, we wanted to plant as fast as we could."

At dusk, when a purple carpet rolled over the valley, they went inside for Sabbath dinner.

After dinner, they returned to their chairs near the vineyard. Flickering yellow candlelight lit the way across the green lawn under a smear of bright star light. Yaakov softly played *Nigun* melodies in the background as the new immigrants shared events of the *Parita's* voyage. They avoided discussing the death of Zosia and the baby, and the challenges faced by the commander as some passengers reached their breaking point. They shared the more interesting bits of the trip.

"During the six days it took to get to Cyprus, the commander allowed only fifty on deck at a time. We danced and sang, even though we were still a little seasick and stiff from our hard bunks, we were joyful," said Yutka.

"I was thrilled to be on the Mediterranean," Elsa said slowly in Hebrew, with René's help. "I grew up in Paris near the Seine and on the Danube in Vienna. Neither is a match for the Mediterranean Sea."

"I agree, neither is the Vistula River," Yaakov added without looking down at the strings as he continued to play.

"Nor the Dreventz River," laughed Yutka.

"When we cruised from Alexandretta back to Cyprus, we saw what we thought was a submarine, but when it came closer, we realized it was a magnificent whale. Actually, a whole pod of sperm whales. One of them came right up to the boat. That big watery eye looked at us as if he were our friend," said Yutka.

"René, how long have you been in Tel Aviv?" asked Zipporah, bringing René into the conversation.

"My parents left France and came here is 1934 when France was falling apart. I was fifteen."

"René is studying medicine at Hebrew University," beamed Elsa. Somehow they understood her rough Hebrew.

"Excellent!" said Srulik. "The Land of Israel needs good doctors."

Zipporah noticed how Elsa and René looked at each other. *Perhaps there will be two weddings,* she smiled to herself.

Chapter 42

Sabbath at the Vineyard

"If Yutka's friends have Sabbath dinner with us often enough, she and Yaakov will have an opportunity to get to know each other," said Zipporah.

Srulik gave her a sly smile and asked, "Should we interfere?"

"Interfere?! When should they see each other?" Zipporah's voice grew higher. "He works in Tel Aviv; she works here at the vineyard." Her arms waved around her like a windmill. "I'm not trying to play *shadchan*."

Srulik laughed out loud. "You're not?"

"Well, maybe a little matchmaking," she grinned. "I can see that he adores her but when they are together, Yutka's typical strength and boldness melts away and she suddenly becomes shy and keeps him at arm's length. They just need to spend time together. Elsa and René both live in Tel Aviv and when it comes to René, Elsa is not shy at all. I'm sure they spend a lot of time together."

Zipporah waited for Yutka after her Hebrew class and walked with her back to Yutka's room. "Yutka, we enjoyed having René, Elsa and Yaakov for Sabbath dinner last week, You should invite them every week. Yaakov and Elsa have no family and I noticed that René and Elsa seem to be inseparable."

Yutka smiled to herself, recognizing Zipporah's conniving. "Yaakov lives with his brother in Tel Aviv. I'm sure they have Sabbath dinner together."

Zipporah couldn't think fast enough, but Yutka let her off the hook. "But I'll ask. It would be nice to have my friends join us every week. And René's parents are currently in England, so I'm sure Elsa and René will join us."

Yutka stopped, held Aunt Zipporah's hands and looked into her eyes. They laughed and hugged but said nothing about Zipporah playing matchmaker. Yutka would be happy to see Yaakov more often.

Chapter 43

Postcards, April 1940

Nine months after Yutka left home, seven months after Hitler invaded Poland, and five months after receiving Mama's letter saying they were fleeing Dobrzyń, a postcard from Yutka's brother Heniek arrived.

> *January 22, 1940*
> *My dear family,*
> *I can tell you we are all alive and healthy. The entire family is OK. Sonya and I live in Mir. Sonya works already in school, papa and mama, the Hirsch's, Zigi, Rozka, Jerzyk, and Rebekah as well as Dr. Max Hirsch and his family are not far from us. They work and are doing well.*
> *Please let us know how the entire family is doing. How are you doing Yutka?*
> *We are sending you our kisses and waiting for news from you. Please send letters to Dr. Hirsch in Trozzyn, Mir, USSR.*
> *Heniek*

Yutka went to her room, pulled paper and pen from a drawer and wrote a letter to her family.

Moi Kochani Rodzina,

Heniek, thank you for the postcard. It took three months to find its way to us. I am relieved to know you are all safe and healthy. I hope you are staying warm and well fed in the harsh Russian winter.

The trip to Tel Aviv took forty-two days instead of seven as planned. We ran out of food and water, but the boat finally landed in Tel Aviv. Somehow, Aunt and Uncle found me among the hundreds of refugees who poured onto the beach. Since then, I have made up for the lack of food, enjoying the bounty of their garden.

Tel Aviv is a beautiful modern city so different from Dobrzyń. The buildings have flat roofs and small windows. The weather is extremely hot in summer and warm in winter, we grow vegetables year-round. I work in the garden and also teach Hebrew and French to the children in the moshav.

Stay well and write soon.
L'hitraot,
Yutka

Yutka wrote letters to her family every week, telling them about the food she grew and cooked and how she was learning to make wine. She wrote about meeting Elsa and the medic who played his mandolin on the *Parita*. She could only hope her family was safe in Russia and that her letters reached them.

Chapter 44

September 1940

Rather than ride his bike or take a bus to the barbershop where he worked, Yaakov often walked several blocks exploring his new environment. He passed undeveloped meadows, citrus orchards, and lots of new construction. The birds in *Eretz* Israel differed from the birds he watched in Poland. He enjoyed the reed warble's loud chirps and clicks as he walked by shallow, brackish water near the beach. He listened to the delicate, sweet chirp of the dunnocks perched in brambles and hedges. A warm rock in a meadow became his favorite place to pause, sit and listen to his new surroundings. He heard the meadow pipits' tiny, almost invisible tweet surround him. His favorite birds, however, were the swifts. They gently dipped from the clear blue sky, catching insects above the grass. In the background, he heard calming waves wash onto the white sandy beach. The war seemed far away from his peaceful perch overlooking the turquoise Mediterranean Sea.

One Monday afternoon, business was slow, so Yaakov closed the barbershop a little early and walked the several blocks home to his brother's house. Part way there, he stopped at his favorite meditation spot, and sat on the warm rock feeling tranquil and safe, listening to the birds, enjoying the warm air and salty sea breeze filled with the fragrance of wildflowers. He thought of the days on the *Parita*, when he feared that hostile anti-Semites might sink the ship. Grateful he had reached *Eretz* Israel, even under the British Mandate, he hoped the war in Europe would end soon without reaching his new homeland.

Suddenly, like a flock of vultures, low flying Italian bombers cast shadows over his tranquility. He heard the pulsing drone and the deep thump of bombs falling on Tel Aviv. Sprinting back to Dizengoff Street, he saw black smoke rising near the barbershop and people running in all directions. Ear-splitting sirens blared, and the air was pungent with smoke. A crater gaped where he had passed only minutes before.

The next day, the morning paper reported that the Italians' intended target was the British refinery in Haifa, but they quickly dropped their bombs on Tel Aviv civilians when the British RAF chased them away. The bombs killed 137 Jews, including children.

Yaakov narrowly escaped. War had reached his new homeland.

Chapter 45

March 1941

Finally, a postcard arrived. Both Heniek and Rozka wrote with tiny script and crowded as much information on the card as possible.
Heniek's portion of the postcard:

Moi Kochani Rodzina,
It has been a long time without getting any news from you. Everything here stayed the same. I am alive, work and earn money. I traveled to the forest and stayed a few weeks of solitude. There is shortage of basic necessities and food, but we try to save and buy only the items absolutely needed. Sonya is getting vacation time and will take our son, Josip to visit her parents.

Rozka's portion of the letter:

The Nazis forced Aunt Rosa into the Jewish ghetto in Warsaw where she has little to eat, and violence threatens on every corner. The situation in Warsaw is not good. We send her care packages with food. Jerzyk attends kindergarten and already fluent in Russian. We are learning the language slowly. Heniek's son Josip grows nicely. The same with Max's

son. Yutka, how do you get along? How about the rest of our family there? We received a letter from Regina Lipka Mishkova. They are also in Warsaw ghetto and our uncle, aunt and Rivka are in Mlava, also a Jewish ghetto. The rest of our relatives are in a ghetto in Kutno. Aunt Regina Lipka is asking us to send food to her there. We are lucky because we have home and bread. Papa is also working and earns money. He is chauffer for Dr. Max Hirsch, taking him to his house calls, using horse and buggy. Please write to us more often at least three times a month. We will do the same. Be well.
Rozka
P.S. Regards from Zigi [12]

Yutka was disappointed to learn they had not received the many cards and letters she had sent.

After spending Sabbath at the vineyard, Yaakov and René boarded the bus back to Tel Aviv early one Sunday morning, but Elsa asked if she could stay for another day or two.

"Of course, but we might put you to work in the garden," Zipporah teased.

Elsa came to Yutka's room and sat on the narrow bed. "I have something I need to talk to you about."

"What is it, Elsa?" Deep lines formed between Yutka's eyes. Sadness always lingered too close to the surface of her skin.

"René asked me to marry him."

"Oh Elsa, I'm so happy for you!" Yutka jumped up to hug her friend.

---

12. The postcard Yutka received in Tel Aviv from her brother Heniek and sister Rozka was written in Polish and translated for her son Sam Regev by a staff member in the Lochamay Hagetaot Holocaust Museum at Fibbutz Lohamei HaGeta'ot (Ghetto Fighters Kibbutz)

Elsa finally grinned from ear to ear. "I loved him the moment I met him, and he felt the same."

"But why do you look so sad?"

Elsa looked at the floor. "Because my parents aren't here with me, I have no one…"

Yutka hugged Elsa again. "Nonsense! You do! You have me and my family. Have you heard anything…?" asked Yutka as they walked outside and sat on the grass, both thinking of the families they left in Europe.

"I have no idea where they are… if they are alive…. They knew I would be staying at Beth Hachalutzot, and they have the address, but I have received nothing."

"It took Mama's letter months to find me, and Heniek's postcard even longer. Maybe their letters are lost in the post…."

The wind rustled the pea vines growing in the garden, and crickets' loud *kree, kree* filled the warm air. Elsa and Yutka rolled onto their backs, pillowed their hands under their heads and stared at the milky sweep of stars and the pitted gibbous moon.

"Hear the owls?" asked Yutka.

"Um-hum," sighed Elsa. Then she sat up, rubbing her eyes. "What are those floating lights?"

"Fireflies," laughed Yutka. She jumped to her feet to grab one out of the warm night air. She let Elsa watch the little insect crawl from her palm to her fingertips where it spread its tiny black wings and took flight. "They come out on warm summer nights. In Poland, my sister and I caught them and put them in a jar with holes in the lid. We watched them twinkle in our room at night. Didn't you see them in France?"

"Not in Paris, of course," said Elsa. "I've never spent a night in the countryside…. What's that scary howling noise?"

"Jackals, I think," said Yutka.

"Did you hear them at night in Poland? Are they dangerous?"

Yutka laughed again, "No, in Poland we had coyotes that look the same but are a little bigger. They're dangerous if you're a rabbit or newborn calf, but they rarely bother humans."

The ceiling of stars swept above them, and the lights of Afula reflected yellow on a scattering of low clouds to the west as the night noises bloomed around them.

Finally, Elsa broke their silence. "René and I have no family, and we are not orthodox… Do you think we could have our wedding here at the vineyard? It's the happiest place I have ever been!"

"I'm sure you can, but let's talk to Uncle Srulik. Maybe he knows a rabbi who will come to the vineyard to officiate."

"Actually, René's friend Saul is an ordained rabbi. He has agreed to officiate no matter where we set up our *chuppah*.

"Would you like for me to make your wedding dress?"

"You can do that? You can sew?"

"*Oui*, I make most of my own clothes." Yutka tugged at the collar of her blouse. "I'm sure Aunt Zipporah will let me use her sewing machine."

In a newspaper advertisement, Elsa found a photo of a dress she loved. Yutka took Elsa's measurements, created a pattern with newspaper and figured out how much fabric she would need.

As they opened the door to the dry goods store in Tel Aviv, they came face to face with Joséphine Edelman on her way out. They all greeted each other with hugs and kisses. Then, at exactly the same time, they all said, "*Ekmek ve su!*" Then they laughed together.

"I think those words will always be the *Parita* survivors' chant," said Yutka in French. "So nice to see you Joséphine. How are Rochelle and Priscilla?"

"They are growing taller, quickly learning Hebrew, making friends, and doing very well in school."

"Do you live nearby?" asked Elsa.

"Just around the block on Ben Yehuda Street," Joséphine gestured.

"It's a wonder we haven't run into each other before this. My *fiancé* lives on Ben Yehuda Street."

"*Fiancé*? I'm so happy for you, Elsa," said Joséphine, giving Elsa a hug.

"Thank you. He is a wonderful man," Elsa's face flushed. "Yutka is going to make my wedding dress. That's why we came to the dry goods store."

"Yutka, you must be quite talented, do you live nearby?"

"No. I live in the Jezreel Valley with my Aunt and Uncle at their vineyard. Have you seen others from the *Parita*?"

"The girls and I saw Nikos, the cook and the red headed Rumanian, Oshrah in Gan Meir Park not long ago. They were married just after we landed. And, we enjoyed a brief encounter with Serioja but that was months ago. He looked quite feeble."

"I'll watch for them. Until the wedding I'm living at Beth Hachalutzot, across the street from Gan Meir Park," said Elsa. "This city is really quite small."

"*Oui*, and Yaakov cuts my husband's hair," added Joséphine.

Yutka blushed when Joséphine mentioned Yaakov.

Joséphine asked, "Have you seen Yaakov since we arrived?"

"Yes, I have. In fact, Elsa's fiancé, René is a good friend of Yaakov's, that's how they met. Elsa, René and Yaakov often come for Sabbath dinner at the vineyard. Yaakov mentioned that he cuts Mr. Edelman's hair."

"I wish we could chat longer, but I need to pick up Rochelle and Priscilla at school."

Elsa, Yutka and Joséphine exchanged addresses before Joséphine hurried off.

"I'm sure we will run into each other again," said Elsa. "I'd love to see the girls."

"Tell them we said, *bonjour*," said Yutka.

✡

Elsa had little money, so they bought yards of inexpensive white muslin, tulle, lace, and white thread.

"How do you know what to do?" asked Elsa, looking at the pile of supplies. Waving her arms, she said, "I wouldn't know where to begin!"

"It seems I came into the world with that skill. I can look at a picture of a dress, cut it out and sew it together," she shrugged.

Uncle Srulik created the *chuppah* at the edge of the vineyard, using vineyard poles, vines and flowers. On the day of the wedding, Aunt Zipporah gathered buttercups, blue globe thistle and eucalyptus to create Elsa's wedding bouquet.

Wearing a black coat, black flat-brimmed hat and long black beard, the rabbi looked on as René signed the *Ketubah*, "...and I will work for thee, honor, provide for, and support thee, in accordance with the practice of Jewish husbands, who work for their wives, honor, provide for and support them in truth...."

Yaakov and Srulik signed the contract as witnesses on Elsa's behalf. Wearing the beautiful long white dress Yutka had created, Elsa walked up the gentle slope between rows of vines naturally decorated with clusters of ripening purplish-red grapes. Independent woman that she was, Elsa walked alone. "I will give myself away," she had told Yutka. She reached the *chuppah* at the end of the row where René waited, grinning like a schoolboy next to the rabbi.

After the *birkot nissuin*, René and Elsa faced their friends and neighbors. Yaakov played his mandolin and sang the traditional, joyful and lively folk song, *Siman Tov U'Mazel Tov*, while guests clapped, sang and danced.

Siman tov u'mazel tov
U'mazal tov vesiman tov
Yehe lanu.
Yehe lanu, yehe lanu
Ulechol Yisrael.

Good signs, and good luck
And good luck and good signs
will come to us.
It will come to us, to us.
And to all Israel.

Chapter 46

The Proposal, April 1941

After the wedding, René and Elsa left for René's apartment in Tel Aviv. Yaakov and Yutka walked through the vineyard. "They looked so happy," said Yaakov.

"Yes," agreed Yutka, "after the hardship Elsa endured getting here, it's wonderful to see her so happy."

Yaakov was certain he wanted Yutka to be his wife. He was getting too old to wait much longer and decided he would take the risk and propose, unless she clearly rejected him.

As he gathered his nerve and took Yutka's hand in his, a bolt of energy flash between them. He was certain she sensed it too, as if their clasped hands completed a prayer. Silently, they walked the length of the vineyard and back to the fig tree.

As they walked, hand in hand, energy flowed freely between them. Her heart pounded and tears burned her eyes. The late afternoon air filled with the scent of sweet citrusy grapes, musky wisteria and burgeoning promise as their hearts melted together. She couldn't deny that he was quite handsome and very romantic, but she was more attracted to his maturity, kindness, and thoughtfulness. She had watched him on the boat, the twinkle in his eyes when he talked about his family, the introspective expression on his face when he played his mandolin. He unselfishly helped others and shared his rations with children.

Suddenly, he stopped walking and took both of her hands in his.

Her heart leaped as he turned to look into her eyes.

"Yutka, do you think..." Yaakov's words caught in his throat. "Do you think we, I mean, you and me, I mean, together, could we be as happy?" Yaakov's voice was quiet, as if he could scarcely produce enough breath to speak.

Grinning, Yutka turned toward him, her dark eyes shining in the moonlight, "What are you saying, Yaakov?" she whispered

"Yutka, I love you. Will you marry me?"

Before her mind could grasp his words, her heart answered, "Yes, Yaakov, I love you. I will be your wife."

He bent to softly kiss her lips.

"Our families cannot be present, and I don't have a lot of money," he paused. "Is next week too soon? We could ask the rabbi to marry us at his apartment."

"I see no reason to wait. I never dreamed of a big, white wedding. In fact, until I met you, I never dreamed of a wedding at all. I'm sure Aunt Zipporah, Uncle Srulik, René and Elsa will join us."

The smile she gave him made his heart ache. "You're so beautiful! I can't wait for you to be my wife."

They silently walked in the vineyard, arm in arm. Yutka remembered the first time she met Yaakov. He sat across from her on the train from Warsaw and tried to make conversation, but she had too many things to worry about. Her thoughts were a stew of emotion: the family she left behind, her uncertain future, crossing borders with counterfeit documents, the voyage across the Mediterranean Sea, breaking the British blockade, and arriving illegally in *Eretz* Israel. She had judged him superficially because of his age and dapper wardrobe. She had treated him rudely. Even on the boat, she was rude when he tried to be her friend. *Thank God he persisted,* she thought, smiling up at him.

"The fig tree has an unusual scent—both decadent and gentle," said Yutka.

"Nothing like the apple and peach trees in Poland…. The scent reminds me, we're far from home."

"But now, *Eretz* Israel is our home," Yutka said softly, hugging his arm, her dark eyes shining like midnight stars.

"We'll make a home here together."

They walked around the thousand-year-old fig tree, carefully stepping over roots that clawed the land like gnarled ancient fingers clutching at life. The trunk looked like a giant heart of coiled ventricles, pumping water and nutrients into the twisted branches that still produced an abundance of sweet, juicy figs. Yutka thought about her *Saba* Fiebush, *He must have walked this very ground.* Yutka had never met her Papa's papa, but she knew he he walked with them on the red sandy soil. *He would be happy we are here.*

They sat leaning against a tall slim root until the early morning hours. For a while they enjoyed intimate silence, her head leaning on his chest, listening to his heartbeat, his hand stroking her curly hair. "How many children do you want to have?" asked Yaakov.

"I've never considered the question," said Yutka. "I guess it would be nice to have a boy and a girl, maybe more? What do you think?"

"At least two. Being an only child would be lonely but having a big family in these uncertain times…. I want to be able to provide for them…"

"Where will we live?"

"We can stay with Arie and Sara until we find our own place. I'll ask my customers and I'll put notices around. I can't afford much."

"We don't *need* much. I'll find a job… and teach Hebrew classes. After all that time on the boat, I think we could be happy anywhere if we're together."

That night before going to sleep, Yutka wrote a postcard to her family in Mir, USSR, announcing their pending wedding.

Moi Kochani Rodzina,

Tonight, Yaakov Polonecki asked me to marry him, and I said yes! We met on the train from Warsaw and again on the boat. He is the mandolin player I wrote to you about. He grew up in Góra Kalwaria where his papa was a rabbi. He has a brother, Arie, in Tel Aviv I will meet soon. His Mama, Papa and his sister are in Poland. He has not heard from them.

Oh, how I wish you could meet him! I will send a photo and a new address once we find an apartment. In the meantime, send letters to the vineyard.

L'hitraot,

Yutka

Uncle Srulik and Aunt Zipporah were thrilled but not surprised when Yaakov and Yutka announced their pending wedding. "*Mazel Tov!*" said Srulik, hugging them both. Behind Yutka's back, Srulik gave Zipporah a mischievous grin, silently saying, *Your plan worked.*

"What date have you set?" asked Zipporah after sending a smug grin toward Srulik.

"Tuesday at 5:00 PM," said Yutka, muffling a giggle.

"*Oy vey*, you give us no time!"

"We'll have the ceremony at Rabbi Liberman's apartment on Ha'Havoda Street, in Tel Aviv," said Yaakov. "Will you come?"

"Of course, of course," said Srulik, wiping his eyes, more emotional than Zipporah, thinking, *I wish my brother Mordechai and Bluma could be with us.*

"Yutka, you have no time to make plans! What about a dress? *Oy vey!*"

"Elsa offered the dress I made for her. I'll shorten the hem and take in the bodice a little."

"And I will borrow a suit and necktie from René," said Yaakov. "We are the same size."

"Yaakov and I both came to *Eretz* Israel with nearly nothing. Our wedding ceremony will be a modest one," said Yutka.

"We'll have a wedding feast at the vineyard next week," promised Zipporah.

Chapter 47

Yutka and Yaakov's Wedding, April 1941

On her wedding day, Yutka's chin-length hair gleamed like blue-black silk as Elsa pinned white carnations in front of the waist-length white tulle veil. "You are beautiful! I've never seen your eyes so bright, like stars at midnight," said Elsa, giving Yutka a hug. "When you offered to make my wedding dress, I admit I hoped you would also wear it soon. I knew you would marry Yaakov the first time I met him on the boat. You both sparkled when you saw each other, even if you denied it, I saw it. I am so happy for you."

They all gathered at Rabbi Liberman's sparsely furnished apartment with its shiny white tile floor, highly polished maple table with four chairs, blue upholstered sofa and wide sliding doors leading to a balcony overlooking orange trees. The bright, joyful space seemed the perfect location for an informal ceremony.

When Arie and Sara arrived, Yaakov introduced them to Yutka. "I'd like you to meet my brother Arie and his wife Sara."

Sara kissed Yutka on both cheeks, but when Arie approached Yutka gasped, "Nice to meet you but, really we've met before," she smiled. "You're a bus driver, yes?"

"Have you been on my bus?"

"Yes, and I was shocked. When I saw you, for a moment I thought you were Yaakov, but I knew the British had taken him to Zarafand."

Yutka motioned to her aunt. "Auntie, do you remember when I nearly knocked you off the bus in Tel Aviv? It was because the driver looked so much like Yaakov. This is Arie, Yaakov's older brother, the bus driver. Arie, this is my Aunt Zipporah."

"Nice to meet you, Arie. You do look a lot like your brother. So happy you could be here today," said Zipporah, thinking, *I wish Yutka's family could be here too.*

Zipporah had known all along that Yutka would marry Yaakov even though he was fourteen years older than Yutka. She could see the love in Yutka's eyes the first time she mentioned the mandolin player, and she had seen love in Yaakov's eyes the first time he came for Sabbath dinner at the vineyard.

Yaakov and Rabbi Liberman sat at the table while Yaakov signed the *Ketubah*. Uncle Srulik and René signed as witnesses on Yutka's behalf.

Then the couple stepped under the canopy in the rabbi's sparsely furnished living room. Rabbi Liberman said the betrothal blessing. Yaakov repeated, "*Behold, thou art consecrated to me with this ring, according to the law of Moses and Israel.*" He placed a plain gold band on Yutka's finger.

At the end of the *Sheva Brachot* René placed a wine glass, wrapped in a white napkin, below Yaakov's right foot. Yaakov had waited until he was thirty-four to find the woman he loved and wanted to marry. He bent his knee and stomped with passion.

The broken wine glass, a traditional Jewish ritual, reminded them of the destruction of the Jewish temples and the tragic event of Jewish history. Missing their relatives however, was enough to mitigate their joy.

> *If I forget you, O Jerusalem,*
> *let my right hand wither;*
> *let my tongue stick to my palate*
> *if I cease to think of you,*

if I do not keep Jerusalem in memory
even at my happiest hour.[13]

After the ceremony, René took photos of the bride and groom that Yutka and Yaakov could send to their families, then they all went out for a light supper.

The following Sunday, when Yutka and Yaakov entered the gathering hall at the vineyard, she wore the white wedding dress, and he wore René's suit and tie. A loud cheer filled the space, "*Mazel Tov!*"

The wedding feast began with multiple blessings. Yutka and Yaakov broke a large loaf of *challah* into pieces and served each guest. Once everyone had a piece of bread, Srulik said the *Hamotzi* blessing over the bread.

> *Praised are you, Lord our God, king of the universe who brings forth bread from the earth.*

Then Srulik poured Yaakov and Yutka each a glass of kosher wine made at the vineyard. When every guest had been served a glass of wine, Srulik said the Kiddush blessing over the wine.

> *Praised are you, Lord our God, king of the universe who creates fruit of the vine.*

First Yaakov then Yutka took a sip of the wine from the same glass. Again, a loud cheer filled the space, "*Mazel Tov!*"

Zipporah had made *krupnik* soup with barley, potatoes and carrots, cooked in vegetable broth. The barley came from a nearby

---

13. Psalms 137:5-6

farmer and the rest from their garden. Their friends and family, both men and women, feasted, danced, and sang well into the night, all in the same large hall, unlike more orthodox weddings where a low removable wall would separate the women.

Later, Yutka and Yaakov walked his brother, Arie and Sara to the bus stop. "We are so happy for you," said Sara with tears in her eyes as she hugged them both. Arie hugged them before boarding the bus back to Tel Aviv.

After everyone else had gone to sleep, Yutka and Yaakov walked across the lawn to the ancient fig tree. "It was a lovely celebration," said Yutka.

"Um hum," mumbled Yaakov as he kissed his wife, took her hand and led her to the guest room where they were staying the night.

Chapter 48

A Married Couple, May 1941

Mr. Newman sat in the barber chair and after pleasantries, Yaakov said, "Mr. Newman, my wife and I are…"

Mr. Newman interrupted, "Did you say wife! *Mazel tov*, Yaakov! You have a wife?"

"Yes, we were married on Tuesday, but we need an apartment or at least a room. Do you know anyone who might be willing to share their flat?" Yaakov asked as he began to cut Mr. Newman's hair.

"As a matter of fact, my wife and I have been talking about renting part of our apartment. It's on the corner of Keren Kayemet Boulevard and Ben Yehuda Street."

The rent was so reasonable, the location so convenient, and it was just down the block from René and Elsa's apartment. Yaakov agreed, sight unseen.

Yutka purchased a mattress with the money Papa had pressed into her hand the night she left home. Then on Friday afternoon before Sabbath, Yutka and Yaakov put the mattress on the floor and brought the rest of their meager belongings to the tiny bedroom, just big enough to walk around the mattress and for the orange-crates-turned-bureau. Yutka and Mrs. Newman agreed on a schedule for the shared kitchen and bath. Yutka was pleased the apartment was on the top floor. She didn't like the idea of people walking around on top of her.

✡

Yaakov placed his mandolin case with its bowlback in the corner next to the stack of orange crates. He remembered his uncle teaching him to tune and play his precious instrument—the introduction to music that changed Yaakov's life. When he thought of his sister Mala and her daughter Halina, who would be five now, memories flooded his mind. He hoped that his uncles, aunts, sister and niece were all safe amid the roundups of Polish Jews he'd read about.

As Yutka arranged her few belongings on the top of the orange crate, Yaakov stood behind her with his arms around her waist, the back of her head leaning against his chest. In the family photo she placed on the crate, her nephew Jerzyk was two and niece Rebekah was a few weeks old. "Jerzyk is four now and Rebekah is two," she told Yaakov as she tenderly touched their faces in the photo. On either side of the photo, she placed the Boy Scout First Aid Kit that Heniek had given her and Mama's copy of *Pan Tadeusz*. With her palm pressed against the book cover, she told Yaakov, "When Mama gave me her copy of *Pan Tadeusz* she said I can return it when we meet again. I hope that day comes soon."

The walls were so thin they could hear the two Newman children crying in the night and often heard Mrs. Newman's scratchy, high-pitched voice reprimanding her husband. Fortunately, Yutka and Yaakov's bedroom had a balcony where they often slept, enjoying the mulberry and orange scented breeze mixed with a whiff of the Mediterranean Sea. Yutka murmured, "The balcony is far more comfortable than the hard pine bunks on the *Parita*." Her head rested on Yaakov's chest.

"And it smells a lot better too!"

They both laughed.

Mrs. Newman occupied the kitchen at all hours, even during time assigned to Yutka and Yaakov, so Yaakov brought home a brazier and Yutka did the cooking on the balcony whenever she could. They awoke early to get ready for work ahead of the Newman family chaos in the bathroom.

Yutka found a job at a towel factory and Yaakov walked her to the bus stop on his way to the barbershop. She posted an advertisement on the bulletin boards in apartment buildings near theirs. In German, Polish and French, she wrote:

> *Learn to read and write Hebrew.*
> *Contact Yutka in 3-B*
> *Pay what you can.*

She set up a small classroom on the flat roof of the building. Although her goal was to make a little extra money, some families could not afford to pay her, but she welcomed them, nonetheless.

On Yutka's twenty-first birthday, Yaakov closed the barbershop early to allow time to walk to his favorite meditation spot to gather a wildflower bouquet. He collected fragrant pink heliotrope, white desert baby's breath, exotic Egyptian caper, and feathery foxtail grass and tied the bouquet with twine. He stopped at the market to buy a loaf of bread and a few oranges and packed them into Yutka's wicker marketing basket, along with a jar of water and the wildflower bouquet.

When she walked into the apartment after work, he said softly, "*Ekmek ve su!*" The phrase Yaakov had shouted from the balcony when he saw Yutka for the first time after leaving the boat, "bread and water!"

"Happy birthday Yutka, someday we will celebrate properly." He bent to kiss his wife.

"Oh, Yaakov. Thank you for remembering my birthday. You are all I need." She stood on her tiptoes to kiss his cheek.

Chapter 49

Last Letter, March 1942

Yutka received a letter from her family.

Moi Kochani Rodzina,

I received your postcard. Yutka, we are very happy to learn you are getting along so well. As for your wedding, follow what your heart is telling you and be happy. Please accept our sincere well-wishing for the wedding.

Aunt Rozia sent us a colored postcard from Warsaw requesting that we send her a care package with food items. I will send it this week. She lives with the Kamiaenicki's, the elderlies. The situation in Warsaw is not good.

Zigi continues to work, and our financial situation is not too bad. Slowly but surely we are buying items to replace the ones we had to abandon. Jerzyk attends kindergarten and speaks Russian. He also speaks Yiddish quite nicely. He learned it from his kindergarten mates. Rebekah is walking everywhere. Her

Polish vocabulary grows every day and Jerzyk teaches her Yiddish. It is a shame you cannot see them. The family has reunited in Mir.
   How is our family in Palestine doing?
   Please give them our regards.
   Rozka

Yutka checked the post every day and continued to write to her family every week, but no more letters arrived from Mir.

Chapter 50

End of WWII, May 8, 1945

Yutka and Yaakov were in their tiny bedroom early one Wednesday morning when Mr. Newman knocked on their door. "Germany has surrendered!" he shouted. "The war in Europe has ended! Hitler is dead!" When Yaakov opened the door, Newman said, "Here, you can have the newspaper, my family and I are going out to celebrate."

Yaakov and Yutka embraced on the balcony as people gathered to sing and dance in the street below. Neither Yutka nor Yaakov felt like celebrating. Now the conflict was over, but they had not heard from their family members for almost three years. Without knowing the fate of their relatives, they had no energy for celebration.

"While the Newmans are out of the apartment, I'll have the kitchen to myself. I'll make a nice meal."

Yaakov opened the barbershop and Yutka made a quick trip to the market for fish and vegetables. Back in the kitchen, she mixed flour and water for a batch of *levivot*, sliced the tomatoes and sautéed the zucchini with onions, tomato paste, salt and a pinch of sugar, then poached the fish.

They ate on the balcony and washed the dishes together before the Newmans returned.

Later that evening, they heard Mrs. Newman's irritating voice loudly complaining, "*Oy vey!* The house, it smells like fish and onions."

"Someday soon we will find our own apartment," whispered Yaakov.

Chapter 51

Tel Aviv, October 1945

As often as she could, Yutka took the bus to visit her aunt, uncle and friends at the vineyard in the Jezreel Valley, a two-hour bus ride from Tel Aviv. One afternoon, while they shared a pot of mint tea, her friend Melina began telling Yutka about her life in Poland during the war.

"Papa owned a textile mill, and the Nazis forced him to make uniforms. Papa worried that neighbors would think he was a collaborator, but he had no choice."

"I worked as a seamstress at the mill. One day the Nazis brought truckloads of blue striped fabric and gave us patterns that looked more like pajamas than uniforms. Some of us sewed the yellow Star of David onto the front of the shirts. That night I asked Papa why we were making these strange, striped uniforms.

"'Melina, the Nazis, they do not tell me why we make certain uniforms. The yellow stars…? This can only mean more bad news.'

"Our big Catholic family lived next door to Ozer's Jewish family in a lovely area of Warsaw. A few weeks after we started sewing the striped uniforms, the Nazis rounded up all the Jews in our neighborhood, including Ozer's parents, grandparents, brother and sister. Fortunately, Ozer was at our house helping my brother with his math assignment, as he often did.

"When Papa heard the trucks in the street and people screaming, he knew what was happening. 'Melina, run upstairs and hide Ozer in the attic, then you and your brother come down here with your books and act like nothing is happening. Now hurry.'

"When Papa went into the yard and talked to one of the German officers he recognized, I peeked beyond the blackout curtain. I heard Papa ask, 'What's going on, *Oberleutnant*?' The officer replied, 'We're just taking care of the Jewish problem, no concern Herr Müller. Have a nice evening.'

"With terror on their faces, Ozer's family joined the crowd of Jews gathered in the street, ready to march, God knows where. I saw Ozer's mama lock eyes with Papa, and he nodded slightly, letting her know that Ozer was safe with us. Papa came into the house, sat in his chair, covered his face with his hands and sobbed. 'What kind of world do we live in?' I had never seen Papa cry. We found out later that the striped uniforms were issued to Jews in concentrations camps, after the Nazis stole their clothing and jewelry."

As Melina told Yutka her story, Yutka wanted her to stop. The story was too frightening, but at the same time, she wanted to know what it was like to hide from the Nazis. Maybe her family also found a place to hide. "Were you worried the Nazis would search your house?"

"Mama and I were worried but not Papa. The Nazis thought Papa was a collaborator. In the beginning, Papa had privileges because of his business, so feeding Ozer was not a burden.

"The Nazis would have shot Mama if they found out how much extra flour, oil and other supplies she secretly stored in our cellar. Hoarding was strictly *verboten*, punishable by death. Of course, Ozer still worried that he was putting our family in danger. One night, Ozer and I were sitting in the attic discussing a book we'd both read, when Papa climbed the ladder to join us. I'll never forget. Papa sat on the cot, patted Ozer's knee, and said, 'Even though my family is Catholic, and you are Jewish, I believe we worship the same God, and He would want us to help you.

Don't worry, Ozer, we will keep you safe.' Ozer never saw his family again."

As Yutka listened to Melina's story, she held her hands firmly tucked between her knees so Melina wouldn't see how she trembled. She held her breath as if that might help. If Melina's Catholic family had been willing to risk hiding a Jew, maybe another brave and generous Gentile family hid her family.

"Every day, when I came home from the mill, I took bread and soup to Ozer and then we sat on the attic floor, leaning against the cold wall, talking for hours in the candlelight."

"What did you and Ozer talk about?" asked Yutka as she poured Melina another cup of mint tea.

"Ozer told me about his dream to immigrate to *Eretz* Israel to help build a new state for Jews so that this kind of pogrom could not happen again. He would have been even more determined if he had known the extent of the slaughter. Whether to become a mathematician or an architect or a farmer in a *kibbutz* was not important to Ozer."

"Did you ever talk about your own dreams?" asked Yutka.

Melina smiled. "Of course. I wanted to have a family, but I was not excited about becoming a housewife like Mama. I wanted to become a writer. Someday I will. Ozer and I both love to read. I brought books to the attic that I had read, like *Sanatorium Under the Sign of the Hourglass* by Bruno Schulz and *The Doll* by Bolesław Prus. We discussed the stories and the authors well into the night.... Then one night everything changed."

"What happened?"

"Papa came home from the mill, and sat in his chair, as always. I heard Mama scream his name. My brother and I ran down the stairs and found them in the sitting room, Papa slumped in his chair with a book in his lap. My brother ran to fetch the doctor, but it was too late. Papa died of a heart attack. He was only forty-five but the stress of working for the Nazis was just too much for his heart. A month later the German army conscripted my brother. Even though he was the head of the household, he had no choice. Christmas had always been a happy time for our family but not 1943. The Germans took over the mill and without Papa, we faced rationing like everyone else. I helped Mama with my siblings as much as I could, and I gave her the meager wages I made as a seamstress but feeding growing children was difficult enough without an extra mouth to feed.

"With all the stress of the war and raising a family alone, Mama worried about the Nazis discovering a Jew in our attic. I convinced her that Ozer had no other place to hide and if she reported him at this late date, they might kill us all. The thought of losing Ozer made me realize we had fallen in love. When the war was finally over, Ozer and I were married and immigrated to *Eretz* Israel with the help of Israeli Jewish Agency."

"Is that when Ozer came to work in the *moshav*?"

"No, at first, we rented a small room from a family in Tel Aviv and Ozer started working in construction. Tel Aviv desperately needs housing for so many new immigrants."

"Yes, we had trouble finding an apartment after our wedding. We share a flat with a family of four. Not much privacy but it's close to Yaakov's barbershop and I take the bus to the towel factory where I work. Did you have a job when you lived in Tel Aviv?"

"No, I was expecting our first baby when we landed, so I began learning Hebrew and converting to Judaism."

As Melina told her story, Yutka's heart ached. She and Yaakov had been married four years but still had no baby. She struggled to hide her sorrow as she listened to Melina.

"While Ozer worked long hours, I studied Jewish history and rituals, but Hebrew will take a long time. I agreed to observe all the commandments of the *Torah*, live a Jewish life with Ozer and raise our children in a Jewish household."

"I'm so glad your love story with Ozer has a happy ending."

"We thought so until a few months ago. A boy at school called our son a *mamzer,* as if Ozer and I never married. I had no idea *Halacha* considered our children illegitimate because I was not born Jewish and have not officially converted."

"Have you asked for a hearing with the Rabbinical Court? They can proclaim your marriage legal under Jewish law."

"Yes, we have scheduled a hearing in Tel Aviv next week. Would you testify on our behalf at the hearing?"

"Of course," said Yutka, jumping up to hug Melina. "I'll be there to support you and Ozer and to testify. Your home is as kosher as any I have ever seen," said Yutka. "The rabbis should welcome you as a Jew and sanctify your Jewish marriage."

When called to testify before the Rabbinical Court, Yutka stood by her wooden chair in the front row. She wore a pale blue cotton dress she'd made for herself. In an attempt to look older, more pious and credible, she wrapped her head with a long rectangular scarf that matched her dress.

Her surprisingly powerful voice filled the room. "When the Nazis took Ozer's family to Auschwitz, Melina and her family hid Ozer and saved his life. Melina studied long hours to convert to Judaism. She and their children are studying the *Torah* and learning Hebrew. Here in Israel, Melina and Ozer follow Jewish traditions and are raising their children as Jews. You should consider Melina and Ozer's marriage legal."

Srulik and Zipporah and other friends also testified. Then the rabbis, dressed in black suits, white shirts and neckties, wearing yarmulkes under their flat brimmed *hoiche* hats, left the courtroom. Yutka and the others waited anxiously for over half an hour to hear the court's judgment.

When the rabbinical judges returned to their table, the room fell silent. The *dayan* announced, "The testimonies about your adherence to Jewish way of life and tradition were impressive, but we did not see any marriage certificate from an ordained orthodox rabbi signed by witnesses. We did not see the *ketubah* which Jewish law requires a groom to provide for his bride signed by the rabbi who officiated the wedding. We are sorry but we have no other choice but to deny your request to consider you a Jewish Couple according to *Halacha*."

Anger and frustration gripped Yutka's heart. She lifted her chin as she rose to her full five feet. Her voice carried throughout the chamber. "You should be ashamed of yourselves!"

Everyone gasped loudly, as if sucking all the air from the courtroom.

Zipporah's sparkling eyes looked at Srulik as she suppressed a proud grin.

The three black hats turned toward this diminutive young Jewish woman in the front row. Yutka folded her arms over her chest and tried to breathe normally. She appeared petite and soft-spoken. No one in the courtroom suspected her strength of character.

The courtroom became deathly still. Yutka's arm swept toward Melina and Ozer as the couple turned toward her on their heavy wooden chairs next to the rabbis' table. "Melina and Ozer married in Poland where the Nazis had murdered the Jews. In such a place, what rabbi should marry them? There were no Jews left alive to sign for them! This woman risked her own life to save a living soul. You are rabbis, yet you forget the *Talmud: whoever saves one life saves the entire world!*"

The room remained absolutely still, except for the squeaking chairs, as the other witnesses turned toward Yutka. Some nodded and murmured support for her remarks.

Others, with their mouths gaping, were shocked by the *chutzpah* from a *woman* no less.

The three rabbis leaned together, their black hats bobbed above their waving, bristly white beards. Finally, the *dayan* looked at Yutka with a grandfatherly smile and announced, "On second deliberation, in light of the compelling plea from Mrs. Polonecki, we have decided to consider Melina and Ozer's union a Jewish Marriage."

A cheer erupted in the courtroom.

Chapter 52

Yaakov's Sister, 1946

Yaakov had just taken the cape from his customer's shoulders when the bell jingled on the door. "Be with you in a moment," he said in Hebrew, in his usual friendly tone.

As he hung the cape on a peg, he looked up and asked, "How can I help you?"

As Yaakov's eyes adjusted to the bright sunlight reflected from the street behind her, he saw the silhouette of a woman with a girl. The woman patted her sleek blonde hair and with a big familiar grin, she said in Polish, "Do you think I need a little trim?"

Yaakov stood, speechless. "Mala?" he whispered. Then he shouted, switching to Polish, "Mala! You're here. You're alive." Tears streamed from his eyes as he grabbed his sister in a bear hug. "How did you…? I thought you…?"

Yaakov didn't notice his customer put his payment on the counter and quietly leave the shop. In Tel Aviv, reunions like this were beautiful and far too rare.

When they released their embrace, Mala said, "You remember Halina."

"Of course, Halina! How should I forget Halina?"

The ten-year-old stood behind her mother, looking at Yaakov with fearful eyes.

Yaakov tried to control his enthusiasm, seeing his niece's trepidation. "You were only three when I last saw you, about this tall," he held out his hand. "Maybe you remember riding on my shoulders in the park or the shadow puppets we made together in your bedroom?"

Without sweeping the hair and whiskers from the floor, he twisted the *open* sign to *closed*, locked the door, and they walked to the apartment.

"I'd like you to meet my *wife*, Yutka. Yutka, this is my *sister* Mala and her daughter Halina. I told you about them."

"You're married!" squealed Mala as she hugged Yutka. "Papa and Mama will be so happy."

For just an instant, he thought his parents had also survived, but Mala's face told the truth, "*Would have* been so happy," she amended quietly.

Brother and sister surrendered to tears and another hug.

Yutka let her own tears fall. Yaakov could see Yutka's pain. She had heard nothing from her own family since Heniek's postcard from Mir, Russia sent four years before.

Later that night, Mala and Yaakov went to the roof, where they could talk without waking Halina or Yutka. "Do you remember Baszka, the Catholic manicurist at the salon?"

"How should I forget? She chased me unmercifully," laughed Yaakov.

"Her crush on you saved Halina."

"How could that girl's crush on me help Halina?"

"When the Nazis invaded Warsaw, I had no trouble passing for a German but my husband… Simi…" she took a deep breath, "Simi looked more Jewish than our papa the rabbi! Fortunately, when they rounded up the Jews in our neighborhood, Halina was at the babysitter's. The Nazis put us in a cattle car headed for Auschwitz. Simi and others helped me shimmy through the train's tiny window. I had to protect Halina."

"Do you know what happened to Simi?"

Mala wiped her tears and quietly answered, "He had a cold when they took him to Auschwitz. A friend reported that he died of pneumonia not long after."

Yaakov's head remained bowed; his elbows rested on his knees. It was difficult for him to watch Mala's face distorted with grief and terror as she relived those years.

"Halina looks very much like Simi," he said, still looking down, his forehead in his hands.

"I asked Baszka, the Catholic manicurist, to take Halina to stay with her sister Mariska and her husband, Sigmund. Sigmund and Mariska were anti-Nazi Catholics and sympathetic to Jews. Halina was only three and Baszka loved to play with her when she came to the salon with me. When Halina walked away with Baszka that day, Halina didn't know what was happening. There was no way to explain to a three-year-old why her daddy left or why she was going away with Baszka. When I knew Halina was safe with Mariska and Sigmund, I got a job as a live-in housekeeper in the house of a rich Catholic family, of course they had no idea I was Jewish. They were Nazi collaborators and hosted German officers for dinners and social events. You should have heard the things they said about Jews! I had to be careful not to react. Once, when they were bragging about how many dirty Jews they had rounded up that day, I dropped a plate full of buttered potatoes. Mistress scolded me, but no one realized why I dropped it.

"Halina lived with Mariska and Sigmund for two years until an old woman in their apartment building, hoping to earn a bounty, informed the Nazis that a Jewish child was living with Mariska and Sigmund. Sigmund saw them coming and hid Halina under the sofa. The solders searched the apartment turning over furniture and stabbing the sofa cushions with bayonets," she took a deep breath. "Somehow, the bayonets missed Halina, thank God."

Yaakov shook his head. "Mala, your story...." He looked up to see his sister trembling. He put his arms around her. "You don't need to tell me...."

"But I must," shaky words poured out of Mala. "I must tell the story to the end. It will help me…." She took another juddering breath and wiped her wet face with the back of both hands. "Halina was almost five years old when the Nazis returned to Mariska and Sigmund's house. Apparently, the upstairs neighbor had reported them again. Sigmund fled out the back door with Halina. They hid under bushes and behind garbage cans. By then, Halina was old enough to understand."

Mala stopped and a smirk covered her face. "Ha! That's not what I mean. No one understood what was happening, but I'm sure Sigmund tried to explain why she had to hide in his truck, especially after see saw the bayonet damage to the sofa cushions.

Sigmund's job was delivering meat from the stock yard to butchers in Warsaw. Halina hid between bleeding beef carcasses while he drove to the Catholic orphanage. I can't imagine her horror as she rode in the dark truck squeezed between the dead animals. Mother Superior seemed to believe him when he said he found Halina, covered in blood, wandering in the street. He gave Mother Superior papers he said he found in the pocket of Halina's bloodied coat and begged her to admit Halina to the orphanage. The forged documents stated that Halina was a Catholic. I'm sure Mother Superior guessed that Halina was Jewish, she looks so much like Simi, but she agreed to take care of Halina when he gave her meat from his truck. I suspect he made deliveries to them more than once, delivering more Jewish children as well as meat. The orphanage didn't have enough food or clothing to go around but… Halina survived."

"How did you find her?" asked Yaakov.

"After the war, while I was still working for the Catholic family, on my day off I walked to Mariska's house and found it destroyed. I sat in the dirty street and sobbed, wondering if they bombed the house with Halina inside." Mala hugged her trembling body and rocked back and forth. "For months and months, I searched and searched then one day I was passing a café, and I heard a woman scream my name. Mariska came running out of the café with flour covering her hands, wearing an apron, nearly knocking me over with a hug, shouting, "Halina is safe! Halina is safe!" She held me tight, so I didn't drop to my knees in the dirt. She knew the name of the orphanage where Sigmund left Halina. Later she told me that the Germans arrested Sigmund after he helped other Jewish children. He died in a camp. I am so thankful to Sigmund. He loved my Halina like his own daughter and died helping others like her."

Yaakov and Mala sat quietly while Mala looked up at the stars, tears rolling into her hair.

"I stood on the street, looking at the dilapidated orphanage where my precious daughter had survived the war. She was there, I saw her looking out the upstairs window. The nuns might not believe that I was Halina's mama, so I asked for a job, working for food and shelter. Halina was seven years old by then and thin and frail, but she still looked like Simi. I think she recognized the old leopard fur coat I wore that day hoping she would remember it."

"I remember that coat," said Yaakov. "Halina loved rubbing her little fingers around the collar. You wore it to special family events."

"It was so unique I think she remembered the fur coat even if she didn't recognize me."

Yaakov understood his sister's pain; Halina didn't know her own mother.

"I started the habit of hugging each child every day. When I hugged her, I saw the small birthmark behind her ear shaped like a bunny, there was no doubt she was my Halina."

Yaakov sat with his elbows on his knees, his face in his hands. Tears trickled between his fingers as he listened to his sister's story.

"The nuns taught the children Catholic rituals. I can't hold it against them, they had no choice. I know Halina's Catholic training was protective coloring so that the Nazis would not notice her when they came to inspect the orphanage. If the children didn't behave like Catholics, the guards would be suspicious, and they would all be in danger."

"It must have been difficult to see her every day and not be able to claim her as your daughter."

"I did my best to bide my time until Halina knew me and trusted me, even if she didn't know I was her mother. Then one day we were in the play yard. Halina and I took a walk and never went back. I'm certain Mother Superior knew I was Halina's mother. Once, our eyes met and I felt like she knew. I don't know how many parents of the children she cared for, Jewish or not, died at the hands of the Nazis.... Just skin and bones, Halina was almost eight when we walked away that day. She had no shoes, and her clothes were ill-fitting rags. Her eyes sunk into dark circles on her face. She still suffers from the effects of tuberculosis."

"Where did you go when you left the orphanage?"

"I did my research ahead of time and learned of a partisan's hideout. We walked all the way, trying to avoid the violence in the streets. Neighbors were accusing neighbors and took it upon themselves to execute collaborators. We passed angry mobs shaving women's heads who they said had slept with Nazis, whether the women were guilty or had any choice. Upset by the sight of the bald women, Halina's bony hands clutched her own head. The nuns had shaved Halina's head to control the lice. I couldn't shelter her from the violence, the pandemonium was horrifying. It broke my heart to see her terror as she kneeled and crossed herself every time we passed a statue of Mary. I never knew there were so many Statues of Mary in Warsaw."

Although Yaakov wanted desperately to ease Mala's pain, he sat as still as he could, allowing his sister to recount his niece's ordeal.

"When we arrived at the camp, the Jewish partisans took away her crucifix and rosary and told her bluntly that she was Jewish. They were so angry at the world they didn't understand why she thought she was Catholic. They were harsh and fanatical. She crawled into my lap, and her bones poked into my legs and chest. I held her while she cried, 'But I am not a Jew! Jews are dirty and they killed Jesus.'

"I feel like she hates me for taking her away from the life she knew for those years, even though she was cold, sick and starving all that time. Now, her Catholic education is making the transition back to the Jewish faith—well—I don't know if she can ever recover."

"We must be gentle with her," said Yaakov. "It will take a long time for her to mend.… How did you find your way to Israel?"

"The Israeli Jewish Agency in charge of helping Holocaust survivors brought us to a special camp. From there we took a boat to Israel. This morning when we came out of our apartment, I noticed an ad for your barbershop pinned to a bulletin board. How should any other barber be named Yaakov Polonecki?" She laughed. "Halina and I will learn Hebrew together. Will you help us?"

"Of course, Yutka and I will help you anyway we can."

Chapter 53

The Vote, November 29, 1947

Like most business owners in *Eretz* Israel on November 29, 1947 Yaakov closed his barbershop to listen to the UN General Assembly's vote on the partition of British Mandate Palestine creating a Jewish state and an Arab state. If they voted yes, Jews would finally govern themselves. If the UN General Assembly declined the partition, no one knew what would happen to the Jews in Israel or elsewhere in the diaspora.

Elsa and René's apartment on Ben Yehuda Street, filled with friends and neighbors huddling around René's mahogany radio cabinet. René adjusted the knobs, trying to reduce the staticky whine, hiss, and buzz, so they could clearly hear the announcer.

Yaakov held a list of the UN General Assembly member countries that he'd cut from the newspaper. He kept the tally as the vote went forward. Guatemala: yes, Argentina: abstain, Lebanon: no, United Kingdom: abstain, United States: yes, Russia: yes, France: yes. Finally, they all held their breath for the deciding vote… Haiti: yes. The reporter announced, "In favor 33, against 13, abstaining 10, resolution 181 of the UN Ad Hoc Committee for British Mandate Palestine passes."

A 2000-year-old dream was reality.

At first, Elsa and René's neighbors and friends fell absolutely still. The emotionally overpowering decision left them numb and speechless. Some stared as if stunned by a powerful electric shock. Some sat on the floor rocking in prayer like a candle flame.

Yutka, Yaakov and Elsa had survived the grueling trip on the *Parita* to *Eretz* Israel, praying for this day to come. Tears streamed down his face as Yaakov hugged Yutka. He whispered, "Until today, others have made decisions for Jews, now we make our own decisions." As the shock abated, their friends openly cried, kissed, and embraced. Commotion in the streets drew them outside. They shouted, *Mazel tov!* and ran out of the apartment and down the stairs to join the celebration.

"You go with them," Elsa smiled up at René. "I'll stay here with the boys."

René bent to kiss Elsa and his sons, then hurried to follow his friends into the street.

After all the excitement, Elsa held her three-year-old on her lap and read to him until he fell asleep. Finally, she tucked him into his crib.

With contrasting emotions, she sat on the floor, leaning on the sofa listening to the radio, nursing their new baby. She still hoped that her family in Austria had survived, but three years after liberation, that hope had faded.

She turned down the volume but continued to listen. In Jerusalem, Jews were crowding the courtyard in front of the Jewish Agency building. David Ben-Gurion stepped onto the balcony. When he raised his hand, the crowd cheered and then Elsa heard complete and utter silence, as if she had unplugged the radio. "Long live the Hebrew state." He asked the crowd to sing *Hatikvah; The Hope* became the Israeli National Anthem.

Elsa kissed the blond head of her sleeping baby boy and quietly sang along in Hebrew as tears wet her face.

> *As long as the Jewish spirit is yearning deep in the heart,*
> *With eyes turned toward the East, looking toward Zion,*
> *Then our hope - the two-thousand-year-old hope - will not be lost:*
> *To be a free people in our land,*
> *The land of Zion and Jerusalem*

✡

The streets of Tel Aviv filled with neighbors and strangers singing and dancing the *horah*, circles inside circles, inside circles, inside circles.

Among the party goers Yaakov and Yutka saw the Rumanian redhead, Oshrah and the Greek cook, Nikos who had been on the *Parita*. "It has happened!" yelled Nikos in broken German, hugging both Yutka and Yaakov.

Yaakov watched Yutka hug Oshrah, then push back and hold Oshrah by the shoulders. Oshrah's eyes glowed. "Yes," she said with her hands on both sides of her belly. "Our baby is due in March. This is our third. Our son is seven and our daughter is five."

"Mazel tov!" said Yaakov, hugging both Oshrah and Nikos. He tried not to remember that he and Yutka had been married six years, but still they had no children. He saw a flash of the same sadness in Yutka's eyes before they all danced the *horah*.

Yaakov broke away from the dancing when he noticed Mr. Bender, the old barber from Góra Kalwaria, shuffling by as if in a dream, leaning heavily on his cane. "*Mazel tov*, Mr. Bender!" Yaakov hugged the old man.

"Our prayers have been answered," said Mr. Bender, his tears streaming with abandon. "When I left Góra Kalwaria I could only hope… But now, in my lifetime, it has happened."

Mr. Bender shuffled on down the street, humming an old Yiddish tune, *Mein Shtetele, Belz*.

Yaakov jumped onto a concrete barricade and watched the celebration.

From the circle of dancing friends, Yutka noticed Yaakov standing above the crowd on a low concrete wall. Their eyes met and she read the twinkle in his eyes. She broke away from the crowd as he jumped down from the barricade. He hugged her close and they hurried back to their tiny bedroom.

Yaakov had waited until he was thirty-four to find the woman he loved and wanted to marry. He was eager to be a papa, but for six years each month brought disappointment.

When Yutka and Yaakov entered their tiny room, Mr. and Mrs. Newman and their children were out celebrating the vote. Yutka and Yaakov were alone in the apartment for the rest of the night. They slept only a few hours.

The next morning, still tired from the celebration, Yutka tiptoed into the bathroom to get ready for work. She splashed water on her face and looked into the mirror. Her face glowed back at her.

She knew. Even this early, she knew, finally they were going to have a baby.

Chapter 54

Hadassah Convoy, April 13, 1948

Elsa's husband, René finished his medical training with a specialty in wound care and joined a clinic in Tel Aviv. A professor had asked him to come to the Medical School at Hebrew University at Mount Scopus to teach a class, so he had been away from home for a few days.

While her boys napped, Elsa prepared *kugle*, not because it was a holiday. *Kugle* was quick to assemble, and René loved it—especially left over. While the *lokshen* cooked in boiling water, she chopped onions, minced garlic and whipped together sour cream, cottage cheese, butter and eggs. She put the casserole in the icebox, ready to bake forty-five minutes before René was due home for dinner.

Listening to Vivaldi's "Four Seasons" on the radio, Elsa nursed their five-month-old baby, then changed his diaper, while her older son played with his blocks on the floor. An announcer interrupted the program.

> "We interrupt this broadcast with a special report. A team of university scientists, doctors, and medical personnel along with a few patients, escorted by Haganah, were on their way home from Hebrew University when an Arab mob attacked them. The

death toll stands at seventy-five. No further details are available at this time. Please stay tuned for our next report."

Staring at the wedding photo next to the lamp, Elsa sat heavily on the sofa with the baby in her arms. Then, as Debussy's "Clair de Lune" filled the room, she stood and paced their apartment, holding the baby as he slept. Turning off the radio, as if turning off her terror, she sat on the floor, robotically helping her three-year-old build towers he loved to knock over. He was quieter than usual, as if he knew his mama was worried.

Elsa nursed the baby, changed his diaper, and put him in his bassinet. Then she put the *kugel* in the oven and set the table. *René will be home for dinner.* She fed her oldest his dinner, read his favorite story as if nothing had happened, and put him to bed at the usual hour.

The baby fussed as the *kugel* grew cold. She held him in her arms as she paced, rocking and humming.

Long after the dinner hour, Yaakov and Yutka came to Elsa's apartment. She opened the door and saw their sorrowful faces.

"Oh Elsa," said Yutka, reaching to hug her.

Elsa looked at them blankly, as if she didn't know why they were there. Then they seemed to swirl and swim in front of her eyes. Yutka took the baby from her arms as Elsa collapsed onto Yaakov. He carried her to the sofa, then placed a cold washcloth on her forehead.

Yaakov answered the door when an official from the University knocked. He had come to inform Elsa that René was among the dead. Elsa stayed where she was on the sofa. Yutka sat next to her, holding the baby. Yaakov thanked the official and closed the door.

"It can't be, it just can't be," she screamed. "We came all this way to avoid the…" Tears erupted. She tried to catch her breath. "My parents are gone at the hands of the Nazis and now my dear

René has lost his life to an Arab mob." She shook her head as if to clear her mind. "What is happening to this world?" still shouting as she gasped for breath.

Yutka paced the apartment. She was wearing one of Elsa's hand-me-down maternity smocks. Tears dripped onto the baby's blue onesie as she cradled him above her swollen belly. Looking down at the sleeping infant, she thought, *How could René be dead? His baby boy is only a few months old. This little boy will never know his wonderful, generous papa.*

Elsa's three-year-old toddled into the room, dragging his special blanket. When he saw his mama crying, he crawled onto her lap and nuzzled his curly blond head under her chin.

"I'm sorry I woke you, precious," she tried to say in a normal tone.

When she hugged him to her, he said, "Mama hug too tight."

Elsa looked up at Yaakov, whispering, "How do I tell him...?" Heavy tears rolled down her flushed face and dripped from her chin. She wiped them away with the back of her hand.

His heart aching, Yaakov bent to rub the little boy's back, *He looks so much like René....*

Yaakov had met René the first day he worked at the barbershop and they had been best friends ever since. René introduced Yaakov to Tel Aviv and from René's apartment balcony he'd found Yutka.

✡

For the next seven days, while Elsa sat *shiva*, Srulik and Zipporah and other friends from the vineyard came to visit and pay their respects. Yutka took time away from work to help Elsa with the two boys and to organize the food that friends and René's medical associates brought. The door remained unlocked so friends could come and go without disturbing Elsa.

Every day, after closing the barbershop, Yaakov went to Elsa's apartment. They talked about René. "I don't know what I would have done if I hadn't met René. He was a kind and generous friend to me when I arrived in Tel Aviv with nothing. Not even the clothes on my back! He was one of my first customers in the barbershop. We chatted while I cut his hair and I told him about the voyage on the *Parita*. He put a big tip on the counter and said, 'Welcome to Tel Aviv. Let me know if you need anything.' Later he gave me trousers and shirts and…"

Elsa listened to her friends talk about René, but she still couldn't grasp that he was gone. She looked around the room at the covered mirror and burning candle, but she believed he would come through the door any minute, give her a kiss, and sit on the floor to play with his boys.

In the weeks after *shiva* ended, Yutka and Yaakov spent a lot of time with Elsa. While Elsa nursed the baby, Yutka sat on the floor playing blocks with the three-year-old, and Yaakov played his mandolin with a tremolo effect that made Elsa both smile and cry.

René's favorite chair remained empty.

Chapter 55

Israeli War for Independence, May 14, 1948

David Ben-Gurion, the de facto leader of the provisional Israeli government didn't publicize the Declaration of Independence ahead of time for fear of intervention by either the British or the Arabs, however the meeting at the Tel Aviv Museum was no longer secret when *Kol Israel* broadcast the ceremony live.

So the Sabbath would not be violated, the formalities began at 4:00 p.m. and finished well before sunset. David Ben-Gurion banged his gavel on the table, prompting the 250 guests to sing *Hatikvah*. On the wall behind the podium hung a larger-than-life picture of Theodor Herzl, the founder of modern Zionism, flanked by two white flags with the blue Star of David between two blue stripes, the design inspired by the *tallit* prayer shawl. Later, they would proclaim the blue and white flag the official flag of Israel. Ben-Gurion read the declaration ending with the words, "Let us accept the Foundation Scroll of the Jewish State by rising and calling on Rabbi Fishman to recite *Shehecheyanu*."

> *Blessed are you our God, King of the Universe, who has kept us alive, sustained us, and brought us to this occasion.*

Guests at the Tel Aviv Museum and everyone listening on the radio said, "Amen."

"The State of Israel is established," Ben-Gurion declared.

Word spread quickly through the new nation.

Finishing his last customer on that Friday afternoon, Yaakov noticed people gathering on the streets. He opened the door. "What's going on?"

"It has happened!" shouted a jubilant passerby. "Ben-Gurion declared independence. Israel is an independent nation!"

Yutka was preparing Sabbath dinner when she heard shouting in the streets. Just then, Yaakov came crashing through the door. He grabbed her and swung her off her feet, then began dancing the tango.

Yutka threw her head back and pealed with laughter, "Yaakov, what has gotten into you!"

"Israel is a free nation, David Ben-Gurion declared independence!" He kissed her hard on the lips. He squeezed her hand and pulled her toward the door. "Let's go celebrate."

"But Yaakov, it is almost Sabbath."

"God will understand," he grinned.

Yutka turned off the oven and, holding hands, they hurried down the stairs and into the street to join the merriment. Again, the streets filled with people singing and dancing the *horah*, circles inside circles, inside circles, inside circles.

They watched Jews climb aboard a British armored carrier as the soldiers joined the celebration. Among the revelers, they encountered Oshrah and Nikos. "It has happened!" yelled Nikos, running to hug both Yutka and Yaakov.

Soon, the Edelman family joined their circle. Yutka hardly recognized the girls, twelve-year-old Rochelle and thirteen-year-old Priscilla, both taller than Yutka.

Later, as they walked back to their apartment, arm in arm,

Yutka looked up at Yaakov through tear-spiked lashes, "I wish *Saba* Fiebush could have lived to see this day."

✡

On Saturday afternoon, Yutka and Yaakov watched David Ben-Gurion and his entourage riding in an open Jeep down Ben Yehuda Street, a direct violation of Jewish law.

"I wonder what is happening to cause Ben-Gurion to breach the Sabbath," Yutka pondered. She couldn't help remembering the testimony she had given in Rabbinical court when she quoted the *Talmud*. She whispered, "*Whoever saves one life saves the entire world.*"

Yaakov was thinking the same thing; it was the only reason Ben-Gurion would breach Sabbath. With creases between his brows, Yaakov agreed, "In this case, not a life but a nation."

Later that day, Yaakov heard the distant hum of approaching aircraft. "Let's head for shelter under the stairwell," he shouted as the hum became a roar. It was the opening salvo of the Israel-Arab war. Egypt, Transjordan, Syria, and Iraq had launched an attack on the newborn country.

They huddled together with their neighbors, listening to the dull thump of bombs landing on Tel Aviv, and the rat-tat-tat, pew-pew of machine gun fire destroying the White City's beautiful buildings. With each bomb blast, the apartment building above them trembled as if a deep earthquake moved the sandy earth.

Early the next morning, Yaakov and Yutka stood on the roof of their building, her back pressed against his chest, watching the black smoke rise too close to their street. The pungent air stung their eyes. The air tasted metallic. "I have no choice," he whispered, his arms around her. "You know it is my duty to join *Haganah*."

"I knew you would," she said as her eyes filled with tears. "But that doesn't mean I like the idea. Please be careful!"

"I'll be at the rear, helping save injured Israeli soldiers not at the front, killing our enemies."

He placed both of his hands on the swell of her belly as she tucked the back of her head under his chin.

"What should we name him?" said Yutka.

"Him?"

"Yes, I'm sure it's a boy."

"How about Shmuel, after my father?"

"That's perfect. I have an Uncle Shmuel on my mother's side of the family."

"And if it's a girl?"

"Maybe D'Vora for my *safta*? But it won't be a girl," she laughed softly.

"Let's hope this war is over before…."

On June 3, when air raid sirens sounded, her belly growing by the day, Yutka ran down the stairs with the Newmans and other neighbors to hide under the stairwell. Someone dragged a pallet to protect them in case of shrapnel. When the all-clear sounded, they climbed back to their apartments, hoping that would be the last of the bombing.

Throughout her pregnancy, Yutka suffered from painful back aches. One afternoon in late August, that perpetual back ache became intense. She lowered herself onto their mattress and tried to rest. The open door to the balcony brought the smell of mulberry and citrus, but the midday heat was unbearable. As the beautiful fuchsia sunset climbed the apartment walls and darkness fell, still there was no relief from the heat or her aching back. When the air raid sirens blasted, she couldn't lift herself from the mattress. She rolled onto the floor, breathless with pain. On her hands and knees, her belly close to the floor, she tried to breathe as she waited for the pain to subside. She grabbed onto the orange crates they used for a bureau and pulled herself to her feet. Then, leaning on the walls, she finally made her way to the stairs. Her water broke on the first step.

Mr. Newman heard Yutka's groan echo through the stairwell. While Mrs. Newman scolded, he climbed back up to help Yutka. "Are you alright?"

She didn't need to answer. Clearly she was in great pain. With Mr. Newman's help, she made her way down the stairs to the make-shift bomb shelter crammed with all her neighbors hiding behind the protective pallet.

The sounds of two terrified children screaming, a panic-stricken woman crying and a man rocking in prayer, helped to mask Yutka's quiet-as-possible moans as the pains grew more frequent and more intense. The scent of gefilte fish and the other's panic made her stomach heave. In her delirium, she thought she was in her reeking, roiling bunk on the *Parita*.

When the all-clear sounded, the neighbors pushed the pallet to the ground, and Yutka rolled onto it. Someone sent word to the midwife, another summoned Elsa who left her boys with her neighbor. Yutka's neighbors, even Mrs. Newman, were sympathetic. While they helped Yutka get as comfortable as possible, Mr. Newman gathered all the men and children and quickly left the area. Someone sat behind Yutka to support her back while Mrs. Newman went to her apartment and returned with tiny diapers, a white baby blanket and clean white towels, just in time to wrap the newborn.

With their hands over their hearts and happy tears flowing, the neighbor women, including Mrs. Newman welcomed the new baby, "*Baruch haba*," just as the midwife and Elsa arrived from opposite directions.

As the neighbors returned to their apartments, Elsa sat quietly with Yutka's head in her lap while the midwife cut the cord, cleaned the baby, and dealt with the afterbirth. The sun came up, and the sky tuned bright except for the lingering feathers of black smoke from the fires. "It makes no sense for you to climb the stairs to your tiny room. Do you think you can make it to my flat?" asked Elsa.

"I need to thank all my neighbors for their help." Yutka looked at her new baby swaddled in the soft white receiving blanket.

"Your neighbors are aware of your gratitude. They were so supportive and understood the situation. Who should have a baby in a bomb shelter?!" she waved her hand over her head.

"I can walk to your place if we go slowly," Yutka said softly.

"I'll run upstairs and ask Mr. Newman to help."

Both Elsa and Mr. Newman were glad that Mrs. Newman and the children were at the market when Elsa knocked. "Of course, I'll help you," he said, looking in both directions as he stepped into the stairwell.

Elsa held the newborn while Mr. Newman helped Yutka to her feet.

They slowly made their way to Elsa's flat with Elsa cradling the newborn and Yutka leaning heavily on Mr. Newman's arm. He asked, "Is the baby a boy or a girl?"

"We have a son," smiled Yutka.

"What will you name him?"

"Before Yaakov left for the war, we agreed his name will be Shmuel."

When they arrived at Elsa's building, Yutka anxiously looked up the stairs. "I'll need to rest before I try to climb all those stairs," she breathed.

"You are so small; would you mind if I carried you up?"

Yutka whispered, "*Toda raba lecha.*"

A foot taller than her, Mr. Newman easily lifted petite Yutka and climbed to Elsa's flat.

"Thank you very much," she said again in Hebrew as Mr. Newman gently lowered her to the sofa.

While Yutka rested and nursed her new baby, Elsa walked with Mr. Newman back to the apartment to fetch the little suitcase Yutka had packed for the hospital and to gather the layette and diapers for the baby.

As he opened the door to his apartment, Elsa thanked him. "*Toda raba lecha*, Mr. Newman."

She went to the Yutka's bedroom, quickly gathered Yutka's things, and left. As the door closed, she heard Mrs. Newman snarl at her husband, "Where have you been while I'm sweating at the market?"

In case of air raids, Elsa and Yutka kept a big diaper bag at the ready, filled with necessities like toys and snacks for the toddlers, diapers, and bottles of water. They tried to keep the toddlers occupied while they prayed that the building wouldn't take a direct hit, but no more bombs fell.

Few knew the new state of Israel had any sort of air force, however a collection of civilian aircraft converted to military use and a quickly acquired variety of obsolete and surplus ex-World War II combat aircraft guarded the skies over Israel and kept the bombing to a minimum. If enemy planes approached Tel Aviv, the hodge-podge air force chased them away.

In late September 1948, there was a knock at Elsa's door. Yutka, holding Shmuel, opened the door to find Yaakov standing there in uniform with a big grin, his cheeks covered in furry ginger. Her tears flowed freely as she introduced Yaakov to his month-old son. They gathered what they needed, said goodnight to Elsa and the little boys, and walked to their own flat.

In mid-October, when the truce failed, Yutka and Yaakov, holding Shmuel, walked back to Elsa's flat before Yaakov reluctantly returned to duty. "It will be over soon I'm certain," he said softly. Yutka tried not to cry as he kissed her goodbye.

Just like before, Yutka knew she was expecting, even before she missed her first cycle. She couldn't wait to tell Elsa.

"You know already!"

"Just like last time." Yutka smiled at five-month-old Shmuel gurgling at Elsa over Yutka's shoulder.

"I'm so happy for you," Elsa squealed, hugging Yutka. "Let's hope Yaakov is home and the war is over before this baby arrives. No more air raid babies. Please!"

Chapter 56

End of the War for Independence, March 1949

Israel won the War of Independence in March 1949. Yaakov completed his service and returned home in April. They settled into life as a family in the tiny bedroom while Yaakov searched for an affordable, bigger place.

When Yaakov re-opened the barbershop, Mr. Newman was his first customer. "Welcome home Yaakov!" he said as he climbed into the chair. "I haven't had a decent hair cut since you left, my wife does a terrible job of it, but don't tell her I said so."

"It's good to be home with my family," grinned Yaakov. "I'd much rather be playing with my son than sewing up wounds!"

"I think you'll be happy to hear, my wife and I found a new apartment and we're moving out in a couple of weeks. Do you and Yutka want to rent the whole place?" Mr. Newman told him what the rent would be. "My father owns the building. He'll give you a good deal."

"Thank you, Yutka will be thrilled. Our room is small for the three of us, and *oy vey* another on the way! I've been looking for a bigger place since I got home."

Yutka was excited to have the entire apartment, relieved that she didn't need to move their meager belongings to a new place, and she liked their neighbors.

"Are you sure you want to stay here on the top floor?" asked Yaakov. "We'll be *schlepping* two little ones up and down the stairs."

"Yes Yaakov, the top floor is also closer for hanging laundry. We will be changing a lot of diapers! Anyway, I don't like knowing people are walking around on top of me."

The Newmans moved out and, without asking, left most of their furniture; Mrs. Newman wanted all new furniture in her new apartment. It was not a style Yutka would have chosen, but she was grateful to have any furniture at all. The Newmans left a rocking chair, highchair, as well as clothes and toys their children had outgrown.

Every day when he came home from the barbershop, Yaakov sat in the rocking chair reading to Shmuel while Yutka prepared dinner.

Yutka went into labor in August. Since there were few telephones in Tel Aviv, Yaakov sent a neighbor boy to take a note to Elsa.

Elsa left her boys in the care of a neighbor and arrived shortly.

While they waited for Elsa, Yaakov read to Shmuel and put him to bed at his usual bedtime. "He is sleeping soundly, and Elsa is here so let's go to the hospital."

"Really Yaakov, we have plenty of time, the pains are still slight and far apart. This is nothing like the last time. It must be a girl."

"When you are safely in the hospital, I'll feel better," he insisted. "I'll hail a taxi, then come back to help you down the stairs."

"Yaakov, I'm fine. I can walk," Yutka laughed as Yaakov hovered around her. He had been at war when Shmuel was born. This was all new to him.

Leaving Shmuel in Elsa's care, he helped Yutka into the taxi then directed the driver to Assuta Hospital. They rode a few blocks north on Dizengoff Street, then turned right onto Ze've Jabotinsky Street. Assuta Hospital was a bright white Bauhaus-style building, untouched by the bombs. As the taxi pulled next to the hospital entrance, and the sun set, the white stucco walls of the angular building turned deep pink, as if foretelling the baby's gender.

Before the nurse pushed her away in a wheelchair, Yaakov kissed Yutka's forehead. "I love you," he whispered.

In the deserted waiting area, he poured himself a cup of stale, burned coffee. The chrome chairs, upholstered with green Naugahyde, were uncomfortable and the scent of disinfectant and floor wax irritated his nose. Tired of staring at the naked green walls, he picked up a week-old newspaper from the coffee table and tried to read but couldn't concentrate. The long fluorescent tubes overhead cast an uncomfortable greenish glow and produced an annoying hum that seemed to grow louder, jangling his nerves even more. He tried to read an out-of-date magazine, but soon tossed it back onto the coffee table. Pacing up and down the hall, he walked to the nurses' station, then returned to his uncomfortable chair, his mind in a whirl of joy and anxiety.

At 2:12 a.m. he heard the squeak of the nurse's rubber-soled shoes as she moved toward him on the highly waxed floor. He thought he heard the broken wail of a newborn. "Congratulations Mr. Polonecki," she said, looking at the dark circles around his blue eyes. "You have a daughter. Mother and baby are doing well."

"When can I see them?" he asked with tears freely streaming down his cheeks covered with ginger fuzz.

"I'll come for you when Mrs. Polonecki is in recovery."

For what seemed like forever, he waited in the hallway, sitting on the edge of the uncomfortable metal chair.

Finally, the nurse led him to Yutka and the baby. He gently sat on the bed next to Yutka and tenderly pushed sweaty curls from her forehead. Tired darkness circled her eyes, but to Yaakov, Yutka had never been more beautiful. Yutka smiled and moved the baby into Yaakov's arms. He curled over the tiny three kilo bundle, kissed her damp forehead and couldn't keep his tears from spilling onto her pink blanket. "Our baby girl is born in the free State of Israel!" he choked.

They named her Chaya.[14]

---

14. *Chaya, Hebrew, life/living*

Chapter 57

Hope, 1949

On his way to the barbershop, Yaakov carried Schmuel and Chaya to Elsa's apartment so that Elsa could look after the babies while Yutka worked at the towel factory three days/week.

On the way home each afternoon, Yutka stayed at Elsa's apartment long enough to listen to a radio program, *Hamador L'hipus Krovim, Searching for Relatives*. Both Elsa and Yutka hoped to hear that their European relatives were alive and searching for them in Israel. The radio announcer gave place of birth and physical clues that might help locate individuals. Some details were not helpful, blond hair/blue eyes, brown hair/hazel eyes, however other designations were more useful, a unique scar, the shape and position of a birthmark, a mole, or the Auschwitz number tattooed on the left forearm. Every day Yutka and Elsa huddled next to the mahogany radio cabinet, hoping for a miracle. "Maybe today will be our lucky day," said Yutka, optimism and hope camouflaged the deep sorrow she was unwilling to concede.

Elsa knew in her heart that her parents had not survived. She had mourned their loss since arriving in Tel Aviv. The announcer's voice blurred in her consciousness, while her heart mourned the loss of her husband, René. She tried to focus her love and attention on the towheaded boys who had their father's hazel eyes, long dark lashes and joyful smile.

✡

One day Yutka was at the market, buying eggs when she overheard two men talking about what had happened in Mir, the town her family fled to after the Nazis invaded Poland.

As she eavesdropped on their conversation, Yutka froze, gazing at the eggs in her basket as if trying to remember how many she needed.

"My brother met a man who escaped, but his reports are grisly," said the man. "Mir ended up on the German front. The Nazis raided Jew's homes, stole everything of value and marched the Jews to a temporary camp. Nazis forced them to dig a deep trench, then every day they marched a group to the pit, lined them up, told them to kneel, then shot them, one by one in the back of the head. Men, women, children, made no difference to the Nazis. Their victims dropped into the gory pit. Some soldiers seemed to enjoy the brutality and even took pictures. My brother said there are no Jews left in Mir."

Yutka dropped her basket of eggs. The egg vendor hurried to catch her before she fainted and toppled his entire egg display. "Are you alright, Miss?" he said as he helped her to a bench. He had been too busy selling eggs to hear the conversation that upset her.

She gathered all her strength and courage, heaved herself from the bench and lumbered toward home, stepping over the orange egg yolks oozing through her wicker basket into the dirt.

When Yutka came into the apartment, Yaakov was pacing back and forth with the baby on his shoulder. "I'm glad you're back. Chaya was getting fussy but when I picked her up she went back to sleep. Is it mealtime?" Then he looked more closely at his wife. "Yutka, you look so pale. Is everything all right?"

"I'll be fine," she whispered as she walked to their bed. "I need to rest."

She never told Yaakov, or anyone else, what she heard at the market that day, as if repeating the story might make it true. She refused to give up hope.

Chapter 58

Holocaust Remembrance Day, December 28, 1949

"Are you coming with us?" Yaakov asked. "Srulik, Zipporah and the others will meet us on the corner of Ben-Gurion Boulevard and Ben Yehuda Street before the siren goes off at 10:00."

"No!" barked Yutka as she prepared to finish the *challah* she was making. He stepped closer to hug her, but she pushed him away, planting a floury handprint on his blue shirt. "My family survived! One day soon they will surprise us, just like your sister."

He picked up sixteen-month-old Shmuel and left the apartment.

✡

Tears welled in Yutka's eyes as the door slammed. She had never been so unkind to her dear husband. She gently lifted Chaya from her highchair, kissed her curly black hair and put her down for a nap, hoping the siren wouldn't wake her.

In the kitchen, Yutka dusted the wooden tabletop with flour and punched down the proofed bread dough. As the siren announced the first Holocaust Remembrance Day, she began kneading with a vengeance, remembering the first time she helped her mama make *challah*.

Five-year-old Yutka's black eyes peek over the edge of the table as Mama dusts the top with flour. Yutka steps onto her little wooden stool.

Mama pinches off a ball of dough, and Yutka eagerly thrusts her little fists into it. As she works, flour settles on Yutka's long, black eyelashes.

As always, Mama separates the big ball of dough into thirds and lets Yutka roll out strands, then Mama braids the strands together. Usually, the dough rises into a long loaf, however, for Rosh Hashanah, Mama twists the braided dough into a round loaf.

"Why did you make a circle?"

"The round loaf means the end of one year meets the beginning of the next." Mama laughs and, with her apron, wipes white flour from Yutka's eyelashes.

Yaakov, with sixteen-month-old Shmuel in his arms, walked down Ben Yehuda Street.

"Hallo, Yaakov," said Joséphine Edelman as he turned the corner onto Ben-Gurion Boulevard. "Good to see you."

Yaakov kissed Joséphine on both cheeks, then shook hands with Mr. Edelman. "Priscilla? Rochelle? Hello, I hardly recognized you."

Priscilla kissed him on both cheeks and Rochelle shook his hand, still the shy one. Nearly sixteen, Priscilla had morphed into a beautiful woman while Rochelle was still a young teen.

"And who is this handsome fellow?" gushed Joséphine. Gently pinching Shmuel's plump, rosy cheeks with both hands.

"This is our son Shmuel," said Yaakov with a proud grin. Anticipating and avoiding the next question, Yaakov added, "Yutka is at home with our baby girl, Chaya."

"Have you seen Serioja," Priscilla asked Yaakov.

"Yes Priscilla, Yutka, Elsa and I visit him every Friday before Sabbath when we can. He's living at the nursing home on Ranak Street."

"I know where that is," said Joséphine. "He was so wonderful to us on the *Parita*. We'll visit him this week and if he's up to it we'll bring him to our home for dinner. He really is an angel."

"I can't imagine that trip without Serioja," said Priscella. "He was like a magical grandfather."

When Yaakov reached the corner of Ben-Gurion Boulevard and Ben Yehuda Street Srulik asked, "Where is Yutka?"

"Yutka refuses to accept that they perished," Yaakov said softly. "She's in the apartment making *challah*."

"She still doesn't believe my brothers and...?" Tears gathered in Srulik's eyes as he looked down at his sandals. "I understand Yutka's inability to give up hope." He closed his eyes and shook his head, as if clearing his mind. "It's difficult to accept that the Nazis should so ruthlessly execute my brothers, their wives and their children."

"I think, deep in her heart, she knows they're gone, but if she admits they were murdered, hope is lost. She fiercely maintains hope," said Yaakov as he kissed his son's warm forehead.

Before the siren blasted, Yaakov turned to Srulik. "There is a ceremony in Jerusalem tonight. The ashes and bones of thousands of Jews from the Flossenbürg Concentration Camp were put in a crypt and brought to the Jerusalem cemetery. I'd like to participate in the overnight vigil, and in the morning prayer service and stay for the Talmudic study session in the morning, in honor of the victims. Would you like to join me?"

"It is good of you to participate, but I have responsibilities at the vineyard I must return to."

✡

At 10:00 a.m. the siren blast announced the first *Yom HaShoah*, Holocaust Remembrance Day.

The sun cast their shadows across the sidewalk: Yaakov, hugging Shmuel, Yutka's Uncle Srulik and Aunt Zipporah, Yaakov's sister Mala and twelve-year-old niece Halina, his brother Arie and sister-in-law Sara, and Elsa with her two boys. Feeling the painful gap left by René, they huddled together in silence. Even the children remained quiet. Traffic came to a halt. People climbed out of their cars and trucks. In commemoration of Jews murdered during the *Shoah*, retailers, bankers, mechanics, bakers, laborers and executives throughout Israel, stopped whatever they were doing. They stood with their heads bowed.

While Chaya slept and the apartment filled with the aroma of baking *challah*, Yutka curled on the sofa holding Mama's poetry book, *Pan Tadeusz*. As if the intensity of her imagination could make them materialize, she watched her mama, papa, sister and brother walk down the gangway from a rescue boat, along with her niece, nephew, her brother's wife and their son. She tried to imagine how grown up the children would be, still believing they survived, even after her letters had gone unanswered for eight years.

As she did each week, Yutka sat at the little desk to write a postcard to her family:

Moi Kochani Rodzina, [my beloved family]

Our little Shmuel learns more Hebrew words every day. Today at breakfast he clearly asked for orange juice and yesterday he made a whole sentence, asking to go to the playground. Chaya is starting to crawl and loves bananas. She has thick black hair like I did at that age and people think she is older than six months.

Last night, before going to sleep, I finished reading your copy of Pan Tadeusz, *again! I can't wait until I can return it to you, Mama.*

L'hitraot, [until we meet again]
Yutka

Epilogue

Early on a sultry morning in June 1999, eighteen years after her beloved Yaakov died of a heart attack, Yutka boarded the bus to Jerusalem. She walked to the Yad Vashem Holocaust Museum and apprehensively told the receptionist, "I wish to give depositions for my family members."

The receptionist leaned closer to hear Yutka's thin voice, then invited her into a small private room furnished with a soft mauve and gray loveseat, two matching chairs and a desk. There was no music. The room was soundproofed. Yutka sat at a small desk with a stack of blank forms, a fountain pen, a pitcher of water, a drinking glass, and a box of tissues.

"Take as much time as you need. Let me know if I can get you anything."

As the door clicked shut, Yutka opened her handbag and carefully took out a stack of photos. She slowly lifted the fountain pen and completed the paperwork. At seventy-eight, she realized it was her responsibility to ensure history remembered her family. Line by line she completed a form for Mordechai, Bluma, Heniek, Rozka, Jerzyk, Rebekah, Sonya and Josip. Each deposition included a photograph, date of birth, and the date and place where the Nazis executed them.

The testimonies were so painful, she never mentioned that day to anyone, including her children, Shmuel and Chaya.

✡

Quote from *My Call of Abraham* by Sam Regev – page 118.

One day I was by the kitchen window looking at the main street below when the Memorial Day siren sounded. My mother who was cooking dinner, gazed out of the window but did not stop. When I asked her why she didn't stop and pay homage to our family and all the people who died in the Holocaust she got extremely angry and admonished me with a very strong and forceful conviction, that her parents and the entire family did not die. She was adamant that they survived the war and we would soon be reunited. I had never heard such a stern voice coming from her. It was triggered by my innocent belief that her family perished in the Holocaust. I learned after that incident not to raise the issue or talk to her about the family.

Deep inside me, a young boy who was born in Israel and not in Eastern Europe, I felt that my family would not rise from the ashes and come back. My mom, however, was in complete denial for a long time, refusing to accept the harsh and painful reality. She finally accepted that her family, the entire Lipka clan was murdered by the Germans. […] I was not aware that she made the depositions at Yad Vashem since I was already living in the USA at that time. I learned about it from a friend in Israel who was in the midst of exploring his ancestry and the fate of his family during the Holocaust and came across her depositions.

The Nazis confiscated the Lipka clan's homes, businesses and bank accounts, however, as the living survivor, Yutka Lipka Polonecki refused to apply for reparation.

Quote from *My Call of Abraham* by Sam Regev – page 38.

Holocaust survivors who immigrated to Israel filed their own personal reparation claims directly to the German government. They were granted a monthly stipend to cover their living and medical expenses. They also received monetary compensation for physical and mental suffering caused by the Nazis. Some were also compensated for their properties stolen by the Germans. My mother was too proud to file such claims as she felt it was below her dignity to do so. No one could compensate her for the loss of her beloved family.

Quote from Sam Regev's memoir *My Call of Abraham* - page 83:

Born and raised in Israel with Hebrew as my native tongue, I felt alienated from anything connected to Poland and the Polish language so I was counting the days until I could replace my last name Polonecki, with a Hebrew last name that would better define who I was and my connection to the land. I chose the name Regev, which is the Hebrew name for the clod of soil created when the farmer ploughs his field.

In 1960, at the age of eighteen, Shmuel Polonecki changed his name to Regev, following the example of David Ben-Gurion (born David Gruen), Levi Eshkol (originally Levi Shkolnik), Moshe Sharrett (born Moshe Shertok), Itzhak Ariel (formerly Itzhak Leibovitz), and Golda Meir (formerly Golda Meyerson).

Photos

Courtesy of Sam Regev

Figure 12
The Lipka family, Bluma holding Yutka, Rozka, and Mordechai, circa 1923. The boy is Kuba, Yutka's older brother born in 1910. Heniek is not in the photo. Kuba went to Brazil before WWII. He is not included in the story. For more about Kuba see *My Call of Abraham*, page 119.

Figure 13
Yutka Lipka (back row left) and her Betar friends, circa 1938

Figure 14
Ger Mandolin Orchestra, Yaakov second left, back row

Figure 15
Jews assembled for deportation in Dobrzyn, September 1939

Figure 16
Yutka's brother, Heniek

Figure 17
Post card Heniek sent from Russia
January 22, 1940 (translation page 185)

Figure 18
Yutka and Yaakov Polonecki, March 25, 1941

Figure 19
Reunion on the beach, L to R: Lala, Daniel, Yutka and Szyjek.

Figure 20
Invitation to the 30th anniversary of the landing of the *Parita*

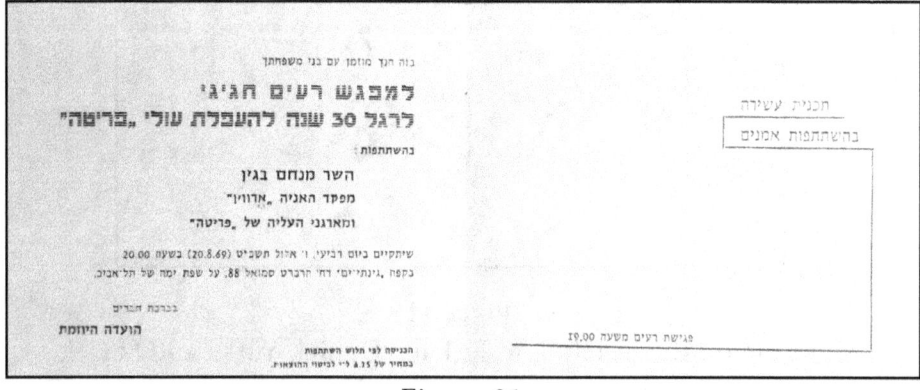

Figure 21
Invitation interior speakers include Menachem Begin and former Commander Itzhak Ariel (aka *Erwin* Leibovitz)

Figures 22
A letter Yutka received announcing a reunion to celebrate the 47th anniversary of the *Parita* landing on Tel Aviv beach.

Figure 23
Yutka and Yaakov years later, date unknown

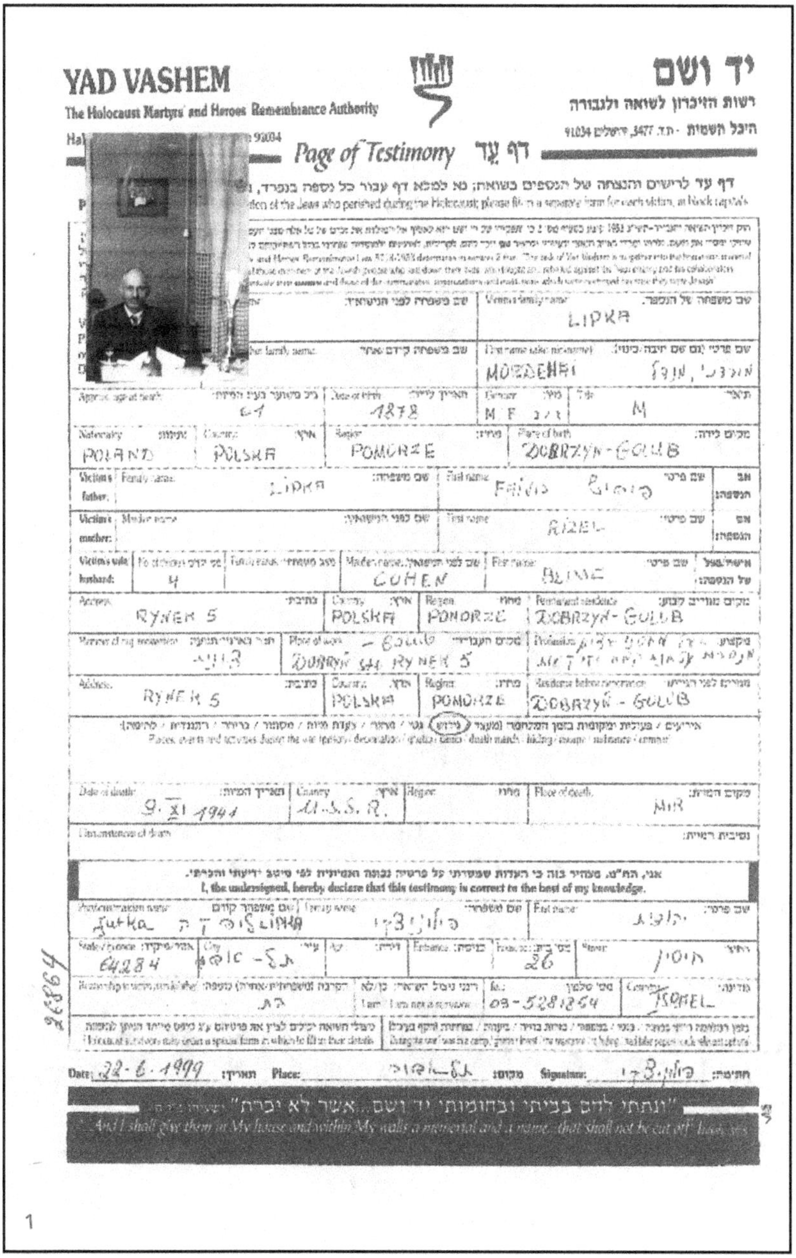

YAD VASHEM

The Holocaust Martyrs' and Heroes' Remembrance Authority

יד ושם

רשות הזיכרון לשואה ולגבורה

Page of Testimony דף עד

Victim's family name	LIPKA
First name	MORDEHAI
Approx. age at death	61
Date of birth	1878
Gender	M
Nationality	POLAND
Country	POLSKA
Region	POMORZE
Place of birth	DOBRZYN-GOLUB
Victim's father: Family name	LIPKA
Victim's father: First name	FAIVIS
Victim's mother: First name	RIZEL
Victim's wife/husband: No. of children	4
Victim's wife/husband: Maiden name	COHEN
Victim's wife/husband: First name	BEIME
Address	RYNEK 5
Country	POLSKA
Region	POMORZE
Permanent residence	DOBRZYN-GOLUB
Place of work	DOBRZYN-GOLUB RYNEK 5
Address before deportation	RYNEK 5
Country	POLSKA
Region	POMORZE
Residence before deportation	DOBRZYN-GOLUB
Date of death	9. XI 1941
Country	U.S.S.R.
Place of death	MIR

I, the undersigned, hereby declare that this testimony is correct to the best of my knowledge.

Submitter's first name	Yutka
Zip code	64284
House no.	26
Tel.	03-5281854
Country	ISRAEL
Date	22-6-1999

"And I shall give them in My house and within My walls a memorial and a name... that shall not be cut off" Isaiah 56:5

1

Figure 24

One of Yutka's depositions, June 22, 1999

Figure 25
Bluma Cohen Lipka, Yutka's mother
1883 to 1942

Chronology

- September 1, 1939, Nazis invaded Poland. WWII began.
- September 13-14, Nazis took money from 270 Jews in Yutka's hometown of Dobrzyń. Some Jews were transported to Bydgoszcz where they endured torture. They were murdered and buried in unmarked graves. Yutka's family survived this round up.
- November 9, Nazis confiscated all of Yutka's papa's land, businesses, and valuables from their home. Yutka's family and the Hirsch family, (her sister Rozka's husband's family) fled to Mir, Russia. Rozka's brother-in-law, Dr. Max Hirsch worked as a doctor while Mordechai Lipka chauffeured him around the community in a horse and buggy.
- Jews in Mir, including Yutka's family members were marched to a camp and forced to dig trenches.
- Dr. Max Hirsch, his wife and children escaped, hid in a nearby forest, and survived the war.
- By August 16, 1942, the entire Jewish population of Mir was murdered in three waves of executions at the shooting pits, including Yutka's mother fifty-seven-year-old Bluma, Yutka's father sixty-two-year-old Mordechai, her twenty-nine brother Heniek, and his wife Sonya, their son one-year-old Josip, Yutka's sister twenty-eight-year-old Rozka, and Rozka's son five-year-old Jerzyk, Yutka's brother-in-law Zigi, and Zigi's mama and papa.
- The Germans murdered an estimated 3,000 Jews in Mir during the German occupation.
- Yutka's aunts, uncles and cousins were lost in Polish ghettos.

Author's Note

In the course of writing this creative nonfiction, I changed some dates, created some characters and of course imagined the dialogue however, the story is true.

Yutka Lipka joined Betar, a Revisionist Zionist youth movement in 1934, at thirteen. Vladimir (Ze'ev) Jabotinsky founded the movement in 1923. Yutka and Yaakov met on the train from Warsaw to Constanța. All true.

Yaakov really was on a friend's balcony when Yutka walked by with her friend Elsa (not the one on the *Parita*) and he yelled, "*Ekmek ve su, Ekmek ve su!*" That phrase became a common greeting for those who survived the voyage of the *Parita*.

Yutka and Yaakov married in March 1941 not 1945. Yutka and Yaakov's son Shmuel was born at Hadassah hospital in 1942 (not in an bomb shelter in August 1948). Their daughter, Chaya, is two years younger than Sam.

Yutka's grandfather, Fiebush Lipka, bought land in the Jezreel Valley in 1909 after attending first Zionist Congress in Basel, Switzerland and listening to Theodor Herzl describe his vision of the reborn Jewish state. Fiebush hoped his clan would plant fig trees, and a vineyard, and realize the prophecy, "But every man shall sit under his grapevine or fig tree with no one to disturb him."[15] Yutka's daughter still owns some of the land

---

15. *Micah 4:4*

Fiebush bought in the Jezreel Valley.

Fiebush Lipka's dream never came true for the Lipka clan in *Israel*. Srulik's vineyard is fictional. However, in 2005 Yutka's son, Sam Regev, realized his great grandfather's dream. He planted a vineyard in the Yakima Valley, in Washington State wine country (page 448, *My Call of Abraham*).

Throughout the 1930s and early 1940s, the Betar organization aided the widespread immigration of Jews to British Mandate Palestine in violation of the British immigration quotas outlined in the *White Paper*. Chartering various vessels, some scarcely seaworthy, Betar helped 40,000 Jews successfully immigrate to British Mandatory Palestine, some traveled via train to Constanța others floated down the Danube River to the Black Sea.

The Greek Boy Scout leader's name is unknown (I named him Adras Alexopoulos), but the event is true and one of my favorite scenes. "The loud, discorded little band marched away from the docks, capturing the attention of police, tourists, and residents, leading them away from the evacuees like the Pied Piper of Hamelin." (page 32). The refugees fled from the train to the Greek fishing boats. The *Parita* waited for them in Château d'If where they climbed aboard unnoticed; then set sail for Constanța to collect 750 refugees who waited there, including Yutka and Yaakov.

The *Parita* cruised from Château d'If, France to Constanța with those fifty French, Austrian and German Jewish refugees already on board.

Mr. and Mrs. Goldfarb are fictional characters, however, the *Parita* anchored next to the *Marco Polo* in Rhodes in early August 1939. Tourists on the cruise ship (names unknown) took pity on *Parita's* passengers, and sent oranges and beer. The tourists were unaware that there were hundreds of passengers below deck. Their contribution was kind and well-meaning but insufficient.

Mr. Edelman and his family are fictional, however, there are reports of a few passengers with unrealistic expectations who required disciplinary action.

Most passengers aboard the *Parita* were between the ages of fifteen and twenty-five, in good health and members of the highly disciplined Betar youth. At thirty-two, Yaakov was one of the oldest passengers on the *Parita*; he was not a member.

Emmanuel Solchansky (later changed to Sella) was a stowaway. He was not a member of Betar but sneaked onto the train going from Warsaw to Constanţa. Betar members on the train hid him under the passenger seats and took care of him until they reached Constanţa.. He may have been the youngest passenger on the *Parita*, however there are conflicting reports regarding whether or not there were younger children on board.

I doubt there was a *family compartment*. Men and women probably bunked in separate compartments

Nikos and Oshrah are fictional characters but there are reports of romances developing between crew members and passengers, as well as between refugees on the *Parita*.

Surprisingly, the *levivot* story is true (page 108). Without permission, the Romanian women spent the night making pancakes. The others ate all the *levivot* before the Romanians came to collect their share. Commander Leibovitz did his best to appease the angry, young Romanians.

Yutka actually did find a leaky pipe and took Yaakov there to take care of a boil on his neck. It was probably the first time Yutka demonstrated her fondness for Yaakov.

Zosia and her baby are fictional characters. As far as we know, no one died on the *Parita's* voyage, but other Betar ships lost passengers during the trip to *Eretz* Israel, especially during winter months, when boats became frozen in the Danube River.[16]

In Israel, Yutka had a good friend named Elsa, however she was not on the *Parita*. The Elsa character is fictional, but her experiences with Betar via Dr. Reuben Hecht are based on actual events.

Her husband, René, is also a fictional character, however, the April 13, 1948, Hadassah convoy massacre was horribly real and

---

16. The Four-Front War *by William Perl, List of voyages, page 367*

happened while the convoy was on its way to the medical school at Hebrew University at Mt. Scopus.

Yaakov's father was a rabbi in Góra Kalwaria. His brother Arie (two years older) and sister-in-law Sara immigrated to *Eretz* Israel in 1933. Yaakov played professional soccer and was a member of the Ger Mandolin Orchestra. (To learn more about the mandolin orchestra, visit https://www.youtube.com/watch?v=IDyW8uyn6Us

He joined the Polish army to avoid an arranged marriage, became an army medic and later became a barber in his sister Mala's salon in Warsaw. He loved nice clothes and always dressed smartly. Due to the love and support of his friend Sigmund, Yaakov's niece, Halina, was kept safe in a Catholic orphanage for four years until Mala (a German-looking beauty) found her after the war. Mala and her family immigrated to Israel and surprised Yaakov at his barbershop. All true, even the leopard coat.

The painter, Bolesław Barbacki was killed by Nazis in August 1941 but did not, as far as I know, paint a portrait of Rozka and Zigi.

Yutka's friends who paid for passage but were told to wait for the next boat died in the Holocaust, except for Lala, (see photo of Yutka and her friends Figure 13).

At the Tel Aviv Rabbinical court, Yutka testified on behalf of her friends (actual names unknown, Melina and Ozer are stand-ins) advocating for the recognition of their interfaith marriage as legal according to Jewish law. This is my favorite story about Yutka and shows her true character (page 220).

Yutka's friends Daniel and Hania Pieniek were real people, however, Daniel went to France to study medicine in January 1939. His sister, Hania went to France in 1931 to go to school. Sam Regev is in touch with Daniel's grandchildren. Daniel's story of survival and his activities as a member of the French resistance could be a book in itself.

After the war Daniel became a surgeon, Hania became a dentist, and they both stayed in France. It is not known how they found each other after the war. Daniel invited Yutka and another Betar friend and survivor, Szyjek, to his home in the French Riviera for a reunion, paying all expenses (see figure 19). The Betar friends stayed close for the rest of their lives.

It is true that on September 9, 1940, Italians, on their way to the British refinery in Haifa, dropped bombs on a Tel Aviv apartment building, killing 137. There is no way to know for certain where Yutka and Yaakov were at that time, however it's safe to guess Yaakov was at his barbershop and Yutka was working at the towel factory.

Between the end of WWII and the beginning of the War for Independence in May 1948, the Israelis created their Air Force from a hodge-podge collection of civilian aircraft converted to military use, and from a quickly acquired variety of obsolete and surplus ex-World War II combat aircraft. On June 3, 1948, pilot Modi Alon shot down the Egyptian DC-3s that had just bombed Tel Aviv, the last bombs to fall on the newborn country during the War for Independence.

While helping Sam Regev self-publish his memoir, *My Call of Abraham*, I noticed he wrote that the Nazis murdered his family "execution style." When I asked how he knew such a gruesome detail, he emailed this image to me, taken in Mir, USSR in 1942, at the same time Yutka's family (Sam's family) was murdered.

Figure 26
Trench execution in Mir where Yutka's family was murdered.

The picture is disturbing on so many levels... the soldier aiming the Luger... the emaciated Jew who knows he's going to die and fall into the pit with the mangled bodies of his dead family members... the soldiers standing around as if watching morbid entertainment... and someone took a photo.

When I hear there are people who believe the Holocaust never happened, I'm even more motivated to write about that time in history; to tell the little-known stories of the people who escaped and the fate of the families they left behind.

I admit, before I met Sam, the horror of the Holocaust seemed sort of "other," something that happened in history. Knowing Sam, I feel as if I also know his family and their story hurts my heart. I compare his grandparents, Mordechai and Bluma, to my grandparents, Cecil and Edith, who owned a dairy farm in Ohio, and probably knew little if anything about what was happening in Europe during the early 1940s. Their daily lives continued as always, watching the sunrise, milking cows, tending the garden, gathering chicken eggs, while the Lipka's fled their homes, abandoned their lives and were ultimately murdered just because they were Jews.

What happened to the Jews is unspeakable, unbelievable, and undeniable. We must do all we can to ensure that history does not forget and repeat itself.

Acknowledgments

How does a Gentile originally from Ohio come to write a book about a Jewish woman who fled from Poland to *Eretz* Israel in 1939?

When I helped author, Sam Regev, Ph.D. self-publish his book *My Call of Abraham,* I was moved by Sam's story about his parents' escape from Europe on one of the *Aliyah Bet* vessels, the *Parita* (Chapter 3). Throughout Sam's memoir, he writes about his maternal family and his mother, Yutka, who, even at seventeen, demonstrated the courage of her convictions, a deep sense of justice, a pioneering spirit, and profound sensitivity. I wish I could have known her. I decided to write a book about Yutka Lipka's journey on the *Parita*.

At first, I was intimidated by the amount of research I would need to do regarding the Jewish faith and the history of the boats that saved over 40,000 Jews from the Holocaust. I found little information about the boats that brought illegal immigrants to British Mandate Palestine before and during WWII.

Sam Regev enthusiastically supplied the gems I needed. He translated journal entries his mother wrote reminiscing about her adolescence in her hometown of Dobrzyń, Poland. He translated letters and postcards she received from family and friends before and after the war, and he translated *The Immigrant's Rescuing Ship, Parita,* (discussed on page 101 of *My Call of Abraham*). He suggested I include chapter and verse from the Hebrew Bible where appropriate.

Yutka's mementos and Sam's translations, details, and support provided deep and personal information, making *YUTKA And the Voyage of the Parita* an authentic account of her life.

Special thanks to Maria Mańkowska, a student in Poland, who translated letters written in Polish.

Thank you to Ruth Lytle who patiently read early drafts (plural) and provided feedback. Thank you also goes to the other beta readers who provided feedback and support, Tess Taft, Rachel Schild, Anne Cameron, JoAnn Raines, Sonja Mathews, Rich Nevin, Lora Sinisi, Judy Drechsler, C. Mark Smith, and Julianna Guy (may she rest in peace).

There would be no book without the support of Sam and Batia Regev. Sam spent many hours hunting for photos, mementos, and documents, reading drafts, discussing his feedback and teaching me about Judaism. Oh so many lessons!

Meanwhile, Sam's wife Batia was a "book widow." The little phrase, Thank You is inadequate to show the depth of my gratitude for Batia's support.

Figure 27
Yutka's son Sam and his wife Batia

Bibliography

- Perl, William R., *The Four-Front War: From the Holocaust to the Promised Land*, by, Foreword by Menachem Begin, Crown Publishing; 1st edition (December 12, 1988)
- Regev, Sam, *My Call of Abraham*, Publishing Partners January 2022
- Ofer, Dalia, *Escaping the Holocaust, Illegal Immigration to the Land of Israel, 1939 to 1941*, Oxford University Press, 1990
- Sella, Emmanuel, *From the Ship Parita to Wall-Street, The life story of Emmanuel Sella, Parita's Child*, Intermedia, Tel Aviv, 1995
- *The Immigrant's Rescuing Ship, Parita,* collection of stories by *Parita's* passengers (in Hebrew) translator Sam Regev
- Wasserman, Tina, *Entrée to Judaism A Culinary Exploration of the Jewish Diaspora*, URJ Press, 2010
- *Dobrzyn-Gollob Memorial Book,* Translation of Ayarati; sefer zikaron le-ayarot Dobrzyn-Golub by M Harpaz (Editor), Allen Flusberg (Translator), The Association of Former Residents of Dobrzyn-Golub, in Tel Aviv 1969 by JewishGen, an affiliate of the Museum of Jewish Heritage—A Living Memorial to the Holocaust
- collections.ushmm.org/search/catalog/irn504953Oral history interview with Elias Cala:
- www.youtube.com/watch?v=IDyW8uyn6Us, Ger Mandolin Orchestra

- https://www.jpost.com/food-recipes/article-692450
- https://www.yadvashem.org/ Yad Vashem, The World Holocaust Remembrance Center website
- https://jwa.org/encyclopedia/article/kibbutz-ha-dati-movement-1929-1948
- https://www.jewishvirtuallibrary.org/the-irgun-rsquo-s-role-in-illegal-immigration
- https://www.jpost.com/aliyah/article-711759

Glossary

Adonai, Hebrew, Lord, or my Master

a sheynem dank, Yiddish, thank you very much.

Alef to tav, Hebrew, First letter to last letter of Hebrew alphabet

Aleichem ha'shalom, Hebrew, Upon you be peace, response to new year greeting.

aliyah bet, Hebrew, second wave of immigration of Jews from the diaspora. The term refers to the clandestine immigration of Jews to British Mandate Palestine between 1920 and 1948 mostly single young people. The first *aliyah* also known as the agriculture *aliyah*, was a major wave of Jewish immigration to Ottoman Syria between 1881 and 1903.

baba ghanoush, Arabic, finely chopped roasted eggplant, olive oil, lemon juice, various seasonings and tahini.

babcia, Polish, grandmother

Balkan Sobranie, expensive brand of cigarette made in Cyprus.

Baruch dayan emet, Hebrew, blessed be the one true Judge, a blessing when someone dies.

Betar (Betarnics), Hebrew, The Betar Movement also spelled Beitar is a Revisionist Zionist youth movement founded in 1923 by Vladimir (Ze'ev) Jabotinsky.

Beth Hachalutzot, an absorption center operated by Women's League for Israel focused on the assimilation, welfare and education of women pioneers immigrating to Israel alone. https://www.womensleagueforisrael.org.il/wp-content/uploads/2019/06/90_en.pdf

birkot nissuin, Hebrew, wedding blessings

bienvenue, French, welcome

boker tov, Hebrew, good morning

bonjour, French, hello.

brava, French, well done (feminine)

British Mandate, a League of Nations decree for British administration of the territories of Palestine and Transjordan. For more information please visit: https://encyclopedia.1914-1918-online.net/article/british_mandate_for_palestine

baruch haba, Hebrew, welcome (male)

bubbala, Yiddish, term of endearment

bulwark, English, the side of a ship above the upper deck, railing

burqas, Arabic, a long, loose garment covering the body from head to feet, worn in public by Muslim women.

challah, Yiddish, egg-rich yeast-leavened bread that is usually braided or twisted before baking and is traditionally eaten by Jews on the Sabbath and holidays

cheder, Hebrew, a traditional primary boy's school teaching the basics of Judaism and the Hebrew language.

chuppah, Hebrew, a canopy beneath which Jewish marriage ceremonies are performed.

chutzpah, Hebrew, supreme self-confidence, nerve, gall

co chcesz, Polish, what do you want?

Da. Da., Romanian, Yes. Yes.

danke, German, thank you.

danke für die suppe, German, thanks for the soup.

dayan, Hebrew, a judge in a Jewish religious court.

Der Judenstaat, German, The Jewish State, pamphlet written by Theodor Herzl published in February 1896 in Vienna www.britannica.com/topic/The-Jewish-State

diaspora, English, the dispersion of the Jewish people beyond Israel. People settled far from their ancestral homelands.

dishdashas, Arabic, a white long-sleeved collarless garment worn by Muslim men.

dreidel, Yiddish, a four-sided spinning top, game played during the Jewish holiday of *Hanukkah*. The four sides are marked with either: **gadol** (great), **nes** (miracle), **haya** (happened), **shan** (over there), **po** (here).

dziadek, Polish, grandfather

dziękuję bardzo, Polish, thank you very much.

Dziękuję ci, Polish, thank you.

ekmek ve su, Turkish, bread and water

Enchanté, mademoiselle, French, Delighted to meet you, miss.

Endecja, Polish, National Democracy, a Polish political movement active from the second half of the 19th century. In the 1930s the ND emphasized its anti-Semitic stance, excluding Jews from Polish social and economic life and ultimately pushing them to emigration out of Poland. Anti-Semitic boycotts, demonstrations, and attacks organized or inspired by National Democrats occurred during the '30s. en.wikipedia.org/wiki/National_Democracy_(Poland)

Est-ce que vos parlez français, French, do you speak French?

eretz, Hebrew, land, country

erev tov, Hebrew, good evening

feh, Yiddish, expression of disgust or disapproval

fiancé, French, husband to be

ganef, Yiddish, Thief, rascal, scoundrel

Gazeta Polska, Polish, newspaper 1929 - 1939

gelt, Yiddish, money (could be chocolate coins wrapped in gold or silver foil)

Ger Mandolin Orchestra, Group of mandolin players in Ger, Poland early 1900s, https://www.youtube.com/watch?v=IDyW8uyn6Us

gerne geschehen, German, my pleasure

gib zich a shukl, Yiddish, hurry up.

gołąbki, Polish, cabbage rolls

gottze dank, Yiddish, thank heaven.

gut yom tov, Yiddish, good year, holiday greeting

guten morgen, German, good morning

gymnasium, school (no longer used in Israel), elementary school = 1-8, middle school = 9 -12 = gymnasium (high school in USA) then university

Hadassah convoy massacre, Israel, https://hadassahinternational.org/hadassah-mount-scopus-marks-1948-massacre-of-medical-convoy/

Haganah, Hebrew, defense, Zionist military organization representing the majority of the Jews in British Mandate Palestine from 1920 to 1948, when it became the core of the Israel Defense Forces (IDF).

Halacha, Hebrew, constitutes the practical application of the commandments in the *Torah*, Jewish Law

halutz, Hebrew, Pioneer, a Jew who immigrated to the Land of Israel.

Hamador L'hipus Krovim, Hebrew, *Searching for Relatives* radio program.

Hamotzi, Hebrew, blessing over the bread.

Hatikvah, Hebrew, "The Hope," Israel National Anthem

hatima tova, Hebrew, a good end

Hava Nagila, Hebrew, a Jewish folk song, traditionally sung at celebrations, such as weddings. Written in 1918.

Hej Sokoły, Polish, folk song "Hey Falcons" https://www.youtube.com/watch?v=jhmEnOoubnU

helzel, Yiddish, handmade sausage using poultry neck skin stuffed with various ingredients including flour, semolina, breadcrumbs or matzo meal, rendered chicken or goose fat, and fried onions, sewn up with thread.

Hessun Ebreo, Italian, No Jews

Holocaust, English, the Nazis genocide campaign to eliminate the European Jews

horah, Hebrew, Jewish folk dance the dancers hold each other's hands and the circle spins usually counterclockwise.

illui, Hebrew, a young *Torah* and Talmudic prodigy or genius

Inser Welt, Yiddish, newspaper in Warsaw

IRGUN, Hebrew, acronym for the National Military Organization. The Irgun was a Zionist paramilitary organization that operated in Mandate Palestine between 1931 and 1948.

ja, German, yes.

jak masz na imię, Polish, what is your name?

je m'appelle, French, my name is.

Judenrat, Jewish councils set up within the Jewish communities of Nazi-occupied Europe on German orders.

judenrein, German, clean of Jews.

kannst du mir bitte helfen, German, can you please help me.

krupnik, Polish, thick soup with vegetable or meat broth, potatoes and barley groats

ketubah, Hebrew, Jewish marriage contract

kibbutz (plural kibbutzim), Hebrew, A socialist community in Israel that was traditionally based on agriculture.

kibitz, Yiddish, make unwanted comments (Not to be confused with kibbutz)

Kiddush, Hebrew, Jewish blessing recited over a cup of wine immediately before the meal on the eve of the Sabbath, wedding or festival.

knäbchen, German, boy

Kol Israel, Hebrew, The Voice of Israel radio station

kolokasi, Greek, yams

kreplach, Yiddish, a kabbalistic food expressing the nature of Divine judgment. A dumpling filled with ground meat or other filling. Similar to Polish uszka, Russian pelmeni, Italian ravioli or tortellini, Chinese won ton, Japanese gyoza.

Kristallnacht, German, a wave of violent anti-Jewish pogroms which took place on November 9 and 10, 1938, throughout Germany, annexed Austria, and in areas of the Sudetenland and in Czechoslovakia recently occupied by German troops. https://encyclopedia.ushmm.org/content/en/article/kristallnacht

kugle, Yiddish, a baked pudding or casserole, most commonly made from Jewish egg noodles or potato. It is a traditional Ashkenazi Jewish dish often served on Shabbat and Jewish holidays.

Kutno, Poland, In June 1940, a ghetto was established in Kutno, and the Jews were given 24 hours to move there. They were crammed into the grounds of the sugar factory, several bombed out buildings, requiring many of them to make outdoor living arrangements, or resort to cellars and buildings unfit for habitation. Some 7,000 Jews were confined in the ghetto, 2,000 were refugees from outside Kutno. The Kutno ghetto was liquidated in the spring 1942. All the members of the Judenrat (Jewish council) and the ghetto police were shot to death in the local cemetery. The remaining inmates were deported to the Chelmno extermination camp. Just 213 Jews from Kutno survived the Holocaust. www.yadvashem.org/holocaust/this-month/june/1940

Latke, Yiddish, potato pancake, see levivot

Lamed Vav Tzadikim, Hebrew, 36 Righteous People serving as the advocates for mankind. Also known as Nistarim (Hebrew for Concealed Ones)

lavash, Armenian, a simple bread similar to sour dough made from flour, water and salt; it is soft, easily folded thinner than flatbread usually shaped into a circle.

l'chaim, Hebrew, to life

Le commandant, French, Commander

leichu l'shalom, Hebrew, go in peace (group)

leichi l'shalom, Hebrew, go in peace (female),

leich l'shalom, Hebrew, go in peace (male)

levivot, Hebrew, potato pancake (pancakes made on the *Parita* were just flour and water) see latke

L'hitraot, Hebrew, see you (assuming they we see each other again soon)

lokshen, Yiddish, Jewish noodles

lubczyk, Polish, Lovage; an herb that tastes sweeter and stronger like celery, with hints of anise and parsley.

l'shana haba'ah b'Yerushalayim, Hebrew, farewell greeting: "Next year in Jerusalem" used by Jews living in the diaspora. Wishful thinking yearning to be in a Jewish state.

l'shana tovah, Hebrew, good year, a new year greeting (Rosh Hashanah)

l'shana tovah tikatevu, Hebrew, May you be inscribed for a good year.

Magen David Adom, Hebrew, Red Shield of David, Israeli equivalent of the Red Cross

mamzer, Hebrew, illegitimate child. If a Jew marries a non-Jew their marriage is not recognized according to the *Halacha* (Jewish law) and the children are considered illegitimate.

marak perot, Hebrew, fresh fruit and juice

mazel tov, Hebrew, an expression of congratulations, best wishes, or good luck.

Mein Shtetele Belz, Yiddish, a song, My Hometown, Blez

Menorah, Hebrew, originally the name for the seven-branched candelabra used in Jewish worship. The nine-branched *Hanukkah* candelabra is called *hanukkiah* in Hebrew, but English speakers came to use menorah for this too.

merci beaucoup, French, thank you very much.

merci pour le pain, French, thank you for the bread.

meshugge, Yiddish, crazy foolish

Metzuda, Hebrew, Israeli red wine label. A blend of Cabernet Sauvignon, Cabernet Franc and Malbec. Named for a fortress (the Metzuda) located on Ashdod Beach, south of Tel Aviv.

Meze, Arabic, (also spelled mezze or mezé), a selection of small dishes served as appetizers, similar to Spanish tapas, Italian antipasti

mishpacha, Hebrew, a close family network of relatives by blood and marriage and sometimes including close friends.

moi kochani rodzina, Polish, my beloved family

mon nom est, French, my name is.

moshav, Hebrew, cooperative agricultural community in Israel

moshavim, Hebrew, plural moshav

naim lehakir otcha, Hebrew, happy to meet you – male.

naim lehakir otach, Hebrew, happy to meet you – female.

năsal cheese, Romanian, traditional Romanian cheese bearing the same name as the village where it is produced in the Țaga commune, Cluj County. It is a smear-ripened cheese made from cow's milk.

nebbish, Yiddish, a noun referring to a weak-willed or feckless person usually male and especially one who is socially inept and lacks self-confidence.

Nigun, Hebrew, "tune" or "melody", a form of Jewish religious song or tune sung by groups. It is vocal music, often with repetitive sounds such as "Bim-Bim-Bam", "Lai-Lai-Lai", "Yai-Yai-Yai" or "Ai-Ai-Ai" instead of formal lyrics.

nie musisz pytać, Polish, no need to ask.

nisht do kein farvos, Yiddish, humbly denying the need for thanks.

Nistarim, Hebrew, Concealed Ones

oberleutnant, German, lieutenant

och-el tov, Hebrew, good food.

Ottoman Empire, one of the mightiest and longest-lasting dynasties in world history. This Islamic-run superpower ruled large areas of the Middle East, Eastern Europe and North Africa, 1299 and 1922

Ottoman Palestine, the Land of Israel was ruled by the Ottoman Turks from 1516 to 1918.

oui, French, yes

pan, Polish, mister.

petite fille, French, little girl

Pikuach Nefesh, Hebrew, that the preservation of human life overrides virtually any other religious rule of Jewish Law (*Judaism Halacha*)

pot au feu, French, soup made with meat, typically boiled beef, and vegetables cooked in a large pot.

Promised Land, *Genius 12, Genius 26:3, Genius 28:13*

quel est votre nom, French, what is your name.

Revisionist Zionism, the Zionist Movement, www.jewishvirtuallibrary.org/revisionist-zionism

Rosh Hashanah, Hebrew, Jewish new year, celebrating the creation of the world. Ten days of introspection and repentance starting with no moon, culminating ten days later on the full moon on Yom Kippur.

Rozhinkes Mit Mandlen, Yiddish, One of the best-known and loved Yiddish lullabies of all time 'Rozhinkes mit mandlen' (Raisins and almonds) was written by Abraham Goldfaden as part of his opera Shulamis in 1880.

rugelach, Yiddish, a filled baked confection originating in the Jewish communities of Poland. It is popular in Israel, commonly found in most cafes and bakeries.

saba, Hebrew, grandfather

safta, Hebrew, grandmother

sabbath, English, a day of religious observance and rest. Jewish people observe sabbath from Friday sundown to Saturday sundown.

sabra, Hebrew, (plural) an informal-turned-formal modern Hebrew term that defines any Jew born in Israel. The term came into widespread use in the 1930s to refer to a Jew who had been born in Palestine (including the British Mandate of Palestine and Ottoman Palestine) In Hebrew, the word *sabra* refers to the prickly fruit of a species of cactus. Symbolic use of sabra, indicating Jews born in Israel are prickly on the outside but sweet on the inside.

schlepping, Yiddish, hauling, carrying

schnootz, Yiddish, dirt, filth

schwarzbrot, German, dark, whole grain bread

Shabbat, Hebrew verb meaning quit. Shabbat (*Sabbath* in English), extends from just before sunset Friday to sundown on Saturday.

shadchan, Hebrew, matchmaker

shakshuka, Arabic, a simple dish made of gently poached eggs in a delicious chunky tomato and bell pepper, onion and garlic, commonly spiced with cumin, paprika and cayenne pepper.

Shehecheyanu, Hebrew, "Who has given us life." A prayer recorded in the Talmud. The prayer expresses gratitude to God for new and unusual experiences.

sheitel, Yiddish, headscarf worn by orthodox Jewish women to signal that they are married and comply with traditional notions of propriety. Orthodox women do not show their hair in public after their wedding.

Sheva Brachot, Hebrew, literally "the seven blessings" also known as birkot nissuin "the wedding blessings."

sheynem dank, Yiddish, thank you.

shiksa, Yiddish, non-Jewish female, could be derogatory.

shir, Hebrew, a song, poetry

shiva, Hebrew, a traditional seven-day period of mourning the death of a family member.

Simchat *Torah*, Hebrew, Rejoicing of the *Torah*, Jewish religious observance held on the last day of Sukkot ("Festival of Booths"), when the yearly cycle of *Torah* reading is completed, and the next cycle is begun.

Shoah, Hebrew, "catastrophe" meaning: the killing of more than six million Jews in Europe by Nazi Germany and its collaborators during WWII. a.k.a. Holocaust

shtetl, Yiddish, Jewish village. Jews were not allowed to live in any other part of a city or town.

shuckling, Yiddish, to shake. Swaying back and forth while praying (like a candle flame) rhythmic movement as a way to concentrate on praying and learning and ward off distracting thoughts.

siman tov u'mazel tov, Hebrew, good luck and good (astrological) sign. Often used at weddings. The celebration of a marriage is one of Judaism's happiest and most joyous communal events.

slik, slang, hiding place for weapons used by the various underground groups during British Mandate

Sochnut, Hebrew, Agency

sprichst du Deutsch? German, do you speak German?

stifado, Greek, rabbit stew

Sukkot, Hebrew, festival of booths (tabernacles), for giving thanks for many things like food and shelter. The holiday celebrates the farmer's yearly harvest which takes place in the fall. Sukkot also commemorates the biblical story of the Jews' escape from Egypt.

sufganigot, Hebrew, deep-fried, jelly or custard filled donuts, typically topped with powdered sugar.

svivon, Hebrew, dreidel: a four-sided spinning top, played during the Jewish holiday of *Hanukkah*.

taboon, Arabic, clay oven where pita bread is baked.

tahara, Hebrew, preparing the body for burial.

tainias, Greek, headband

tak, Polish, yes

tallit, Hebrew, a fringed garment, a Jewish prayer shawl

Talmud, Hebrew, an intergenerational rabbinic conversation that is studied, not read https://www.myjewishlearning.com/article/talmud-101/ includes: whoever saves one life saves the entire world

Tanakh, Hebrew, Hebrew Bible

tante, Yiddish, Aunt (mother's or father's sister)

tarboosh, Arabic, a red felt or cloth hat with a silk tassel, worn by Muslim men

tashlich, Hebrew, casting off, a ceremony performed on Rosh Hashanah when Jews symbolically cast off their sins of the previous year by tossing chunks of bread into flowing water

Theodor Herzl, father of political Zionism. (May 2, 1860 - July 3, 1904) https://www.myjewishlearning.com/article/theodor-herzl/

Toda raba lecha, Hebrew, Thank you very much (to male)

Toda raba lech, Hebrew, Thank you very much (to female)

Torah, Hebrew, the Five Books of Moses (also known as the Pentateuch) the core of Jewish faith and source of the main laws and ethics.

treif, Yiddish, non-kosher meat

tshulent, Yiddish, traditional Eastern European Jewish stew. An entree served on Sabbath includes beans, potatoes, meat, herbs and spices. Cooked overnight to avoid starting a fire on the Sabbath. (see recipe: marciabreece.com/wp-content/uploads/2024/04/Tshulent.pdf)

Tu as survécu, French, You survived.

Vallos In 1934, the first attempt to bring in a large number of illegal immigrants by sea happened when some 350 Jews sailed on the Vallos, a chartered ship, without the permission of the Jewish Agency, who feared illegal immigration would cause the British to restrict legal immigration.

verboten, German, forbidden

verklempt, Yiddish, (pronounced "fur-klempt") overcome with emotion.

Vielen dank, Fräulein Yutka, German, Many thanks, Miss Yutka

wszystkiego najlepszego, Polish, best wishes

walizka, Polish, suitcase

White Paper (in this context), English, a policy paper issued by the British government led by Neville Chamberlain in response to the 1936–1939 Arab revolt in Palestine.

witam, Polish, hello

Yehi zichra baruch, Hebrew, "May her memory be a blessing" (a blessing when female dies)

Yehi gichro baruch, Hebrew, "May his memory be a blessing" (a blessing when a male dies)

yeshiva, Hebrew, traditional Jewish educational institution focused on the study of Rabbinic literature.

yom tov, Hebrew, good day

zayt nir moykhl, Yiddish, I'm sorry, please forgive me

Zebulon, Hebrew, A school that taught students how to operate large sailing boats and navigation. Named after Zebulon who was the tenth son of Jacob, written in Genesis 49:13

zfat cheese, Hebrew, a semi-hard salty cheese originally from sheep's milk

Zion, Hebrew, "Israel" In the Old Testament, the name Zion is used to refer the Promised Land and the city of Jerusalem, the source of the term Zionism.

Zionist, Hebrew, a person who believes in the development and protection of a Jewish nation in what is now Israel.

zloty, Polish, coin, a monetary unit

Γεια σας, με λένε, Nikos, Greek, Hello, my name is Nikos.

Χωρίς Εβραίους, Greek, No Jews

Благодарю вас, Russian, I express gratitude for the assistance you provided.

Recipes

The following recipes can be found at marciabreece.com/recipes-yutka-and-the-voyage-of-the-parita/

    Baba Ghanoush (page 178)
    Gołąbki (page 11)
    Halloumi (page 133)
    Helzel (35)
    Kreplach (36)
    Kugle (233)
    Levivot (Latkas) (page 109)
    Lokshen (page 233)
    Marak Perot (page 74)
        Marak Perot (recipe version 2)
    Pot Au Feu (page 67)
    Sufganigot (page 174)
    Greek Stifado (page 133)
    Tshulent (page 35)

About the Author

I loved my corporate career, a fast paced, grab onto the rocket and scream yee–haa, kind of career. After my two children started college, I had the opportunity to live in "exotic faraway places" like India, Taiwan and Hong Kong, however there was nothing glamorous about 24-hour flights. From my flat in India to my home in Seattle was a 48-hour trip via train, taxi and airplane. Once, I crossed the international date line and enjoyed a 48-hour birthday with champagne, and a plane full of strangers singing "Happy Birthday."

I loved it—until I didn't. A line from Mary Oliver's Poem said it all, "…are you breathing just a little and calling it a life?" ("Have You Ever Tried to Enter the Long Black Branches?")

I started writing a memoir, and enrolled in the Port Townsend Writers Conference. I was moved to jump off the fast track and spend more time writing so I naively jumped into another high energy opportunity. I bought a hobby farm and opened a B&B on Washington's Olympic Peninsula. I'm a morning person and I love to cook so it sounded like a good idea at the time. After my zany corporate career and single motherhood, caring for five llamas, several ducks, a pair of Toulouse geese and oh-so-many goslings, two (boy) rabbits, two (girl) sheep, and twenty-some chickens, seemed doable. I served very fresh eggs for breakfast.

Farm chores and inn keeping however, left little time for writing, even in the slow winter months. After six years I sold the farm and moved to a beach cottage that couldn't have been more rural—or quiet.

There was an eagle's nest in a tree above my bedroom and a bear devoured my birdseed. My dogs and I walked the Hood Canal beach teeming with sea life during low tide and we listened to the owls and coyotes every night. You might say I turned 180° from tending to the needs of guests and the chaos of my farm and B&B. Before that, over-populated big city career and before that, caring for my family. I discovered that all I really want to do now is write.

Now I'm in a small place on Discovery Bay, closer to Port Townsend, WA., still rural with eagles and heron flying overhead and owls calling in the night. (No bears lately.)

I absorb the surrounding quiet, making creativity possible, both in my writing and in the design work I do for other authors. I may have hated this kind of life when I was younger—who knows—but I do know, it's what I need now.

To learn more, visit my website www.marciabreece.com.

Book Club Discussion Questions

1. What feelings did this book evoke for you?
2. At age 17, with war certain, do you think you could have made the decision to leave your family and travel alone?
3. How are food, wine and music important in the story?
4. How did Yutka handle her grief and fear?
5. How would you describe Yaakov?
6. If you could ask Yutka (or one of the other characters) a question, what would it be?
8. How would you feel about living on a *kibbutz*?
9. In 1939, some Jews believed the establishment of the free state of Israel should wait for the coming of the messiah. What are your thoughts?
10. How does illegal immigration in *YUTKA And the Voyage of the Parita* differ from today's immigration issues?
11. What other books did *YUTKA And the Voyage of the Parita* remind you of?
12. Which character in the book touched you the most? Why?
13. If you were making this story into a movie, who would you cast?
14. Which character in the book would you most like to meet?
15. Which places in the book would you most like to visit?
16. Did the story and characters remind you of people you know?

www.ingramcontent.com/pod-product-compliance
Lightning Source LLC
Chambersburg PA
CBHW070128080526
44586CB00015B/1601